The Spirit of Marikana

Wildcat: Workers' Movements and Global Capitalism

Series Editors:

Peter Alexander (University of Johannesburg)
Immanuel Ness (City University of New York)
Tim Pringle (SOAS, University of London)
Malehoko Tshoaedi (University of Pretoria)

Workers' movements are a common and recurring feature in contemporary capitalism. The same militancy that inspired the mass labor movements of the twentieth century continues to define worker struggles that proliferate throughout the world today.

For more than a century labor unions have mobilized to represent the political-economic interests of workers by uncovering the abuses of capitalism, establishing wage standards, improving oppressive working conditions, and bargaining with employers and the state. Since the 1970s, organized labor has declined in size and influence as the global power and influence of capital has expanded dramatically. The world over, existing unions are in a condition of fracture and turbulence in response to neoliberalism, financialization, and the reappearance of rapacious forms of imperialism. New and modernized unions are adapting to conditions and creating class-conscious workers' movement rooted in militancy and solidarity. Ironically, while the power of organized labor contracts, working-class militancy and resistance persists and is growing in the Global South.

Wildcat publishes ambitious and innovative works on the history and political economy of workers' movements and is a forum for debate on pivotal movements and labor struggles. The series applies a broad definition of the labor movement to include workers in and out of unions, and seeks works that examine proletarianization and class formation; mass production; gender, affective and reproductive labor; imperialism and workers; syndicalism and independent unions, and labor and Leftist social and political movements.

Also available:

Just Work? Migrant Workers' Struggles Today
Edited by Aziz Choudry and Mondli Hlatshwayo

Southern Insurgency: The Coming of the Global Working Class
Immanuel Ness

The Spirit of Marikana

The Rise of Insurgent Trade Unionism in South Africa

Luke Sinwell

with Siphiwe Mbatha

PlutoPress
www.plutobooks.com

First published 2016 by Pluto Press
345 Archway Road, London N6 5AA

www.plutobooks.com

British Library Cataloguing in Publication Data
A catalogue record for this book is available from the British Library

ISBN 978 0 7453 3653 4 Hardback
ISBN 978 0 7453 3648 0 Paperback
ISBN 978 1 7837 1968 6 PDF eBook
ISBN 978 1 7837 1970 9 Kindle eBook
ISBN 978 1 7837 1969 3 EPUB eBook

Typeset by Curran Publishing Services, Norwich
Text design by Melanie Patrick

Simultaneously printed in the European Union and United States of America

Contents

Glossary of South African Organisations

This section is intended particularly for those who are unfamiliar with the South African political context.

AFRICAN NATIONAL CONGRESS (ANC)

With its anti-apartheid credentials, the ANC has remained the hegemonic political party in South Africa since the first democratic elections in 1994. Especially under the leadership of the charismatic Nelson Mandela (but also under his successor Thabo Mbeki), the ANC had historically been viewed countrywide as a liberator of black people, rather than their oppressor. After the massacre, this began to change dramatically as many across the country, including mineworkers themselves, have come to see the ANC as an anti-working-class and even murderous organisation. Hence, the votes which the ANC received in the 2014 national elections declined significantly in each province except Kwa-Zulu Natal. Jacob Zuma, who is the president of the ANC, lambasted the strikes in the platinum belt, and at different points in time essentially blamed the strikers for the deaths of 34 of their fellows on 16 August 2012.

ASSOCIATION OF MINEWORKERS AND CONSTRUCTION UNION (AMCU)

The union was founded after a spat within the National Union of Mineworkers (NUM). Joseph Mathunjwa, who was a leading branch chairperson of the NUM in the late 1990s at Douglas Colliery, had a fall-out with Gwede Mantashe, then general secretary of the NUM (Mantashe is now the general secretary of the ANC). Workers believed Mathunjwa was being undermined, and they went on strike underground in his defence. They then asked him to form a new union. It was officially registered in 2001 and by 2012, in the lead-up to the Marikana massacre, it had a growing, but relatively small, presence in the platinum belt particularly at Karee, one of the shafts at Lonmin.

While the AMCU did not initiate the strike action at Lonmin or any of the three major platinum mines in 2012, workers joined the AMCU en masse throughout 2012. The union's dominance was a product of support from the independent worker committees. By 2013 the union dethroned the NUM as the major miners' union in the Rustenburg platinum belt, and had about 120,000 members. In 2014 the AMCU led workers in what became the longest strike in South African mining history. The union's official T-shirts are green, and for many across the country they symbolise the necessity for independent working-class mobilisation. As this book goes to print, it is at best questionable whether the union, with its apolitical stance, will position itself as a vanguard of a broader and long-term working-class fight for a socialist future in South Africa and beyond.

CONGRESS OF SOUTH AFRICAN TRADE UNIONS (COSATU)

COSATU has been one of the most important organisations of the working class in South Africa since it was formed in 1985. The federation joined in a tripartite alliance with the ANC and the South African Community Party (SACP) in 1990, and played a major role throughout the transition period and into democracy. More recently, the general secretary, Zwelinzima Vavi was expelled, the NUM declined and the NUMSA, currently the largest South African union, was expelled from the federation, so COSATU is now in crisis nationally. Many mineworkers in the belt continue to believe that the NUM, COSATU and the tripartite alliance itself (see below) played a key role in the Marikana massacre.

DEMOCRATIC LEFT FRONT (DLF)

The DLF was initially formed as an anti-capitalist umbrella organisation under the title Conference of the Democratic Left (CDL) in 2008. From its inception, it opposed the ANC's neoliberal programmes. In 2011 a national conference brought together activists and in particular leaders of civic bodies from all over the country, and the CDL was renamed DLF. The organisation responded quickly and decisively following the unprotected strikes in the platinum belt in 2012. The DLF was instrumental in the formation and activities of the Marikana Support Campaign (MSC) as well as the Gauteng Strike Support Committee (GSSC).

DEMOCRATIC SOCIALIST MOVEMENT (DSM)

A socialist organisation in South Africa, the DSM was working with leaders in the platinum belt as early as 2009. When Amplats workers went on strike in September 2012, the DSM sought to build a strike committee which would unite workers from various companies in the platinum belt and beyond. They also formed a political party, the Workers and Socialist Party (WASP), in 2013. The party received just over 8,000 votes in the 2014 national elections.

ECONOMIC FREEDOM FIGHTERS (EFF)

This recently formed political party supported the mineworkers' demand for R12,500, and AMCU members are today sympathetic to the party. Julius Malema, commander in chief, indicated that he and his colleagues chose to launch the EFF at the mountain in Marikana since mineworkers had died there while fighting for their economic freedom. The EFF is anti-capitalist in its orientation and sustains what is arguably the most important youth movement since 1994. The party earned about 6 per cent of the votes (over 1 million) in the 2014 national elections. It is the official opposition in the North West and continues to pressure the ANC on the streets and in Parliament.

MARIKANA SUPPORT CAMPAIGN (MSC)

MSC was officially founded after the Marikana massacre. It works in direct consultation with the mineworkers who survived the massacre as well as with the families (primarily the widows) of the workers who were killed. In seeking justice for the mineworkers, it combines fundraising and legal work with mass mobilisation and direct action.

NATIONAL UNION OF MINEWORKERS (NUM)

A powerhouse of COSATU since its inception, having led hundreds of thousands of mineworkers from the 1980s during the anti-Apartheid struggle, the union organised massive strikes for wage increases and other improvements in the work and living standards of mineworkers. Cyril Ramaphosa, now deputy president of the ANC, was central in the formation of NUM and its exceptional activities. Many of the former leaders of the NUM became national leaders of the ANC in the post-apartheid period. By the late 1990s, particularly in the Rustenburg platinum belt, which had been a stronghold of the NUM, mineworkers began to conclude that shop stewards' partnership with management had undermined the union's relationship to the rank and file. From 2012, with the rise of independent worker committees and the exponential growth of the AMCU, the NUM has been substantially weakened (it is arguably defunct in the Rustenburg region), and some workers call it the National Union of Management. Indeed, some mineworkers simply told us they 'hate' the NUM. There were a number of times when my research team and I were in the platinum belt and people told us that it was dangerous to wear red T-shirts (which is the colour that NUM members wear).

NATIONAL UNION OF METALWORKERS OF SOUTH AFRICA (NUMSA)

NUMSA is one of the most radical unions in COSATU. Founded in 1987, it has a strong tradition of shop floor organising and education campaigns. After the massacre (when workers began leaving the NUM en masse and joining the AMCU), the NUMSA became the largest trade union in South Africa with approximately 350,000 members. At the end of 2013, the union made a decision to end its ongoing support of the ruling ANC. One key reason given was the assertion that the ANC had killed workers in Marikana. This set the stage for a historically monumental process which led to the union being expelled from COSATU and forming a united front to bring together workers and community members across the country. As this book is being written, this process has only just begun.

TRIPARTITE ALLIANCE

Formalised in 1990, the internationally renowned powerhouse COSATU joined the South African Communist Party (SACP) and ANC in order to highlight the link between the ruling party (ANC), the Communist

Party and the workers of the country. When the ANC adopted neoliberal programmes in 1996, the other two bodies in the alliance (COSATU and SACP) showed their discontent, but in the end they could not change this decision. The tripartite alliance showed its true colors when each of its three major formations opposed the 2012 and 2014 strikes in the Rustenburg platinum belt.

OTHER BRIEF NOTES AND DEFINITIONS

Amplats, Impala and Lonmin

Amplats is the abbreviation of Anglo Platinum, the largest platinum mining company in the world. Its Rustenburg operations are relatively spread out compared with those of the two other major companies. Amplats Rustenburg operational shafts, which are on the Western limb of the Bushveld complex, include Khuseleka, Khomanani, Thembelani, Siphumelele and Bathopele. It also has operations in Northam in Limpopo province, and internationally (whereas Lonmin is confined to the North West of South Africa). On the Eastern Limb of the Bushveld complex, Amplats has a range of mines as well. It also has an exceptionally large open pit mine, Mogalakwena, at Mokopane on the Platreef in the north, which did not join the great strike of 2014. In the lead-up to the 2012 strike, Amplats had an estimated total of 54,000 employees.

All three mining companies undertake a substantial degree of conventional mining, meaning that they generally require mineworkers to physically go underground and blast rock formations apart in order to extract minerals.

Impala, which is only briefly discussed in this book, is the second largest platinum mining company in the world with about 33,000 workers. With the exception of a small shaft in Limpopo, Impala's operations are situated within a limited geographical space in and around Rustenburg.

Lonmin is slightly smaller, and is the third largest platinum mining company in the world with approximately 28,000 workers. It was also the site of the Marikana massacre. Its major operational shafts, which are close to each other (workers can walk from shaft to shaft), include Eastern, Western and Karee.

Apartheid

A system of white supremacy, and racial segregation, which was instituted in South Africa from 1948. While Apartheid officially ended more than two decades ago the vast majority of black people are still excluded economically, politically and socially. In the contemporary period, mineworkers tend to refer to the term apartheid as any system of oppression.

The Migrant Labour System

The migrant labour system involves recruiting men from rural areas, especially the Eastern Cape (South Africa), Swaziland and Lesotho, to come to the mining areas to work. Because of the struggle by the workers, the system has been reformed particularly since the end of Apartheid. Instead of workers being confined only to hostel compounds, now they receive housing subsidies, which means they have the option of living wherever they can afford to. Health and safety policies have also been improved dramatically. However, the very structure which removes predominantly men from their rural homelands to the mining areas still remains a key component of the political economy of mining, which is coupled with relatively low wages. Hence, women and children are left behind in their rural communities and just the men go to the mines. Migrant labourers tend to eke out an impoverished life at the mines, living in shacks and often with no electricity and running water. This is partly because they have to maintain two homes, one at the mines where they work and another for their family. The areas from which these workers come have not changed since the dawn of the industrial revolution in South Africa.

The Right to Strike

The right to engage in strike action is enshrined in the South African Bill of Rights, and as such there are no 'illegal' strikes. However, the Labour Relations Act (no. 66 of 1995) draws a distinction between 'protected' strikes, which comply with its provisions, and 'unprotected' strikes, which do not. Workers engaging in protected strikes cannot be dismissed nor can civil legal proceedings be brought against them, whereas an unprotected (or 'wildcat') strike can constitute a fair reason for dismissal. Despite this, the 2012 unprotected strikes in the platinum belt were uniformly portrayed as 'illegal' in media, political and union circles, primarily because they developed outside and against the formal structures of the NUM.

Acronyms and Abbreviations

AMCU	Association of Mineworkers and Construction Union
ANC	African National Congress
ANCYL	African National Congress Youth League
CCMA	Commission for Conciliation, Mediation and Arbitration
CEO	chief executive officer
COSATU	Congress of South African Trade Unions
DA	Democratic Alliance
DLF	Democratic Left Front
DSM	Democratic Socialist Movement
EFF	Economic Freedom Fighters
EXCO	Executive Committee
GEAR	Growth Employment and Redistribution
GLWC	Greater Lonmin Workers' Council
GOG	Gift of the Givers
GSSC	Gauteng Strike Support Committee
IFP	Inkatha Freedom Party
KZN	Kwa-Zulu Natal
LOA	living out allowance
LPD	Lonmin Platinum Division
LRA	Labour Relations Act
LRS	Labour Research Services
MEC	minerals energy complex
MEWUSA	Metal and Electrical Workers Union of South Africa
MSC	Marikana Solidarity/Support Campaign
NACTU	National Council of Trade Unions
NEC	National Executive Committee
NSC	National Strike Committee
NUM	National Union of Mineworkers
NUMSA	National Union of Metalworkers of South Africa
RDO	rock drill operator
RDP	Reconstruction and Development Programme
SACP	South African Communist Party
SADF	South African Defence Force
SANCO	South African National Civics Organisation

SAPS	South African Police Service
SRC	Students' Representative Council
TCC	Thembelihle Crisis Committee
TEBA	The Employment Bureau of Africa
UDM	United Democratic Movement
WAU	Workers Association Union

Leaders

This section provides brief details of some of the most extraordinary individuals in the platinum belt during the period under investigation. Undoubtedly I have not included many others who played an equally indispensable role. The first name which appears is the name applied in the text when I refer to the individual. Their real full name is given in parentheses. Some of the names used are pseudonyms, as noted below.

'Bhele' (Tholakele Dlunga): an RDO from Western Platinum, he was among the first leaders of the 2012 strike at Lonmin. Bhele had seen for quite a long time that the NUM had betrayed the workers. He was tortured by the police after the 2012 Lonmin strike ended, and because of his commitment to the struggle, he was elected an AMCU shop steward in 2013.

'Magqabini' (Bulelani Magqabini): worked closely with Mofokeng in the lead-up to the 2012 unprotected strike at Lonmin. They both approached Karee manager Mike Da Costa on 21 June 2012 to put forward what they called a request (rather than a demand) for monthly net pay of R12,500. According to the minutes (see Appendix B) that they took at this first meeting, they initially had no intention to strike. Magqabini was on leave when the Marikana massacre took place. He is now an AMCU official.

'Mambush' (Mgcineni Noki): was an avid soccer player and an RDO at Karee, Lonmin mine, who became the spokesperson of the Lonmin workers between 9 and 16 August 2012. His demeanour was transformed completely after workers were shot at by NUM members on 11 August, according to family members. He was gunned down below the infamous mountain by police along with 33 others in what is now known as the Marikana massacre. (He was found with 14 bullet holes in his body.) Because of his attire during his brief time on the mountain, he became known as the 'man in the green blanket'. Mambush would become symbolic of the independent working-class power which was unleashed in the platinum belt and beyond in the months and years which followed the massacre.

'Mofokeng' (Alfonse Ramaola Mofokeng): in the lead-up to Lonmin's unprotected strike of 2012, he was a member of the NUM. Mofokeng was a humble and articulate RDO at Karee. An uncelebrated historical figure, he conceptualised the now infamous living wage figure of R12,500 while on leave, then discussed it in the changing rooms after work with another RDO, Bulelani Magqabini, who was also based at Karee mine. They approached management, first as a group of two and then with others, on multiple occasions before uniting with RDOs from Lonmin's other shafts (Eastern and Western). Mofokeng had previous experience in the three major platinum mines and was formerly secretary of the Mouth Peace Workers Union. In the aftermath of the massacre, he joined the AMCU, but did not become an office holder.

'Rasta' (Magubane Sohadi): an RDO at the Eastern shaft, he became a leader during the early stages of the strike at Lonmin and experienced the massacre at first hand. He was among those who decided to stay on strike despite the killings, and became a member of the newly formed workers' committee which sought to welcome visitors and organise funerals for the dead. In 2013 he was elected an AMCU shop steward.

'Sobopha' (Siviwe Sobopha): a winch operator at Karee mine, he joined the strike days after it started and became a leader during his time on the mountain. On 16 August, he handed Mambush money which he and others collected to buy food for the workers on the mountain shortly before the massacre occurred. He presently lives in a corrugated iron shack, like many others, with no running water or electricity.

'Zakhele' (a pseudonym): an outstanding organic intellectual, leader and organiser in the mines who was born in 1960 in Flagstaff, Eastern Cape. He was at the forefront of the 2012 strike at Lonmin and later supported the AMCU enthusiastically like many others. He then became the chairperson of the Greater Lonmin Workers' Council (GLWC), an autonomous organisation formed to hold the AMCU accountable to the rank and file who had seen their own blood, and that of their brothers, spilled at Marikana. As the NUM had betrayed the workers who brought it into power, he feared the AMCU could do the same.

MINEWORKERS AT AMPLATS

'Chris' (Zukile Christopher Mbobo): became a key figure in the formation of the worker committee at Amplats. In 1978, he was 17 years old and already working at the mines. His teeth were smashed out by opponents when he was trying to bring the NUM, which was then viewed as a liberator of black mineworkers, to the mines in the mid-1980s. Later he came to view the NUM as an enemy of workers. Chris worked closely with S. K. Makhanya in the early stages of the mobilisation at Amplats, and throughout the contemporary mineworkers' movement in the country. He shifted around from mine to mine, and during the 2012 strike wave he was working at Amplats in the Khuseleka shaft. He was living in Freedom Park, alongside many Impala employees, and was acutely aware of the new developments at that mine, which witnessed the first set of unprotected strikes in the platinum belt. The discussions taking place across the mines played an indispensable role in fuelling the resistance. When he went to work at Khuseleka, he told his fellow workers about what was happening at Impala. His stature as a key leader of the strikes in 2012 and 2014 led the company to lay charges against him.

'Desmond' (a pseudonym): became a shop steward of the NUM at Amplats in early 2011. He believed that if the NUM could harness its power properly, particularly given its majority status and its relationship to the ANC, it could make real changes in people's lives at the mines. However, he soon came to the conclusion that the NUM had sold out. When Amplats workers sought to unite under a common non-union affiliated plan for strike action, he joined in (although he was not a member of a workers' committee) and in 2013 he became a shop steward for AMCU.

'Edwin' (a pseudonym): a vocal and articulate mineworker from a relatively small mechanised shaft called Bathopele, he was a leader of the NUM until a falling out. When he was called in to lead the workers of his shaft independently from trade union affiliation into strike action, he did so. In 2013, he felt betrayed by the AMCU's National Executive Committee (NEC) and he did not support the great strike of 2014.

'Gaddafi' (Gaddafi Mdoda): as part of a new generation of mineworkers, he had seen the way that his uncle suffered as an ordinary worker at Khomanani when he was growing up. He became a core leader at the same mine during the 2012 unprotected strike at Amplats, and the following year he hesitated to join the AMCU since he believed the union could undermine the democratic nature of the workers' committee of which he was part. Although he became a key leader of the AMCU in 2013, he has now reverted to his earlier job as a stop timber.

'Lazarus' (Lazarus Khoza): a friendly and at the same time very serious and unflinching representative of the workers, first under the workers' committee at Khuseleka in 2012 and then under the banner of the AMCU in 2013 and 2014. He believed that the slaying of mineworkers at Marikana made the workers at Amplats more courageous. His brother, Jacob Khoza, was also a foremost leader of the workers at Khuseleka shaft in 2012 and led workers as an AMCU shop steward in 2013 and 2014.

'Mabanana' (Godfrey Lindani): an energetic young mineworker in his late 20s at the time of the uprisings, he was chosen by his fellow colleagues to be a leader of Khomanani shaft at Amplats. Despite personal issues at the time, he could not say 'no' and he became a core leader of the 2012 unprotected strike at Amplats. As a member of the workers' committee, he recalls being called 'faceless' by management and the government. At this time of writing, he no longer works at the mine but runs a small business in Rustenburg.

'Makhanya' (S. K. Makhanya): Then in his early 30s, he conceptualised the demand for R16,070 at his Reconstruction and Development Programme (RDP) house in Siraleng and pioneered an independent workers' committee, alongside his trusty older comrade Chris. This committee united all the shafts at Amplats, starting with the nightshift winch drivers at Khuseleka, the shaft where he worked. He was arguably the quintessential leader of the contemporary mineworkers' movement between 2012 and 2014, first as a member of the workers' committee and then as a branch chairperson of the AMCU. Today he is an ordinary worker at Amplats.

'Tumelo' (a pseudonym): alongside Chris and Makhanya, he was a winch driver at Khuseleka platinum mine who helped provide the impetus for the workers' committee at their shaft. While at first he questioned the way in which the AMCU leadership seemed to be undermining the autonomy of workers following the 2012 unprotected strike at Amplats, Tumelo nevertheless became a branch organiser of the union in 2013 and played an important role throughout the mineworkers' movement.

OTHER KEY FIGURES

'Bheki' (Bheki Buthelezi): defied barriers first as a major community organiser in the Ward Crisis Committee in a black township called Umlazi in Kwa-Zulu Natal (the committee had occupied the local government councilor's office in 2012), and then as a leader of the Democratic Left Front (DLF). Although he had never worked in the mines, he was called on many occasions to act as a representative of the mineworkers. He first arrived in Marikana on 17 August, just out of a community struggle in Umlazi, to join the mineworkers' struggle. He was soon tasked by the DLF to organise on a full-time basis. He lived in Rustenburg in late 2012 and throughout 2013 and much of 2014, dedicating his relentless activism and offering solidarity and a socialist perspective to the mineworkers in Rustenburg and beyond.

'Da Costa' (Mike Da Costa): a witness in the Marikana Commission of Inquiry since he was the manager at Karee mine who engaged with RDOs on multiple occasions prior to their decision to hold a mass meeting of Lonmin's shafts (including Karee, Eastern and Western) on 9 August 2012, when the unprotected strike began.

'Malema' (Julius Malema): a notable orator and political strategist, he was expelled from the ANC Youth League for his calls for nationalisation of the mines. He was central to the formation of the Economic Freedom Fighters (EFF) in the aftermath of the Marikana massacre, and he became the party's commander in chief (equivalent to president).

'Mathunjwa' (Joseph Mathunjwa): became president of the AMCU in 2001. On 16 August he went down on his knees in front of the 3,000 workers on the mountain and begged them to leave as he had received information which suggested that they would be killed. Minutes later, the massacre took place. Mathunjwa vowed to fight alongside the workers, uniting the three largest platinum mines in the world in Rustenburg and Northam under the AMCU in what culminated in the longest strike in South African mining history.

'Steve' (Mawethu Joseph Steven, also known as Steve Khululekile): the foremost leader of the NUM at Karee mine until 2011, he was respected and known by workers at Lonmin more generally. When the NUM refused to reinstate him in May 2011, virtually all employees at Karee went out on an unprotected strike. He was expelled from the NUM and then became the foremost regional AMCU recruiter in the Rustenburg platinum belt. He was murdered in 2013 before he could speak at the Marikana Commission of Inquiry.

Timeline of Key Events

At the South Africa platinum mines, independent worker organising can be traced back to the mid-1980s. Violence has historically been prevalent in these mines. In 1997 at least five workers were killed by the police during an unprotected strike at a mountain in the informal settlement of Sefikile in Northam (where the platinum belt extends to Limpopo). Maintaining the hegemony of the NUM was never easy as the union had to contend with, among others, the Mouth Peace Workers Union throughout the late 1990s and early 2000s. There were major violent confrontations between the two unions, including murders, during this period.

2009

A wave of unprotected strikes hit the platinum sector in areas such as Aquarius Platinum Kroondal Mine and Crocodile River Mine (see the map, p. xxviii) in which workers at each company engaged in sit-ins as a tactic to bring management to the bargaining table. NUM vice-president Piet Matosa had one of his eyes gouged out by a rock when he sought to convince workers on an unprotected strike at Impala Platinum to return to work.

2011

May 2011: Virtually every mineworker at Karee shaft (Lonmin) went on an unprotected strike in support of the very popular NUM chairperson 'Steve', who had been removed from his position by the union. The NUM opposed the strike action, to the dismay of many workers, and 9,000 were sacked by Lonmin management. Most were rehired, but 1,400 were not. The AMCU and Steve began to work together. Alongside the majority of workers at Karee, Steve created the path for the AMCU to become established in the platinum belt. The AMCU began to spread, slowly and unevenly, to other mines in the belt.

June/July 2011: Lonmin's Karee mine recruited Magqabini and Mofokeng among others as RDOs to fill the gap in the workforce created when the 1,400 were not rehired. (They separately decided to join two different unions.) These two key individuals were the 'spark underground' who would begin mobilising independently, worker by worker, less than a year later to fight for a basic monthly wage of R12,500.

2012

January 2012: An unprotected strike at Impala (the second largest platinum producer in the world) began in mid-January, led by the RDOs. By the end of January the unrest at Impala had spread, and virtually the entire workforce had downed tools.

March: The Impala strike ended on 3 March with workers winning a pay increase to R9,000. Discontent with the NUM had come to a head at Impala because the union had opposed the popular unprotected strike. By the end of the strike, management had fired 18,000 of the striking workers, effectively ending their union membership. About 11,000 other Impala workers resigned as NUM members by 30 March.

April: The mass dismissals and the response of the NUM to the unprotected strike created the conditions for the AMCU to extend its membership at Impala, particularly at Freedom Park (where many Impala employees lived).

April/May: Ad hoc committees begin organising at Amplats (specifically at the Khuseleka shaft), claiming basic pay of R16,070, and Lonmin (at Karee shaft), claiming R12,500. These committees remained independent of the unions.

June/July: Ad hoc committees at Amplats (Khuseleka) and Lonmin (Karee) approached management at these shafts on multiple occasions, but did not yet engage in strike action.

9 August: Mass mobilisation at Lonmin extended beyond the confines of Karee shaft. About 3,000 RDOs from all three major shafts (Karee,

Eastern and Western) adopted the demand for R12,500 and held a mass meeting. Unprotected strike action began that evening.

10 August: Thousands of Lonmin workers approached management offices and were told instead to take their grievances to the dominant union at the mine (the NUM).

11 August: Workers marched to NUM local offices in Wonderkop, Marikana. The strikers were fired on by NUM security staff with live ammunition, and many believe that two were killed. The workers decided to arm themselves in self-defence, and made a strategic decision to head to the Marikana mountain.

12 August: Each day, more and more employees came together at the meeting place on the mountain with the primary objective of speaking to their employer about their wage demands. Although management had engaged with them previously on multiple occasions, no representatives came to the mountain. The workers marched again to the NUM offices on 12 August. They were again shot at by security staff, and two Lonmin security employees were killed.

13 August: An armed battalion of workers went to the Karee mine to press workers not to go to work. The police were waiting for them at a railway line and attacked them. Two police officers, two security officers and four workers were killed in the ensuing violence. Some of the worker leaders were later charged with the murders of the police officers.

14 August: The police, with a heavy presence at Marikana, sought to negotiate with the workers on the mountain through their leaders or 'Mountain Committee'. The committee asked to see only their employer, but still no employer representative came.

15 August: The police presence at Marikana intensified further, and two leading union officials attempted to speak to the workers on the mountain. Joseph Mathunjwa, president of the AMCU, came there in his own car and addressed the workers directly. He was sympathetic to their case. Senzani Zokwana, president of the NUM, arrived in a large armoured police vehicle which he did not leave. He said the workers should go back to work.

16 August: Police opened fire on the striking workers, and 34 were killed, in the largest episode of state violence since the Soweto uprisings of 1976. The Marikana massacre is already viewed as a major turning point in South African history. An ad hoc group of 10–20 mineworkers met that evening and decided to continue the strike for a living wage, so their colleagues would not have died in vain.

17 August: The striking workers formed a committee to deal with visitors and another to organise funerals for their dead colleagues in their mostly rural home areas.

8 September: Leaders of workers at the Amplats Khuseleka shaft initiated a plan to unite workers from all the company shafts in the Rustenburg region, including Bathopele, Thembelani, Khomanani and Siphumelele.

12 September: An unprotected strike of Amplats workers began with the night shift of 11–12 September and by the next day was in full swing.

18 September: Following a crackdown in Marikana by 1,000 South African Defense Force (SADF) forces, Lonmin workers agreed a 22 per cent rise in pay, which was accepted at a mass meeting at the Wonderkop Stadium. The Lonmin strike came to an end as a result.

End September: In response to the victory at Lonmin, approximately 100,000 unprotected and protected employees came out on strike nationwide.

1 October: The Marikana Commission of Inquiry began. Very few Lonmin workers and no representatives of the dead men's families were called on to attend. It seemed even at this stage that the commission's objective of 'truth, restoration and justice' was unlikely to be met.

5 October: The Amplats unprotected strike continued. The strikers were summoned to disciplinary hearings, and Amplats CEO Chris Griffith announced that the company would dismiss the 12,000 workers who failed to attend them. In response the Rustenburg worker committees extended the strike to company operations in Northam, Limpopo.

13 October: A National Strike Committee was launched in Rustenburg, with the DSM activist group at the forefront, attempting to coordinate the major strike actions taking place across the entire country.

27 October: In the midst of the industrial mobilisation, cosatu attempted to 'reclaim Rustenburg' by holding a mass rally. It had little impact.

10 November: Amplats workers held a rally of 10,000 people at Olympia Stadium in Rustenburg, with the support of the DLF.

14 November: The Amplats workers' committee met with cosatu leaders including Zwelinzima Vavi and Sdumo Dlamini, who attempted to convince them to end the strike.

18 November: The Amplats strike ended with an agreement for a salary adjustment of R400 and a promise from management to negotiate further early in 2013.

End November and December: The Amplats workers' committees (in both Northam and Rustenburg) were given 'interim access' to the union offices so that management had a legitimate structure to engage with.

2013

January: Amplats announced its intention to lay off 14,000 workers and put further wage negotiations on hold.

February: Now that the vast majority of workers at Amplats and Lonmin had joined the amcu (an ongoing process particularly from 2012) there were major tensions between the worker committees and the union, especially at Amplats in the Rustenburg region, where the committees were most deeply entrenched.

Mid-2013: After a bitter struggle over union recognition, which witnessed intimidation and murders of both num and amcu representatives, the amcu signed recognition agreements at Amplats and Lonmin.

16 August: The first commemoration of the massacre at Marikana, attended by at least 10,000 workers and largely organised by the Marikana Solidarity/Support Campaign (msc).

Timeline of Key Events

13 October: The Economic Freedom Fighters (EFF) political party was launched.

16–20 December: The NUMSA union held a Special National Congress which decided to no longer officially support the ANC, citing the ANC's involvement in the Marikana massacre as a key reason.

2014

23 January: The start of the longest strike in South Africa mining history. A protected strike under the auspices of the AMCU, it united workers from the world's three largest platinum mining companies. After five months it ended with an agreement to a pay rise of approximately R1,000 (about 20 per cent) over each of the next three years.

2015 TO PRESENT

The Marikana Commission of Inquiry reported, finding that the police had needed to intervene, and shoot, because of striker violence. The future of the AMCU, particularly its ability to unite with a broader range of forces outside its relatively narrow constituency, increasingly came into question. The struggle for fair pay and living conditions for South African mineworkers, and for the poor and working class more broadly, continues.

Acknowledgements

This book is dedicated to the people of Marikana and to those who fight at their side.

Like any book, this was a collective endeavor. Hendrick More assisted throughout most of 2013 as a translator, a guide and an exceptional travel companion. Without Bheki Buthelezi, who dedicated a significant portion of his life to the everyday struggles of the mineworkers, we would not have met many of the key leaders in and around Rustenburg. We are grateful to Dunbar Moodie for his invaluable comments on multiple drafts of the manuscript. A special thanks goes to Peter Alexander and the South African Research Chair in Social Change for providing the intellectual space for a project of this nature. Immanuel Ness offered mentorship and much needed moral support throughout the final stages of the project. We would also like to thank Thapelo Lekgowa, Bongani Xezwi and Botsang Mmope for their participation in the early stages of the research process and *Fats1000*, Bonginkosi Masiwa, Marcelle Dawson, Shannon Walsh, David Moore, Prishani Naidoo, Gavin Capps, Elke Zuern, Noor Nieftagodien, Mondli Hlatshwayo, Claire Ceruti, Mosa Phadi, Sam Ashman, Eddie Webster and Trevor Ngwane for their various contributions.

Luke would also like to thank his loving wife Mukelwa Sinwell and their son Harugumi Joseph Sinwell. Siphiwe would also like to acknowledge his wife Thokozile, his sister Nomakhazane, and his two children, Sboniso and Nonhlanhla without which he believes he would not have been courageous enough to pursue his dreams in difficult times. Lastly, he thanks Luke for the opportunity to join this project.

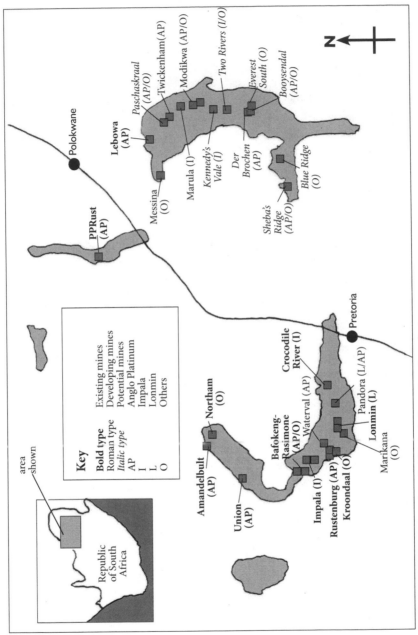

Map 1 Approximate location of South Africa's platinum deposits and mines

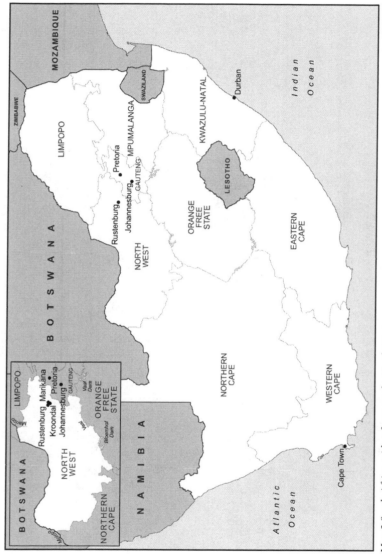

Map 2 South Africa, with a focus on the North West

1

Introduction

Mgcineni 'Mambush' Noki, who became known as 'the man in the green blanket', is an iconic figure of the contemporary South African strike wave at the three international platinum mining giants – Amplats, Impala and Lonmin.[1] After being attacked on 11 August 2012 by members of the then dominant union at Lonmin mine, Mambush and others armed themselves with traditional weapons and fled to the now infamous mountain at Marikana to wait for their employer to address them about their wage demand of R12,500 per month. (This was equivalent to about $500 at the time.[2]) Mambush's family later recalled that he always made peace at his rural village in the Eastern Cape whenever there was a quarrel, but now he had been pushed into an all-out war. A rock drill operator (RDO) with a penetrating voice and a wide frame, he was selected to be on the militant, and at the same time defensive, worker committee. When the workers in Marikana effectively removed negotiations from the offices to the mountain, Mambush acted as their spokesperson.

Embodying the uncompromising characteristics of a warrior, he became a hero practically overnight. Yet almost as quickly as he became a recognised leader, he was targeted by police, who shot 14 bullets into his body. I could not interview him or tell his story comprehensively.[3] Fortunately, however, Mambush was just one among many in the platinum belt. He represented the unflinching determination of mineworkers to engage with management not only for themselves and their families, but for future generations of exploited and oppressed people across the world.

The case study which this book showcases is a testimony to what scholar-activist Frances Fox Piven has tirelessly demonstrated in her eminent work: that when ordinary people organise collectively, outside of the framework of elites and mainstream political authorities, progressive changes in the structures of society become possible.[4] Drawing primarily from original interviews with the individuals who led the strikes at Amplats and Lonmin, this book details how mineworkers united with each other, and in some cases died, while fighting for basic dignity. It illuminates the micro-processes through which the idea of a 'living wage' of R12,500 and then R16,070 first emerged from conversations between two sets of workers in changing rooms at each mine, and then spread like wildfire across the industry. It soon shook an entire nation. Mineworkers, through their ad hoc independent worker committees, challenged what they considered to be the 'pocket unionism' exemplified by the National Union of Mineworkers (NUM), bringing a new radical political culture to the mines – one based on worker needs rather than bosses' interests, and informed by notions of direct democracy.[5]

At Amplats and Lonmin in particular, worker committees galvanised an innovative conceptualisation and expression of power. If the culture and forms of power that they exhibited were not qualitatively new, they were far more strident than anything that had been witnessed in the recent past. When we comprehend more completely what transpired during and ahead of the 2012 unprotected strikes at Amplats and Lonmin, it becomes apparent how and why the first half of 2014, under the banner of the upstart Association of Mineworkers and Construction Union (AMCU), witnessed the longest strike in South African mining history. Yet despite the overwhelming significance of worker committees, they have been given very limited scholarly attention.

Since the burgeoning of trade unions internationally from the mid to late 1900s until the present, they have been the preferred topic of scholarly work by labour historians.[6] Industrial sociology in post-apartheid South Africa has also been dominated by investigations into formalised unions which operate within the framework of the tripartite alliance.[7] Sakhela Buhlungu in particular has noted the anti-democratic nature of unions, the tendency for shop stewards to drift away from workers and become part of the bureaucracy, rather than to represent them, as well as the discontent that has resulted from this. He has also called the victory of 1994 – in which the federated Congress of South African Trade Unions (COSATU) gained great influence as a partner with the ruling African National Congress (ANC) – *A Paradox of Victory*.[8] COSATU and its affiliated unions were largely institutionalised by capital and its allies in the 'class compromise' which resulted from the transition to democracy. COSATU had major achievements after its establishment in 1985, and played a key role in formulating the people-centred Reconstruction and Development Programme (RDP) – only to see it jettisoned in the name of market principles and international investors under the Growth Employment and Redistribution (GEAR) policy document of 1996.

The NUM, which once courageously backed the blacks oppressed in the struggle for liberation from white apartheid rule,[9] became a pocket union. Its former general secretaries, political heavyweights including former deputy president Kgalema Motlanthe, general secretary of the ANC Gwede Mantashe and deputy-president of the ANC Cyril Ramaphosa, a billionaire who sat on the board of directors at Lonmin at the time of the Marikana massacre, lambasted rather than defended the strikes of 2012 and 2014. The NUM's close ties to big business and the ruling party, and primarily its failure to respond to the concerns of ordinary workers at the local branch level, became its Achilles heel. The union is now virtually defunct in the platinum belt, with one leader in a play on words calling it the 'National Union of Management'.

The tendency of social scientists to focus on formalised structures in the workplace and elsewhere has meant that they pay little attention to 'informal' worker organisations – in this case worker committees. Independent worker committees are arguably the most neglected features surrounding the Marikana massacre, an event that is likely to become as important symbolically as the Soweto uprisings and the Sharpeville massacre, as a turning point in South African history. According to Philip Frankel, author of the authoritative text on the Sharpeville massacre, 'Marikana has [already] become a moral barometer against which future developments in mining and wider South Africa will be measured for many years to come.'[10]

Worker committees are fundamental for understanding the strike wave along the Rustenburg platinum belt, where these independent organisations at one time asserted an overwhelming degree of power. Only empirical research can uncover the hidden details which shed light on the nature of these committees and their political trajectory. At this stage, scholars and the general public know very little about them or their relationship to unions. The Marikana Commission of Inquiry, initiated to unpack the causes of the events between 9 and 16 August

2012 in Marikana, also proved inadequate to explain the role of these committees, in part because of the limited period within which it sought to understand and explain the strike and the immediate events surrounding the massacre itself.

The formation of independent worker committees, and the strikes they helped organise and sustain between 2012 and 2014, were by no means isolated events. They are a reflection of ongoing contestation over union representation at the platinum mines which dates back at least to the early 1990s. Moreover, the NUM's services to its members in the Rustenburg region had consistently been rated by researchers as among the worst in the country.[11]

Inequalities between the rich and the poor, unemployment and poverty did not end in 1994, but arguably became more deep-seated than they had been under the apartheid government.[12] Subsequent to the democratic transition in the 1990s, which saw unions like the NUM incorporated into the tripartite alliance, employer and employee relations tended to be characterised by the idea of corporate or 'pocket' trade unionism. The disempowerment of the NUM during the period following the transition to democracy paralleled what scholars and commentators have called 'the death of labour and class-based movements'.[13]

However, these movements were soon revived on an international level. With the deepening crisis of capitalism epitomised by the world economic crisis from 2008, something had to change. In response to the crunch of the drained economy and the increasingly precarious nature of working-class jobs, labour discontent began to spread. Beverly Silver, who has undertaken extensive investigations into the relationship between the shifts in globalisation and worker's movements since the late 19th century, noted that in 2010, 'the world's major newspapers were suddenly filled with reports of labour unrest around the world'.[14] This was followed by unprecedented protests against austerity internationally, and mass uprisings in Egypt against authoritarian rule. By 2011 the so-called 'Arab spring' seemed to offer hope that ordinary people could transform politics, society and labour relations through mass action. Later that year, the Occupy movement took hold in the United States, and in the state of Wisconsin, public sector workers organised en masse to demand that the bargaining rights of unions be re-established.[15]

New forms of workers' power were beginning to take shape during this period, as we witnessed the unravelling of the trade unions founded on the events of the Durban strikes of 1973 and the emergence of black trade unions throughout the 1980s. As a response to the events surrounding the Marikana massacre, South Africa found itself at a crossroads of trade unionism. In the Western Cape, farm workers initiated unprecedented unprotected strikes in 2012 to demand higher wages. AMCU soon became the most obvious example of the rupture inside the trade union movement, dethroning NUM in the platinum belt and creating circumstances that led to the National Union of Metalworkers of South Africa (NUMSA) emerging as the largest trade union in the country.

In South Africa, the creation of independent committees in the platinum belt was a worker response to the shifting nature of the political economy both nationally and internationally. The prices of platinum, and commodities generally, boomed in the 1990s, but the gains went to shareholders – many of whom are overseas – and not to workers. This left mineworkers overstretched. They were digging out platinum from underground, working overtime, while their wages remained largely untouched.

In the lead-up to the 2012 strike wave, mining companies themselves exhibited some of the most profound inequalities between employees and chief executive officers (CEOs), leading one political economist to aptly describe the insurgency in the Rustenburg platinum belt as a 'local battle in a global wealth war'.[16] Economists at Labour Research Services (LRS) conducted a survey on mining company CEO salaries in 2011, which found that the average CEO made R20.2 million per year, or R55,000 per day. This made the worker demand for R12,500 per month seem like a pittance. In 2011 the 'wage gap between the CEO and the average worker in the mining industry was 390 to 1'.[17]

Inequality and tough working and living conditions are not in themselves an adequate explanation for a revolt by mineworkers. In fact, another set of more immediate structural issues played a critical role in harvesting the workers' insurgency. In the two mines under consideration, the work process involved conventional rather than mechanised mining. This means that the mines required drillers (and other categories of worker) to create the conditions for the removal of the platinum, and gave workers including RDOs more power in the workplace.[18] Unlike the gold and coal industries, managers at the platinum mines had also developed a tendency, going back to the 1990s, of engaging directly with worker committees over wage demands.[19]

In 2011, for example, in an attempt to prevent the emergence of further unprotected strikes, Lonmin initiated a policy whereby management could engage directly with workers outside of the formal bargaining structures (see Chapter 2). By engaging directly with them, management suggested to workers that they had power independently from their trade unions. These decisions by management backfired, at Lonmin and elsewhere. The following year witnessed the major wave of unprotected strikes in 2012 which largely forms the basis for this book. Workers formed independent committees at Impala in early 2012, and these were very effective at obtaining concessions from the employer. This led workers at Lonmin and Amplats to form worker committees which engaged directly with management and subsequently led unprotected strikes (see Chapters 2 to 4).

In 2012, RDOs were being paid $511 per month (about R5,000). Most were the main wage earners in their families, responsible for up to 15 dependants. When they fell into debt (as many did, not surprisingly), there was extensive use of garnishee orders by debt collection agencies to recover the money owed, which exacerbated their situation. The pay for one of the most arduous and dangerous jobs on the planet was insufficient to say the least, and these 'exploitative debt relations' made things even worse.

It would seem that the structural conditions existed for mass mobilisation. The workers digging out metal in the mineshafts were ready to erupt. But the structural conditions in late 2011 and early 2012 can only partially explain why people embarked on unprotected strikes in exceptional numbers. 'Someone had to blow the whistle,' in the words of one activist. No observer or participant could have predicted the spirit and sheer magnitude with which mineworkers would come out to make their demands over a sustained period of time in both 2012 and 2014.

AN ACTOR-ORIENTED APPROACH

Scholars have argued that the migrant labour system (see prelims) – whereby most workers had homes and families elsewhere in rural areas, and travelled long distances to the platinum belt for work – and the social and economic position of RDOs are (structural) causal factors requiring attention.[20] These are valuable contributions and provide a crucial starting point from which to understand the platinum belt strike wave. However, considering these factors fails to address the role of locally specific factors and triggers. Existing approaches have fallen short in revealing why the origins of the strikes can be traced back to certain moments in time, and specific shafts of a mine and not others.

Understanding these dynamics requires a sociological examination of mineworkers centrally involved in the strikes. A primary step to piecing together a narrative which helps explain the origins of the strikes is to identify key leaders and to uncover hidden histories. This work lies behind the development of the argument of this book. A great deal of self-organising from below has been underexplored; in effect, it is written out of history. As the prominent historian Philip Bonner has noted in relation to the study of social transformation more generally, 'These bottom up processes are generally subterranean, slow moving, and barely visible, often only exploding after long periods of gestation into public view.'[21]

It is necessary to add here that structures, and indeed institutions and more ephemeral patterns of social relations, are of course part of people's enactment of agency.[22] Agency is not something which merely results from structural factors, however, although agents obviously make history within a specific social and economic context over which they have little control. This book takes as a starting point the 'organic capacity of the working class', or ordinary people in the conscious process of what Marx has described as 'making their own history'. Colin Barker and his colleagues captured the essence of this approach when they indicated that:

> The very social relations of production are themselves the product of ongoing agency, even if in alienating forms, on the part of those who currently suffer their continuation .... There is no absolute line of division between movements seeking 'reforms' within existing structures and movements that threaten to surpass their limits. Rather, movements operate on the boundaries between forms of opposition that remain contained within the limits of the system, and those that potentially transgress them.[23]

Another salient concern which emerged during the course of writing is the tension between individual and collective agency. Without the unity of a collective, the individual is virtually powerless in labour relations, whereas without individuals' motives, energy, experiences, creativity and dreams – in short, their agency – the collective also cannot exist.[24] The book focuses on individuals and their relationship to the collective in an attempt to uncover the leadership practices of a few key organic intellectuals who played a significant role in the development of the 2012 and 2014 strikes, and perhaps more crucially, in the events immediately prior to them.

As 'organic intellectuals' in the Gramscian sense these individuals developed counter-hegemonic ideologies rooted within the material conditions and discourses of their fellow workers. According to the Italian Marxist revolutionary Antonio Gramsci, 'all men [sic] are intellectuals'.[25] Of specific interest in the pages that follow are 'articulate knowledge specialists who are found in all sectors of society'.[26] More specifically they can be described as 'framing specialists: women and men who develop, borrow, adapt, and rework interpretive frames that promote collective action and that define collective interests and identities, rights and claims'.[27]

At the core of an organic intellectual's ability to be effective at achieving counter-hegemony, and therefore also unity among the working class, is arguably the notion of 'leadership'. In part because of attempts to avoid 'great man' theories of history, leadership has tended to be neglected in the study of collective mobilisation, and more specifically of social movements.[28] Barker and colleagues point out that:

> Few academics want to revive conservative 'agitator' theories which imply that there would be no strikes, no militant movement activity, were it not for the malign trouble-makers who cause them. We must, it is argued, pay proper attention to the real grievances motivating movements, just as we must avoid treating movement members as nothing but mindless sheep.[29]

Regardless of scholars' emphasis, however, labour and other movements are inextricably intertwined with leadership which conceptualises a common set of demands, unites sympathisers and exerts power in solidarity.

While the dominant perception of the strikes of 2012 and 2014 is that they were spontaneous uprisings which involved employees who used primarily violent techniques and intimidation to maintain solidarity (among other employees or non-strikers), the pages that follow should indicate to the reader that something very different may have been far more relevant. By this I mean democratic leadership and the element of persuasion. 'Persuasive argument' is, according to Barker, 'inherently "dialogical" in function, it seeks understanding and agreement. It presumes that an initial proposal may be modified by the listener's response. It encourages the further critical self-development of the follower.'[30] While these workers (through their committees) provided the way forward, they were led by (and directly accountable to) the rank and file. Referring to Foucault's conception of 'pastoral leadership', Dunbar Moodie elaborated the way in which NUM stalwarts (including Ramaphosa) applied this form of leadership in the mid-1980s:

> the pastoral leader does not dominate. Instead, he gathers his followers together, guides and leads them. This is fundamentally beneficent power, directing the conduct of its followers, individualising them in a complex mutual relationship of responsibility. For the pastoral leader, wielding power is a duty, pursued with zeal, devotion and endless application, offering care to others but denying it to oneself. Leadership is defined not as an honour but rather as a burden and effort. The leader puts himself out for, acts, works and watches over all his followers.[31]

Paradoxically, the failure of the NUM to apply this method in recent years created the conditions for a new form of organisation of pastoral power to emerge.

Existing accounts of the strike at Lonmin give precedence to Mambush, and imply that he led the workers throughout, yet – as this book shows – he was not one of the RDOs who actually initiated it.[32] While the initial involvement of many mineworkers sprang from the moment, the involvement of a handful of those who became leaders at various points before, during and after the strikes was anything but spontaneous. Without their efforts to engage within (and where necessary create) informal networks for the mobilisation of the strikers, it is not unreasonable to conclude that events would not have occurred at the moment and in the manner in which they did. Without their strategic intervention, events might have shifted onto another track, taking a different course.

Indeed, for socialist activists working closely with the workers in the platinum belt, it appeared that the unprotected strikes of 2012 were the pinnacle of resistance, and that a swift decline in mobilisation was likely to follow as a result of workers' and their leaders' decision to join what appeared to be a top-down, authoritarian union. AMCU was opposed to the unprotected form of strike that worker committees led and sustained in 2012. It seemed to many observers, myself included, that under the banner of the new union, unprotected strikes were not an option, and worker militancy would soon perish. Such assumptions conform to the current Marxist critique of trade unions as 'managers of discontent', limited by their incorporation into bargaining structures and dependent on management support.[33]

The empirical research provided below indicates, however, that the core politics that underpinned the militant strikes of 2012 have remained constant over time, despite workers' decision to join a union and to engage primarily in protected strikes (hence the 2014 strike which has been stronger and longer). Put in a different way, this study demonstrates that when the rank and file takes on an insurgent character, the trade union's bureaucratic or official power (at the national, regional and branch level) becomes marginal, but only relatively so, as the events reveal. Just as the exclusive nature of the NUM provided the structural basis for new forms of organisation to emerge (that is, worker committees), worker committees created the political space, or at least the possibility, for the flourishing of an insurgent trade union (AMCU).[34] The discourse in which various stakeholders sought to enact their agency had shifted with the introduction of worker committees. The new structural context constrained certain practices and ideas, and enabled others. There had been a narrow arena in which workers reluctantly accepted that they should strike to demand a pay increase of about 10 per cent under the auspices of the NUM. The new politics now created an open space to engage around what workers thought they needed in order to live decently. In other words, instead of being based on what management would likely consider rational, mineworkers based their demands on the amount of money which they considered a living wage. (They settled on R12,500.)

Gramsci's analysis of the emergence of trade unions and their relationship to the mobilisation of rank and file workers is instructive in terms of AMCU's burgeoning following workers' resolve to fight for a 'living wage' in the Rustenburg platinum belt from 2012. He cogently pointed out that 'The trade union is not a predetermined phenomenon: it becomes a determinate institution, that is, it assumes a definite historical form to the extent that the strength and will of the workers who are its members impress a policy and propose an aim that define[s] it.'[35]

AMCU is the product of the militant labour struggles – in this case the relatively short-lived but extremely potent worker committees – in the platinum mines. Leaders of the worker committees at Amplats, Implats and Lonmin organised independently from unions and embarked on unprotected strikes. When these strikes ended, worker leaders, in dialogue with management, believed they needed a union to represent them. They chose AMCU. The union began to champion the radical wage demand of R12,500, since rank and file workers had died on the mountain in Marikana waiting for their employer to come to negotiate for that amount. Joseph Mathunjwa took the demand of R12,500 and made it his union's pillar. In a sense, AMCU and Mathunjwa's rise to prominence in the platinum belt has been drawn out of the blood of the 34 mineworkers killed during the Marikana massacre. One prominent AMCU T-shirt proudly worn by mineworkers in the platinum belt reads, 'Never Forget: We Died for a Living Wage … The Struggle Continues.'

The analysis presented below indicates that AMCU is neither the saviour nor the enemy of the working class. Rather, the union as an entity in itself is riding on the wave of the insurgent fervour of the rank and file. The fact that the dominant view of both the state and society at large is that unprotected strikes are 'illegal' (or anarchic) leads us to delegitimise any organisation associated with this behaviour. The committees did not need to sign a paper granting them formal collective bargaining rights in order to gain legitimacy in the eyes of management (who negotiated directly with leaders of the committees during and after the 2012 strike) or the workers (who put their trust in them to negotiate on their behalf). With the exception of some former members of the committee, most workers did not see a firm break with the politics of the worker committees, but rather viewed AMCU (in particular its face and spokesperson, Mathunjwa) as the embodiment of their struggle.

The concept of insurgent trade unionism assists us in analysing the relationship between the past, when workers went on unprotected strikes with their committee at the helm (2012), and the present, when workers go on protected strikes under the AMCU banner (2014). What we witnessed in 2014 was not an ordinary trade union, but one that came into power following a mass upheaval. The notion of insurgent trade unionism both highlights the diversity of existing trade union experiences and practices, and demonstrates how they change over time as a result of shifting structural circumstances. Most importantly it reveals the ways in which trade unions may be driven from below by the rank and file's collective, and in this case insurgent, agency. It also, however, points to new struggles, both within the union and with management.

ENCOUNTERING THE SPIRIT OF MARIKANA

Let me provide some context by explaining briefly how this book evolved. I first went to the Rustenburg platinum belt, and more specifically Marikana, on 18 August 2012 – two days following the massacre. At that time it was unclear even to the most diligent activists and scholars what had actually transpired during the mineworkers' strike at Lonmin. Thapelo Lekgowa and I had been tasked by the South African Research Chair in Social Change with undertaking 'quick-response' academic research on the biographies of the 34 men who had died. Television images at the time (and to some degree since) portrayed the mineworkers as bloodthirsty and violent savages. We wanted to humanise the workers by describing who they actually were: their circumstances, personalities and their (mostly rural) homes of origin. In late August 2012 Thapelo and I met the worker committee below the mountain in Marikana. The men were still on strike. After an extensive discussion with key leaders, they gave us details of the funerals in the rural areas and we went to those that we could go to. Thapelo and I visited people's homes and joined the families in their grief. This, I believe, has had a lasting effect on both of us. Soon afterwards City Press coordinated groups of journalists to take photos of most of the dead men, and to write short biographies of them. We decided it was unnecessary to duplicate this work, and that we should not make researching the mineworkers' families our central task.

By this time, Peter Alexander and his fieldworkers had already begun to provide a critical and alternative view to the dominant one promoted in the media. They suggested that the workers had not been charging at the police, as was claimed, but most were running away from them. This was proved by their being shot in the back or the back of the head, when if they had been facing the police, they would naturally have been shot in the front. (This theory was later confirmed.) I had previously done extensive scholarly work on the politics of service delivery protests, and decided that it would be most useful to place the moment of the massacre in its historical context. This meant tracing chronologically the events of the days and weeks (and eventually months and years) preceding the actual day of the massacre, from the perspective of the workers who had survived. In the meantime, I proceeded with a group of researchers, Thapelo Lekgowa, Botsang Mmope and Bongani Xezwi among others, to record the voices of mineworkers without probing the precise forms of organisation that were created by them in order to forge a social movement. Our preliminary findings were reported at length in an edited collection with Peter Alexander entitled, *Marikana: A View from the Mountain and a Case to Answer.*[36] The research was completed in about three months, and the book came out in late 2012 (and again, in other versions, in 2013): we issued it as quickly as possible because all the contributors wanted urgently to influence popular opinion in favour of the workers.

This present book is an expansion on the work that was done in 2012. It is not about whether the mining companies could afford to pay a living wage of R12,500.[37] Nor is it about the structural changes in capitalism which in part prompted the insurgency.[38] It does not claim to provide a history of the people who have worked at the platinum mines, and it does not reflect the (broadly defined) culture in the mines during the period under investigation. Dunbar Moodie's seminal *Going for Gold* looked at these issues, and concluded that historically whoever had power in the compounds also had control in the mines.[39] At the time of his research most workers lived in compounds, but after 1994 a living out allowance (LOA) was introduced. Following this change, workers have tended to take the allowance and to find their own accommodation, often in informal settlements which have proliferated in the Rustenburg region, and in houses built under the RDP. This changed the pattern of informal organising from the one Moodie reported: subsequently it occurred outside the hostels, next to the workplace and in the changing rooms.

The book does provide some historical background regarding individuals who became leaders in the 2012 and 2014 strikes, but I do not attempt to provide any detailed historical analysis of the rise and decline of the NUM, with the exception of the fairly immediate context in which committees emerged as a response to the shortcomings of the union. It is worth noting, however, that the history of union organising and hegemony in the mines, including the emergence of Mouth Peace Workers Union from 1997 (and its later dominance at certain periods in the late

1990s and early 2000s), shows that battles such as that between AMCU and NUM over union hegemony have been relatively normal occurrences.

It is perhaps most relevant to point out that this book does not advance an argument about the sociology of the massacre itself. The earlier book to which I contributed does this, by examining the events surrounding the massacre from the perspective of the mineworkers who survived it. Rehad Desai's film *Miners Shot Down* (2014) also offers a devastating analysis of the role of the NUM, the police, Lonmin and the ruling ANC.[40] More recently, Greg Marinovich provided an incisive account of the 'real story of the Marikana massacre' and some of the key events and figures that surround it.[41] By now, I think most of those who look into what happened in Marikana will conclude that 16 August was no accident. It was a premeditated attempt to destroy the independent working class organisation which was fermenting at Lonmin.

At the commission of inquiry, Cyril Ramaphosa claimed that 'we are all to blame'. His testimony has unfortunately exemplified the government's approach to dealing with the killings at Marikana. As time passes this looks less and less like a diplomatic explanation that can reasonably be taken at face value, and more like a malign attempt to cover up the truth. From day one the workers have known that truth. The families of the dead men knew from the start that they died fighting for their rights, and this was repeated in early September 2012 during the funerals (see Chapter 3). As the symbolic meaning of Marikana becomes sharpened and engrained in ordinary people's minds, the idea that it was an unfortunate tragedy will become a thing of the past.

To a certain extent the book employs a biographical approach in order to understand the events under investigation. The strength of this approach, according to Brigitta Busch, 'lies in the change of perspective from the observed object to the perceiving and experiencing subject'.[42] Rather than bend a singular argument in relation to an abstract generalisation, the book follows the ethnographic tradition exemplified by David Graeber, as it lays bare the mineworkers' 'cultural universe' in relation to the movement that they initiated and sustained.[43]

Like any good ethnographer, we needed to be patient and on many days we waiting hours to speak, or simply to spend time, with people. Our intention was not only to collect archives, conduct in-depth interviews and then simply report our findings to an academic audience. We spent as much time as possible with mineworkers in their own social settings: cooking together, eating, driving, having informal conversations, listening to speeches at mass meetings and, in the most trying of times, we visited leading mineworkers while they were in jail (on trumped-up charges of public violence). During a relatively short period of time in 2013, we lived with one of the key activists (Bheki Buthelezi) in his spare room in Siraleng, a mining community just outside of Khuseleka, Amplats. During the great 2014 strike, we played a small role in organising in an attempt to extend the strength of the workers.

While in the field we were mostly unaware of the fact that we were challenging traditional approaches to social science that create a stark divide between the researchers and researched. Shadowing Michael Burawoy's distinctive approach, this book is a product of the extent to which we believe that we 'share a common world' with those that we study. The pages which follow are a result of 'a collaborative enterprise between participant and observer'.[44]

It should be clear by now that this book is unapologetically based on the perspective of mineworkers and strike leaders, and their experiences of organising at the mines. Identifying leaders was not a straightforward task. Some workers claimed to be a central part of the leadership structure, but later, when we were able to see mobilisation on the two platinum mines holistically, we concluded they were not. Only by engaging with a wide range of workers over an extended period of time, and also obtaining official documents and notes, did my colleagues and I eventually discover (after more than a year in the field) which people were the core organisers at specific moments. After a significant degree of patience and perseverance, we also uncovered the ways in which leadership changed over time and was multifaceted.

In each interview, we asked workers when they came to the mine, when they first joined a union (in most cases they had joined the NUM at some point in their career), and what their experiences were with the NUM and other unions. We probed the circumstances under which they began to feel betrayed by the union, and paid attention to the sequence of events in the lead-up to the 2012 strikes. We also investigated what followed, with the transition of the committees to the AMCU and then the great 2014 strike. We also questioned interviewees about other key events. With some critical exceptions, there is very little written material on the origins of ad hoc committees in the platinum belt. This meant that it was an arduous and painstaking task to reconstruct the events accurately.

For the actual period when the men were on strike, there are news reports – but these accounts are largely ahistorical and provide an impersonal characterisation of the strikers and the forms of organisation which they sustained. We realised that to reconstruct the lead-up to the strikes at Amplats and Lonmin there needed to be empirical research based on producing very detailed oral histories. Participant observation offered an invaluable tool for understanding the texture of mobilisation at the mines between late 2012 and the end of 2014. Where possible, we used documentation (affidavits and workers' notebooks and saved files) to supplement the interview evidence.

Siphiwe Mbatha came to Marikana one day after the massacre in order to show solidarity with the mineworkers. He provided invaluable assistance in making contacts, translating and interviewing. He conducted more than half of the interviews which colour the text of this book, so he has made a major contribution to it. I could not have written this book without his careful attention to the project. This work, and his unflinching dedication and focus, mean that he deserves to be named as co-author.[45]

Generally, we were able to obtain more thorough information about the workers' mobilisations at Amplats than at Lonmin. This was primarily because the leaders at Amplats were more accessible, while Lonmin branch leaders tended to duck and dive. They were more cautious, and some were very fearful of outsiders. In the most extreme cases informants did not survive to tell their stories. The death of a man we call 'Steve' was a particularly heavy loss, since this critical individual could have provided a detailed account of the emergence of AMCU at Lonmin and in the platinum belt more generally (see Chapter 2). He was murdered (by a person or people not yet identified or charged) during the ongoing bloody tensions at the mine in 2013.

The book is divided into six chapters. Chapter 1, this introduction, provides context for the (almost exclusively empirical) material that follows. The following three chapters form the core of the book.

Chapter 2 describes the origins of the worker committees at both Amplats and Lonmin. This contains perhaps the most contentious material: it indicates that the process began with a conversation in a changing room between two individuals at each mine. Two workers conceptualised the demand for a living wage of R12,500 at Lonmin while two other workers at Amplats conceptualised a living wage of 16,070. In two distinct processes, unfolding under relatively similar circumstances, these two sets of workers proposed to a small number of workers that they should take action to try to achieve their demands. In doing this they embarked on a path that would eventually unite virtually the entire workforce at first Lonmin, and then Amplats.

While there were clearly links between the two strikes, each had an independent dynamic. We therefore chose to divide the material on the 2012 unprotected strikes into two separate chapters. Chapter 3 discusses the emergence of the strike at Lonmin, and hones in on the stubborn bravery which led workers to continue striking following the Marikana massacre. Two things characterised the period following the massacre: mourning over the death of their colleagues, and intensified strike action. The chapter also introduces how left-wing organisations, including the Democratic Left Front (DLF) and the Democratic Socialist Movement (DSM), intervened decisively in order to provide solidarity following the massacre.

Chapter 4 gives a history of the 2012 unprotected strike at Amplats. This has received less scholarly attention than the Lonmin strike, although it occurred at the largest platinum mining company in the world and lasted longer. It demonstrates the way in which leadership, in collaboration with the rank and file, extended strike action and the demand for R16,070 from one shaft (Khuselcka) to the entire Rustenburg region. When CEO Chris Griffith announced the dismissal of 12,000 workers who had not attended the disciplinary hearings to which they were called for participating in an unprotected strike, the employees united yet again and extended their strike to Northam.

Chapter 5 investigates the ways in which leaders in the platinum mines have transitioned from informal to formal organisations – in this case from a worker committee into AMCU branch structures. By disaggregating and highlighting conflicts between the branch structures and the AMCU National Executive Committee (NEC), it reveals that the union is not a homogenous entity, nor is it necessarily more militant than the NUM. As the chapters before begin to suggest, and as I hope Chapter 6 demonstrates, the AMCU is best understood as an insurgent trade union.

Chapter 6 moves forward to consider the great 2014 strike, providing the context and outlining the democratic negotiations which characterised it.

To a certain extent we as researchers have lived through Marikana, and we have dreamed of it at night, but our experiences are nothing compared with those of the men who risked their lives underground and on strike, including on the infamous mountain at Marikana. To them, the strikes literally became a matter of life and death. Many of the workers we have engaged with continue to vow that they would die, if not to realise their demand for a living wage, then for the rights of workers more generally. We have experienced Marikana and the platinum belt strike wave a step removed from these realities. Nevertheless we believe we have been closer to the action, both in physical proximity and in spirit, than virtually anyone else known to us who has done (or is likely to do) extensive research on this topic.

This detailed ethnographic story of the micro-politics of resistance which culminated in the strikes of 2012 and 2014 at Amplats and Lonmin provides a classic example of how seemingly ordinary workers developed a critique of the hegemonic discourse of their employers (and their pocket trade union), formed a counter-discourse based on their own lived experiences, and then undertook a series of actions in order to transform their reality and – unintentionally, at least at first – the political face of South Africa.

2

The Spark Underground

'They opened their eyes. Now they could see that they were being oppressed.'[1]

The 2012 worker committees and the concomitant strikes at Lonmin and Amplats were led by seemingly ordinary rank and file mineworkers. Though the conditions were ripe for mobilising a wide range of employees who had emerged as leaders in various shafts, the worker committees can be traced back to one or two individuals at each mine. These individuals were popular or organic intellectuals in the Gramscian sense (as discussed in Chapter 1). The strikes did not occur magically or with the flick of a switch, but required immense leadership, dedication and organisation. Eric Batstone and colleagues indicate that 'strikes do not just happen. As a form of collective activity they require the development of a degree of unity among those involved.'[2] They further assert that 'Particular individuals or groups are likely first to introduce the idea of a strike and then to persuade their fellows of the validity of this course of action.'[3]

In the case of the platinum mine strike wave of 2012–14, we are indeed able to identify precisely the 'particular individuals and groups' who introduced the idea of the strike demands and then 'persuaded their fellows of the validity of this course of action', but some background is necessary first. The 2012 unprotected strikes at Amplats and Lonmin took place on the back of an unprotected strike at Impala (the other major platinum producer) which began in mid-January of that year and was led by the RDOs.

RDOs are the workers who actually drill into the rock at the stope face into which explosives are inserted in order to blast out the rock-containing

19

ore. Since the introduction of the current (known as Paterson) pay scales in 1973 they are some of the least well-paid underground workers although they do the most dangerous work. Almost as dangerous, however, is the job of the winch drivers, who operate the scraper winches that haul the broken rock down into trams that move it to the shaft for hoisting.

By the end of January 2012 at Impala the unrest had spread beyond the confines of RDOs and virtually the entire workforce had downed tools. They won an increase to monthly pay of R9,000, and the strike ended on 3 March. Discontent with the NUM had come to a head at Impala because the union had opposed the popular unprotected strike. As was not unusual in South African mine strikes, substantial violence was used against strike breakers and several deaths occurred. By the end of the strike, management had fired 18,000 of the striking mineworkers. This effectively ended their union membership. About 11,000 others had resigned as NUM members at Impala by 30 March 2012. The perceived shortcomings of the union at each of the three major platinum mining companies, especially its failure to defend workers subject to dismissal for engaging in unprotected strikes, provided the structural conditions in which informal worker committees took hold.

At one specific shaft at both the Amplats and Lonmin mines, workers began organising independently from each other in small groups from April to August 2012, meeting first underground and then above ground. Two RDOs provided the impetus in May 2012 for a demand for a R12,500 basic wage at Lonmin. They were both workers who had replaced those dismissed during an earlier strike over NUM leadership at Karee mine in 2011, so they had only been with the company for a year when they began organising. They initially met in the changing rooms after work, and worked out what was, in the initial stages, merely a request. Thereafter, they met in small groups with five to ten RDOs until their numbers reached about 100. At that point, on 21 June 2012, they all marched to the management at their mine – Karee – and presented what had then become a demand. The manager eventually informed them that the R12,500 could not be given to workers at Karee only. Any decision about wages had to be for all three of Lonmin's mines (the others were Eastern and Western). This provided the worker leaders from Karee with the impetus to unite all the shafts at Lonmin, leading to a mass meeting of RDOs on 9 August 2012, which set in process the events leading up to the infamous massacre at Marikana.

A similar organisational process, completely independently of the events at Lonmin, took place at Amplats, in Khuseleka mine, where two winch drivers who worked together during the night shift were at the forefront of organising workers. As was the case at Lonmin, they drafted a memorandum in the changing rooms, this time for a wage demand that amounted to R16,070. Other shafts at Amplats were also organising informally but there was not as yet any plan for uniting all the shafts into company-wide strike action.

The following chapters introduce these largely uncelebrated leaders at both Lonmin and Amplats, and demonstrate how they established independent bodies – worker committees – and at the same time also ushered in a new union, AMCU, which Impala workers had already joined en masse. The balance of this chapter hones in on the 2011 strike at Karee mine, which provided part of the impetus for the formation of the worker committee at Lonmin. I go on to discuss events at Lonmin leading up to the Marikana massacre, before turning back to developments at Amplats, which were well under way prior to the police killings of 16 August 2012.

LONMIN: THE 2012 STRIKE AND THE EMERGENCE OF AMCU

To a significant extent – albeit indirectly – the 2012 strike at Lonmin resulted from the complex and tumultuous internal dynamics within the NUM itself. The situation in Karee mine in early to mid-2011 highlighted divisions within the NUM, and in particular the relationship between the branch and the regional offices. One man, who was born in the early 1980s and arrived at Lonmin in 2006, eventually joining the NUM at Karee mine, told us this mine had five NUM branch leaders in 2011.[4] One was Mawethu Joseph Steven, also known as Steve Khululekile, who was popularly known as 'Steve' to the workers. He became a prominent shop steward in the mid-2000s and was the NUM branch chairperson at Karee. He was a leader who was, according to the *Daily Maverick*, 'a thorn in the side of the NUM'.[5] Whenever the NUM branch met with the regional office, he would stand up for the interests of workers – regardless of the outcome and its implications. He had a 'loud voice' and was largely perceived to be a genuine representative of the workers.[6]

One worker, Tholakele Dlunga (nicknamed 'Bhele') from Western Platinum, had come to know Steve while he was active at Lonmin. He recalled that Steve became 'an enemy of the NUM and then they decided to like chase him away from the organisation NUM because he was very vocal with issues of the workers'.[7] From the perspective of Bhele and many other workers, Steve spoke 'the truth'. When he blamed the NUM officials for filling 'their [own] pockets' this led to his expulsion. Bhele described his leadership style as follows:

> He did not like for someone to eat alone and [he] always used to say that 'when you are a leader the people that you are leading are the ones leading you'. And [he also said] 'if you are a cook, you do not cook for yourself, you cook for other people. So you cannot cook and eat alone … you had to make sure that they were full first before you ate.[8]

Another worker remembered that the workers 'really trusted [these five men in the branch and especially Steve] at the time. Whenever the workers sent them to say something they said it as it was'.[9] Despite his admirable qualities Steve did not play by the rules, however, nor was he entirely democratic. In 2011, he decided for himself that he would not be challenged for the role of branch chairperson, and informed the regional NUM office of this. The office staff perhaps unsurprisingly responded that it would be 'unconstitutional' not to have an election for the position. Steve then held a mass meeting at Karee, and a man named Bongani attempted to stand against him. Steve addressed the workers and allegedly said, 'Comrades, you said that anybody who tried to contest my position is a spy. And now there are people who are showing; you must deal with him.' Bongani was then taken to a room and then stoned to death.[10]

NUM regional representatives subsequently held a mass meeting with the workers at Karee. The workers stoned the regional office holders, who fled the mine. According to a communication from the regional secretary of the NUM to Lonmin:

> the branch has been dissolved as we speak and that has been communicated to all committee members in a meeting held on the 12th May 2011 with them at the regional office. In the same meeting, Steve Khululekile and Daniel Mongwaketsi [the branch secretary] were suspended from all union activities.[11]

Over the next week, the NUM office at Karee was closed. Lonmin management responded to the NUM, telling its officials that about 700 workers had marched to the vice president of Karee on 17 May and demanded that 'the Karee Branch particularly Steven should be reinstated by the Region'.[12] The workers reported that they:

> found out that the region had called our [NUM] branch officers and suspended comrade Steve and comrade Dan and divided our branch committee. They were told that when they return they must not talk to the workers, they were not allowed to say anything to the workers. We as workers wrote a memorandum and took it to the management requesting for leaders because we didn't know what was happening to our leaders.[13]

Steve approached the workers to say he had been fired and asked them, 'What are you going to do about it?'[14] On 18 May all the workers at Karee went on an unprotected strike. The following day representatives of the regional NUM office met with the strikers, who said, 'All we wanted was our leaders and for our office to be opened so we could continue with our work'.[15] The regional leaders attempted to address a mass meeting at Karee, but the workers refused to engage and simply dispersed.[16] In the end, all 9,000 striking mineworkers were suspended. Most applied for re-employment and were rehired, but 1,400 were considered 'trouble-makers' and were not.[17]

According to Joseph Mathunjwa, who became president of AMCU from 2001, from 2010 until just prior to these incidents the union had a small presence among subcontracted shaft sinkers at the Karee mine. Mathunjwa was born in 1965 and was from, in his words, 'the family of priesthood under the Salvation Army'. He completed his matric, but there were no resources to further his education and he began working in construction at Witbank. He then spent a short time at Tweenfontein Colliery until he became employed at Douglas Colliery. He recalled that in 1986:

> I didn't wait to join a union to express how I see things. Firstly, when I realised when we were confined in the hostel, [with] no transport for black workers to take them to the locations [townships], to stay with their families, I was the first black person who jumped into a white [only] bus in 1986, forcing my way to the location. Subsequent to that I was the first black person at Douglas who led a campaign [for] workers to have houses outside the mine premises. So I led many campaigns.[18]

The NUM was present at Douglas Colliery. However, its officials were not focused on people's homes or living conditions, but rather, he recollected, 'on disciplinary hearing[s]'.[19] Mathunjwa became known by management at the company for addressing a wider range of concerns than the union officials raised. It was not long before workers approached him to be part of the collective organising force, the NUM. He joined the union, but because of the forceful way in which he dealt with issues management transferred him to a more isolated area where he did not have regular contact with the mass of workers. In spite of this impediment he was elected as a shaft steward for the NUM. He soon waged a battle against management regarding bonuses for workers who go underground, which the workers won.

Mathunjwa's involvement as an organiser in the mines took a new turn when the existing branch committee was voted out because they were failing to address the needs of the workers. By the end of the 1990s, Mathunjwa had been elected as the new chairperson of the branch. He believed that NUM officials in concert with management attempted to 'sabotage' him, and he was 'sort of dismissed'. The workers, however, responded that 'No, we have to do something, because Joseph was fighting for our cause. So an injury to one will be an injury to all!' The workers went to work but stayed underground for ten days in protest. Mathunjwa commented, 'it was difficult. Sometimes there was no food, no water. They had to drink the water from the roof. They sacrificed.'[20]

Gwede Mantashe, who was then general secretary of the NUM, called Mathunjwa to a disciplinary hearing. He refused to attend it on the grounds that he believed that Mantashe was a biased party. Mathunjwa was then expelled. He recalls the key events that followed:

> the workers called a meeting. They said they are going to resign from NUM, which, of course, they did. They called a meeting, and I was called in. They said I must go and look for a union, which they might join, which I did. I called different unions for interviews. The workers were not happy. So they mandated me to form a union. It's not that I formed a union, I was mandated [to do so].[21]

The AMCU was registered in 2001, with only one branch at the time, at Douglas. It had one basic office in Witbank, and Mathunjwa was the main organiser. 'There was no secretary. I was doing everything – recruiting, going to CCMA [the Commission for Conciliation, Mediation and Arbitration], holding mass meetings – for quite some time.'[22] So a new union, whose formation had been prompted by an internal spat within the NUM, was now in its embryonic stage. Mathunjwa was at the helm, largely holding the AMCU together on his own. This was to have a strong influence over the way in which he organised at later stages, when the union had a much larger support base.

Let me fast-forward to the main story. It became evident that a similar process to the one at Douglas in the late 1990s was getting under way at the Karee mine in mid-2011. It was the view of the striking mineworkers that the NUM had in fact dismissed its own members, and increasingly they saw it as a pocket union. They sought to have their branch leader Steve reinstated. This put the NUM in a difficult position, since Steve had undoubtedly contravened the union constitution. The AMCU was now well positioned in Karee to fill the vacuum left by worker dissatisfaction with the NUM. The two unions continued to battle to sign up a majority of the workers at the Karee mine between 2011 and mid-2012. The workers who had been dismissed and rehired were up for grabs. As one worker explained:

> at the time AMCU was recruiting, NUM was also recruiting on the side. The reason NUM was recruiting here in Karee during that time when they were firing workers and re-electing some of the workers, everything was new then. If you had joined NUM it was cancelled then you had to start afresh and rejoin and there was nowhere to run to. You've been re-employed which means you have no union, you have nothing. So to the workers, it was evident [to us] that NUM cannot be trusted if you can sleep knowing that you have a union then the next day you are fired and your union has cancelled you and you don't have a union anymore. The workers' terms were cancelled by NUM. They said we should be fired instead of defending us and representing us to the employer, you see?[23]

Dumisani Nkalitshana, who was then an organiser for the AMCU, visited the Karee mine following the dismissal to engage with the fired workers. He agreed to take their case to the CCMA. One worker at Karee highlighted the process through which AMCU began to garner support and obtained an access agreement at Karee mine from 2011:

> they explained that this is AMCU, it's a registered union that stands for the workers. Then the workers started registering with AMCU ... and then when AMCU realised that the number of members was increasing

AMCU challenged the employer and said 'here is the stop order, we have got members' ... it was [then] discovered that [having] the majority of AMCU [members] allows them to get certain office[s] although they are still recruiting and don't have too many members.[24]

By the time of the 9 August 2012 strike, NUM had barely 20 per cent membership at the Karee mine while AMCU had over 50 per cent. Across the three Lonmin mines (Karee, Eastern and Western), however, NUM represented 58 per cent of the total workforce.[25] This was to change drastically in the months to follow.

THE SPARK UNDERGROUND AT LONMIN

Alfonse Ramaola Mofokeng – perhaps the unacclaimed architect of the R12,500 demand at Lonmin – is a humble and articulate Sotho man, born on 9 December 1979 in Botshabelo, the third largest town in the Free State. He speaks slowly and precisely, highlighting to the listener the significance of each word, and repeats himself often for clarity. Possibly because of the harshness of conditions underground, he looks older than he actually is. Like many other black men who later came to work at the mines, he was unable to complete his matric because of financial and other difficulties. He did not finish standard 5 (equivalent to US grade 7), and went to work at a farm called Montic Dairy at the age of about 14. In 1999 he was contracted to work at Goedgevonden Colliery in Mpumalanga, and within five years he had become an RDO at Bleskop mine (Khuseleka 1). When he arrived there, he joined Mouth Peace (the Mouth Peace Workers Union) because 'NUM didn't have the truth.'[26]

Officially founded in 1997, and at one time the majority union at Anglo Platinum, Mouth Peace still had strong representation among rock drillers at the time Mofokeng arrived. Mofokeng's ability to represent the interests of workers materialised for the first time, and between 2006 and 2009 he acted as a Mouth Peace shop steward and became deputy secretary of the branch. During that time, he recalls, he learned a great deal about leading workers and the channels through which they could press for changes outside of established bargaining structures. In about 2010, he became an RDO at Impala, but he explained that he 'didn't last long because ... the money it was so little.'[27] This was, of course, prior to the 2012 strike at Impala.

Following the dismissals of May 2011, which led to the selective re-hiring of workers, Lonmin representatives went in search of workers, especially RDOs, because the decision to not take back some perceived troublemakers had left gaps in their workforce. The positions were soon filled, and Mofokeng was among those who took them. In mid-2011 he arrived at the Karee mine and joined NUM, the dominant union at Lonmin:

> When I arrived I was part of those people to try to build NUM in Karee in [the second half of] 2011. But in 2012, I saw that the NUM does not get the membership in Karee. It's where I thought about this. I found that AMCU has got the majority in Karee and NUM does not have the majority but I was a member of it.[28]

Mofokeng had spent less than a year working at Lonmin before concluding that workers deserved more money for the tough work they were undertaking day after day. He had gained experience working in the three largest platinum mines in the world. His attitude was also shaped by his coming from Impala, where RDOs were then (in 2012) making more money than they did at Lonmin. At Karee the machinery they used was lighter and designed for single operators,[29] but Mofokeng was nevertheless further disappointed that at Karee, unlike in the other shafts – Eastern and Western – RDOs had no assistants to carry the cumbersome machines:

> I found the money at Lonmin, it's small. As the money is so small, it was clear that Lonmin doesn't have the truth. It was apartheid. They don't treat people equally. And they are doing the same job. Those that they [management] liked, they gave them assistants. And there are those that they … don't give assistants. That's the thing that hurt my heart the most, when I look at my salary. The money, it's small … after deduction, it comes to R4,000, R3,900. That's the thing that triggers me. And then I end up calling the guys and say, 'Hey… let's approach the management about this money.'[30]

Prior to meeting with others and discussing whether they should demand a rise to R12,500, he thought about the situation himself:

> This 12,500, when I was on leave at home [in May 2012], I thought, I sat down, I took my pay slip and said, 'No, this is not the money I

have to get when I am drilling.' So I saw that I got 5,000 at that time. It's when I demanded 12,500, which I thought was a maximum before we approached the management, and I thought the time when we approached him it's where we are going to sit down and see what we can do. But I know and I took the understanding that when I meet him, maybe it can come to be 8,000 or 7,500.[31]

Mofokeng met a Xhosa man named Bulelani Magqabini in the changing rooms in late May 2012 after completing a tough day's work underground. They had both been working at Lonmin for less than a year, but that day they began a process of uniting workers – one that has gone down in history. Mofokeng recalls, 'I started to talk with other guys here about going to approach management because we work hard.' He told the workers, 'We don't have to meet these union guys because we will confuse ourselves. Because there are two [unions] we don't know which will agree and which will disagree. It's our right to approach management if things are not going well.'[32]

Magqabini did not have any notable previous experience as a leader of the miners. He was born on 24 August 1976 in the Eastern Cape in Dutywa, where he began his schooling. He then moved to Germiston and continued his education. In 1999 he took his matric, but failed it. He attempted to join the South African Defence Force (SADF) but without success, and in 2001 he began doing contract work at a gold mine in Klerksdorp where his aunt's husband was employed. Once Magqabini had gained enough experience he became a permanent employee at Klerksdorp between May 2004 and 2011. During that time, he was a member of NUM.[33]

Magqabini had also begun working at Karee in May/June 2012. He and Mofokeng chose to join different unions. Magqabini remembered that when he first arrived at Karee:

People were joining AMCU. Then I also didn't waste my time, I joined AMCU. At that time we were joining it in private. There was this other place here in block 8, we used to join there in the hostel. I didn't go to NUM, I just went straight to AMCU .... I heard that during the first strike [in 2011] NUM was the one that said workers must be let go. [Those were] the people who were replaced by us. So they fired people when they were fighting for their rights. So AMCU was still a new union and it was promising and it cares for the workers. So I wanted to give them a shot and see what they have for us.[34]

The NUM became increasingly unpopular at Karee, and over time the AMCU developed a stronghold primarily because it had a strong new regional organiser in Steve. Mofokeng, however, decided to join the NUM. He believed that as a new employee, he would find it beneficial to be part of the dominant union at Lonmin.[35]

Mofokeng recalled that during a conversation he and Magqabini had in late May when the two RDOs had first met in the changing rooms, 'we reached a point where we talked about combining workers'.[36] The two men agreed that 'even if it can be like five RDOs, it will be fine. Five to ten people and discuss about this issue'.[37] At the outset they had no intention of striking. Their main concern was that management take note of the hard work that they were doing underground as RDOs with no assistants. They also discussed what basic salary would adequately compensate them for their work, and agreed on a figure of R12,500. Mofokeng explained:

> We sat down, me and Magqabini, two of us. And then we said, because we see that we are earning 4,500, some 4,900, [we thought our salary should be] 5,000 plus [an additional] 5,000 .... We took the wages we are earning, we multiply it times two. And then we saw that if we can take the salary that we are getting and multiply it twice, that this will be an amount of money that can satisfy us ... according to the work we are doing .... That's why when I spoke to the workers I said, '12,500 is the money that can satisfy us'.[38]

In fact R10,000 was approximately twice the then salary of an RDO, but the two men reckoned that it was worth asking for the additional R2,500 by calling on management's 'sympathy' for the workers: 'He can put some other cents that come from him [and] when it combines with this R10,000, it will be like R12,500.'[39]

Magqabini knew another RDO whom he called to discuss their concerns. Here I shall call him Mandla. Mandla was older and had far more experience working at Lonmin. He was born in the late 1960s in a village called Ndabakazi in the Eastern Cape. He went to primary school in his village, but left after completing standard 4 in 1984. His father was not able to assist his family, and Mandla had the responsibility of being the eldest child, so he left school to do construction work. He stayed in Alexandra Township from 1988 until 1990, when his cousin from Rustenburg paid him a visit and persuaded him to move in with him at

Wonderkop, hostel number 1, and look for a job at the mines. In 1991 he obtained a job at Lonrho (before it became Lonmin) at a time when people at the company were beginning secretly to join the NUM. He recalled that 'the Boers [that is, the white management] did not want it [the NUM] but the NUM became recognised between 1993 and 1994'.[40]

Mandla worked at Bob mine (as the Eastern mine was previously known) until 2009, took a nine-month break and then came back to Karee in 2010. He participated in the strike demanding the reinstatement of Steve in 2011. He described the process of selective rehiring after the strike:

> If your boss did not like you he would put your name on a list of those to be fired or not re-employed. But I was lucky because as for me at work I do speak if I don't like something but I also do my work well. I think they realised that I might be talkative but I also do my work properly. Plus I was not often absent.[41]

He was thus was able to remain at Karee. Following the strike the workers there had no union for several months until Steve began to recruit them to the AMCU. Karee soon became the only Lonmin shaft at which the AMCU was dominant.

When the three mineworkers met, Mofokeng realised that '[Mandla] even him, he was aware of this issue that we are talking about. That Lonmin is robbing us, the money that they are giving us [is too little] and we are working hard.'[42] The three men called a meeting with other Karee RDOs. They organised by word of mouth, and at the first meeting there were indeed the five or ten people that Mofokeng and Magqabini had hoped for. They discussed the fact that at Karee, RDOs were paid the same amount as other workers at the Eastern and Western shafts, but unlike the workers there they were not given an assistant. Mofokeng explained that 'Karee was worse. They make it exceptional by not giving it assistants. Karee was working very hard …. That's why I end up doing what we are doing, because they [management] do it on purpose.'[43]

Many of the RDOs were hesitant to join, perhaps believing that nothing would come of it. Others feared they would be fired. Based on his conversations with the rank and file, Mofokeng explained, 'The previous year people were fired and they were confused about what I was doing because they thought that when this strike starts again it will happen again.' He told them in response that 'it would not repeat again'. He later pointed out (following the 2012 strike) that 'No one is gone, everyone is there, with the exception of those who were killed, [but] no one was fired'.[44]

The organisers produced pamphlets to mobilise RDOs for a second meeting, which was held around early June. About 45–50 RDOs attended, and the question of a R12,500 basic salary was the main issue of concern. Michael Da Costa, who took the senior manager post at Karee 3 shaft from 2009, recollected that he had seen an A4 sheet of paper preparing for what would be the third meeting of RDOs on 21 June.[45] He further confirmed that there was 'no indication thereon of any trade union involvement' and that other staff with whom he worked had also seen these posters, but that previous meetings had been fairly small.[46]

Da Costa was concerned that he might have to deal directly with the issue. He noted that following the 2011 strike at Karee, 'Lonmin implemented a "Line of Sight" strategy in terms of which management would, where possible, communicate directly with employees to improve the effectiveness of direct management communication and to identify problems and issues quickly and to resolve them at the lowest possible level'.[47] Da Costa also knew that RDOs at Amplats and Impala were being paid more than they were at Lonmin, making this a potential hotspot for grievances. The facts that RDOs at Impala had sought to engage management directly earlier in the year and that RDOs at Amplats were in talks with management regarding salary increases were also on his mind.[48]

LONMIN MANAGEMENT CONSIDERS THE DEMAND FOR R12,500

Mofokeng recalled that at the third informal meeting of RDOs which took place at Karee hostel on 21 June, the consciousness of the workers began to shift. He could not have realised at the time the significance that his seemingly minor organisational tactics would later have not only for Lonmin as a company, but for South Africa as a country. He was the spark underground which would eventually ignite the entire workforce at Lonmin. More than 100 RDOs were present at the meeting, and the mood no longer signalled quiescence. 'They started opening their eyes. Now they are seeing that they were oppressed,' he explained.[49] The RDOs at Lonmin, in the Karee mine in particular, had been undertaking strenuous labour, some for merely months and others for decades. Their earlier experiences highlighted for them that their unions were inadequate, and that at any rate the unions would divide them (given the membership pattern at Karee).

The workers decided during the meeting to march with their grievances to management. According to Da Costa this march took place at 5.00 pm, and 300 RDOs were present.[50] The security personnel, however, did not allow them to enter the premises. Da Costa said that a security worker had informed him that 'the crowd requested me to meet them outside of my office and to address them directly'. He did not agree. Instead, he sent 'a message to the crowd, informing that that I would not address a large crowd on such short notice'. Da Costa then asked them to put their issues in writing so that they could be responded to in due time. Security, however, told him that the workers were claiming to be illiterate and were therefore requesting to see him in person.[51]

As Mofokeng recalled, 'I know [sic] exactly what I was planning.' When questioned about which union he belonged to, he once again reiterated:

At that time when I approach[ed] Da Costa, I know exactly that I was the member of NUM because AMCU at that time did not, did not deduct my money. At that time AMCU did not deduct my money when I started this thing. I was a member of NUM at that time.[52]

Despite the fact that he speaks clear English and is able to read and write as a former secretary of Mouth Peace, he explained that he 'told them that the memorandum that I have is in my mind. I just gave a plan to these guys [RDOs]. I was not known in this company. I was a new recruit, but from that time I took that space because I know what I wanted.' He told Da Costa 'the memorandum was in my mind, it's just that I didn't know how to write it.'[53]

Magqabini detailed how he and Mofokeng were chosen to engage with management: 'we came to the office as a mass but only two people got inside and talked with him [the manager of Karee]. It was me ... and Mofokeng .... The workers elected us at the gate to go and talk to the management.'[54] The meeting therefore involved one NUM member, one AMCU member and Michael Da Costa. Da Costa himself noted that the representatives of the RDOs had indicated to him that they did not want to involve union structures in the deliberations since this grievance was a matter for RDOs only. Da Costa described the meeting as one that was respectful, not aggressive and non-confrontational. Nevertheless, when Mofokeng requested a R12,500 basic salary for all RDOs at the Karee mine, Da Costa was flabbergasted since this amounted to a wage increase of 150 per cent:

> I once again expressed my dissatisfaction with the situation and indicated [to] them that RDOs earn approximately R9,000 per month. In this regard I was referring to their total package. I had thought, when the figure of R12,500 was first mentioned, that the demand related to the total monthly package. Magqabine [sic] and Mofokeng immediately stated to me that RDOs earned approximately R5,000 per month. At that stage, I realised that they were seeking an increase in their *basic salary* to R12,500 per month.[55]

Mofokeng was clear that he had intended to get this type of response from the management:

> Because I know when I saw these things in NUM and in Mouth Peace. It's where I saw that when you approach a management [official], you approach him with a clear mind. In a sense that's when he comes to what you are talking about. He thinks about this [only then] and you have already thought about this then he comes, you are coming, then you approach each other. Then it's happening the way it's happening now.[56]

Indeed, when Mofokeng put the demand on the table, he already understood that Da Costa would indicate that he was unable to meet it completely: 'We were not even looking for him to give us this 12,500, but we were trying to talk to him, just to raise our [salaries] … Maybe if it was to be at least 8,000, but we demanded 12,500.'[57]

This appears to have been the first time that management learned about the demand for R12,500. Da Costa insisted that such an increase would need to go through proper channels and would have to be dealt with during wage negotiations. The next negotiations were set to take place at the end of 2013. Da Costa summarised his conversation with the two RDOs as follows:

> I asked Magqabane [sic] and Mofokeng how they had arrived at the figure of R12,500. They simply stated to me that that amount seemed like a good and reasonable amount. I then asked them whether they realised that if they were to be paid a basic monthly salary of R12,500

RDOs would in effect earn more than team leaders. In response, they stated to me that I should not complicate the issue. They said that team leaders do not do much work anyway, whereas RDOs worked in tough conditions and wished to be compensated for the difficult circumstances in which they worked.[58]

Magqabini took care during the meeting to insist this was 'not a strike, but a memorandum of requests', that the intention was 'not to have a negative impact on production', and that this was why they were approaching the management directly. Moreover, he said that he understood that 'wage negotiations are for everyone and [that] this is specific for RDOs due to hard labour'. Da Costa stated he needed to consult with Lonmin management, 'as the demand is unreasonable', particularly given the 'tough economic conditions' and the fact that other mines were closing as a result. The meeting lasted for about an hour, and the two RDO representatives were told to come back in two weeks to find a way forward regarding the issue.[59] Mofokeng and Magqabini left the room and joined the workers, who drifted away from the offices.

Da Costa also decided to involve other executives at Lonmin given the potential graveness of the concerns raised:

> Immediately after the meeting, I contacted Mark Munroe ... who is Lonmin's executive vice-president for mining. I reported the incident to him and told him about the request which had been made by Magqabine [sic] and Mofokeng. Munroe informed me that he would table the issue at Exco [Lonmin management's Executive Committee]. He request that I prepare a note in this regard .... I did prepare a note, which I understand was tabled at the next Exco Meeting held on Monday, 28 June 2012.[60]

Prior to the second meeting with management, the workers decided to elect five representatives to speak for them. They chose Mofokeng, Magqabini and Mandla since they were trusted to represent the workers, and two others.

These five visited Da Costa on 2 July to further pursue the negotiations. Da Costa informed the five RDOs that he 'could not give them any final answer on the issue since the Exco was still dealing with their demand'.[61] In his opinion the meeting 'remained relatively cordial', but 'the RDO representatives were becoming increasingly more assertive on the issue'.[62] Da Costa agreed to set up a task team to examine the work they were doing. He told them that he was unable to give them the R12,500, but that there was indeed an amount he could give to RDOs at Karee (since they did not have assistants like Eastern and Western). This appeared to the workers to be a delaying tactic, and their underlying feeling from the meeting was that Lonmin was not going to give them what they were asking.

They reported back directly to the masses when they finished work at 3 pm that day. Magqabini remembered, 'we had a meeting in the hostel. We told them that management doesn't have money'.[63] The workers were disgruntled. They decided to wait for Da Costa and others at the entrance to the building of their offices. They soon learned that he was not there, and instead they found the human resources manager at Karee, Tumelo Nkisi. The workers told him that 'we are not going to work tomorrow'. Nkisi pleaded, 'Guys please don't do that …. [Rather] come back [at a later stage].'[64] He convinced the RDOs to leave, and come back in three weeks' time.

Over the next few weeks, the issue of RDOs requesting more money was raised with the Lonmin Exco. Da Costa was asked by Mark Munroe, Lonmin's executive vice president for mining, to give the RDOs an allowance if that was likely to prevent a strike. While Da Costa did not engage directly with union representatives at this time, Nkisi reportedly did speak to the branch secretaries of both the NUM and AMCU at Karee. Perhaps because the RDOs were not being led by a union, and Lonmin had engaged directly with workers, the two indicated that this was Lonmin's problem rather than their own.

On 23 July, 500 people marched and waited outside Da Costa's offices. The same five RDOs went inside. Da Costa told them that Exco would not agree to the R12,500 demand, but that they were considering providing an unspecified amount to RDOs. Da Costa described the RDOs at this meeting as being more aggressive than previously. He 'could sense the potential for strike action'.[65] The five RDOs went back outside to provide feedback to the marchers, and asked Da Costa to address them. Lonmin security was 'anxious' about his doing this, and at first he refused. However, he changed his mind. Initially, he spoke in English, but upon request switched to Fanagalo, in which he was fluent. For the Farlam commission, he recapped the speech which he gave to the 500 marchers on 23 July:

I told them that that manner in which they had approached the whole issue was wrong, because it had to be dealt with through established structures. I further told that that Lonmin would and could not agree to an increase of R12,500 to their basic salary, and that the matter should be dealt with in the recognised bargaining structures. I then mentioned to the crowd that the issue which had been raised with me was referred to Exco and that Exco had decided on an RDO allowance.[66]

He was reportedly asked by a mineworker, 'What do we do tomorrow?' and subsequently, 'How do we return to work when you have not given us what we want?' He then responded that they must go back to work, and that a failure to do so would result in the workers undertaking an illegal strike. Eventually security forces ended the meeting, and encouraged the marchers to leave the area. The crowd, however, continued to ask questions about the allowance, while others asked about the R12,500. Da Costa told them he would have an answer regarding the allowance within a week.

The decision to give the RDOs an R750 allowance was signed by Exco on 27 July.[67] Da Costa later met with representatives of UASA and Solidarity (two other major trade unions in the mines under investigation), who were 'supportive' of the RDO allowance, but advised him 'there was a risk of the RDO allowance upsetting the collective bargaining structure, and having a knock-on effect on other job grades'.[68] They could not have been more correct. The NUM regional office made a similar point.

Since the AMCU had a significant membership at Karee, Da Costa and Nkisi arranged a meeting with AMCU representatives on 29 July 2012. They met with Steve, who had become a regional organiser, and four other AMCU representatives. These representatives told the two managers that if Lonmin wanted to give the RDOs an allowance, they should do so. Significantly, Da Costa recalled that he got the distinct impression that 'AMCU was trying to portray to me that it (as a union) was not involved in the matter.'[69]

The fourth and final meeting of the RDOs with Da Costa took place on 30 July, a week later. Da Costa requested Mofokeng to come alone, but Mofokeng thought it was wise to bring another person, so he called Magqabini and the two of them went to the meeting.[70] Da Costa then offered the RDOs at Karee money to compensate for the fact that at Karee the single-person drills did not require assistants, but he went beyond that. The offer was R750 for unassisted RDOs, R500 for assisted RDOs, and an additional R250 for assistant RDOs.[71]

It might have been expected that this increase would have kept the RDOs at bay, given that the RDO worker committee had largely been set up because at Karee the RDOs had no assistants. But by now the R12,500 had become engrained in their minds, and in the minds of those workers waiting for the report back. At this stage, it seemed, it was already R12,500 or nothing. The two RDOs therefore responded to the offer by saying that 'you [Da Costa] can give us your R750 but what we are saying is that we need R12,500'.[72] Mandla recalled that the two reported to Da Costa who told them that:

[all] he had was R750 ... so they called me and we called a meeting to inform the workers that the boss was only offering R750. They [the workers] decided that they were not going to refuse the amount but they were going to continue to demand R12,500. Da Costa said that's all he has and the R 12,500 was not within his reach. And [he] gave an example that if he paid the Karee miners R12,500, Wonderkop would want R16,000 and Eastern R21,000 – it will [therefore] confuse the company. [He said] 'I have R750. The R12,000 [short for 12,500] is for Lonmin.' So we left Da Costa.[73]

The representatives apparently interpreted Da Costa to have indicated that while the R750 could be given to workers at Karee, the R12,500 that they were requesting could not be determined for Karee only, but was a matter for all of Lonmin to consider.

So the management's attempt to quell the workers with an offer of R750 per month backfired. The relatively speedy unilateral decision indicated to workers that the company had money sitting in its coffers. The isolation of RDOs at Karee would soon be broken, and this would have major ramifications for the development of the strike. When the representatives reported back to the RDOs at Karee, those RDOs decided to invite the RDOs from Eastern and Western to join them in a collective struggle for R12,500.

3

The Spirit of Marikana is Born

People have died already so we have nothing more to lose ... we are
going to continue fighting for what we believe is a legitimate fight for
living wages. We would rather die like our comrades than back down.[1]

To a significant extent management's response to the RDO representatives
was responsible for extending the demand of R12,500 beyond the one
shaft, Karee, where it was first independently popularised. According to
Mofokeng, 'we told all the shafts... that we need to unite. So that we
can fight for this 12,500 [together] because of the hard work that we
are doing.'[2] RDOs at Eastern and Western Platinum in Lonmin were not
indifferent, they also desired more money and were gradually becoming
disillusioned with the NUM.

A young man I shall call Thomas, who worked at the Eastern shaft,
was one of these workers. Born in mid-1981, he grew up in Qumbu
in the Eastern Cape and left school after finishing standard 9 in 1999
because he lacked money for food and transport. Like others in his community, he lived far away from his school and walked 45 kilometres each
day to get there, leaving at 3.00 am each morning in order to arrive at
7.50 am. Dissatisfied with the low wages he had received from other jobs,
he signed up at Lonmin in April 2011 and became an RDO. He joined
the NUM at Eastern because it was 'the only union that was working in
the mine [at the time]'.[3] There were regular mass meetings with RDOs
and the NUM shop stewards, and he was one of the ordinary members
who stood up at meetings in May and June 2012 in order to demand
that the NUM leaders negotiate for better wages and working conditions.
Many workers, including Thomas, hoped the NUM would provide positive feedback regarding their demands, but its officials never did so. He

recollected, 'I am waiting a long, long time. Thereafter waiting I take [the] decision on 9 August [2012] to organise the RDOs to come in the stadium to talk about what to do …. [Because] this money is so small. It's not enough.' The idea emerged of holding a mass meeting of all RDOs, and Thomas (no doubt with others) informed the leaders of the NUM branch committee at Eastern that there needed to be 'a central meeting'. He sought to give them confidence. Believing they were in a position to assist, he told them, 'NUM you can do it.'[4]

The union failed to respond, however, and workers took it upon themselves to unite with other shafts. Bhele (mentioned in Chapter 2) was another who helped organise a meeting which took place on 9 August. He was born on 27 June 1978 in a poor rural village called Libode in the Eastern Cape, where he is a pastor in the Zionist Christian Church. Like many of the other workers who held leadership positions in recreational spaces and at schools where they grew up, his position as a pastor informed his involvement in workers' politics at Lonmin. He started in the mines at Anglo-American Platinum and in 2005 began working at Lonmin. By 2006, Bhele had become involved in wage negotiations along with the NUM. He was also a union safety representative between 2009 and 2012. According to Bhele:

> These issues of money stretch far back. We have been complaining for a very long time. We even tried to meet with our leaders, the NUM, to discuss the matter. In August we decided we were going to take further steps …. We got tired of waiting and started meeting as workers.[5]

On 7 August Bhele and other representatives met with the RDOs at Karee, and the leaders from the Western mine, including Bhele, then proceeded to speak to the management to request basic pay of R12,500. They were hoping to obtain a significant increase if not the entire demand. Bhele remembers being told that they 'cannot give us the increase. [Shaft manager Etienne Haman told us that] we will have to speak to Ian Farmer who is the mine manager and that there will have to be an agreement amongst all the mines.'[6]

Zakhele was also involved in the early stages of this process. Born in 1960 in Gabajana, Flagstaff in the Eastern Cape, he was recruited with 18 other men by The Employment Bureau of Africa (TEBA), and obtained his first mining job in 1981 at Leslie mine in Mpumalanga.[7] In

2006 he was upgraded to an aid, in which post he was responsible for fixing winches, locks and other machinery. Zakhele's core job, however, was as an RDO. By 2012 he was earning a salary of R7,000, but after deductions (these almost certainly included the loan-shark-like garnishee orders that plague mineworkers in the platinum belt) he was left with a mere R3,000. This sum left his family in severe poverty, as was also the case for many other mineworkers.[8] Referring to mineworkers as 'slaves', Zakhele maintained that:

> we are oppressed, but it is us that dig up the platinum and precious metals. When they talk about the economy of the country, they mean the gold, platinum and silver and diamonds in this rich land. But we do not see the wealth of our land at all .... We want our kids to go to universities and become leaders of this country ... so we must not be taken for granted because in a day they talk of billions that come out of the mines.[9]

While the NUM had been able to negotiate salary increases above the rate of inflation for workers in the platinum mines virtually every year since 1994, the mineworkers were still in a very difficult situation. They endured one of the most difficult and dangerous jobs on earth. The migrant labour system contributed to a situation whereby when workers arrived home, they did not eat and sleep in well-built houses, but in zinc shacks which are often very cold in winter and boiling hot during summer. They wanted a fair share of the income from the mines in return for their hard work: not what Zakhele and others considered a slave wage, but rather a living wage. The NUM had not proved that it would act to try to obtain this. In fact, Zakhele suggested that the union he had once supported had now become a sell-out bosses' union:

> So we decided to go on strike [on 9 August], but still we did not get the right response as machine operators. We had heard [previously] that the employer does want to respond to the machine operators, but [that] there was some stumbling blocks between us and them. The previous union, the NUM, was the stumbling block. They were defending the whites [bosses at Lonmin] saying, 'do not give the workers increases' etc. We had taken it up with them as our leaders and gave them time to negotiate the increase and upgrade until we ended up taking it upon ourselves as the workers of Lonmin.[10]

The worker leaders settled upon 9 August to provide feedback to workers about the various exchanges they had had with management representatives at the different mines and shafts. At a mass meeting that day, workers decided they would strike the following day, and march to confront management at the Lonmin Platinum Division (LPD).

The days that followed have been well documented by the Marikana Commission of Inquiry and by academics and journalists. Workers marched to LPD on 10 August and were met by a white security officer who told them to wait. After a few hours, they were informed that they needed to bring their issues to the NUM, their official union. They were told that Lonmin was not in a position to negotiate directly with informal worker leaders.

On 11 August, the workers assembled at the nearby Wonderkop stadium, a central meeting place in the village (Wonderkop) in which many Lonmin mineworkers live. They then marched to the NUM offices in the hope that the union would agree to pursue their demands. Mofokeng recalls that there were nine NUM men waiting for the strikers at the offices, and he saw that two of them had guns. As the marchers approached the NUM offices, Mofokeng was at the front. The gunmen opened fire. Mofokeng recalled that when the guns went off, unlike the other workers, 'I was [too] lazy to run ... I just stood.' He put a hand in one of the pockets of his coat. Some of the NUM men approached him with axes, and he believed they wanted to kill him. They asked him, 'Which side are you on?' He responded, 'I am with the NUM.' To a certain extent he was telling the truth, as he was indeed a member of the NUM. He was also, however, the one who had initiated the action which culminated in the strike. Fortunately they said to him, 'OK, just pass,' and proceeded to chase other workers who had taken part in the march.[11]

According to another worker, 'we got there [the NUM offices], the leadership of NUM came out and shot at us, they beat us and they killed one guy and the other one went to hospital. We ran [away] as workers.'[12]

The shooting by NUM officials was the key turning point in the 2012 strike at Lonmin. The workers then went back to the Wonderkop stadium, but found it locked. From that point, the striking workers also began to carry weapons. A worker recalled that 'the reason we decided to go to the mountain [is] because when you are sitting in that stone there you can see anything that [is] coming from behind, and you can see things that are coming from the front ... we were sleeping there until the 16th.'[13] Since the NUM had attacked the strikers once, the workers believed they would do so again. What began as a peaceful affair now became bloody and warlike. The demand for R12,500 was quickly becoming a matter of life and death. Now the workers were stationed at the mountain and a new, larger and more militant committee was chosen to represent and protect them.

Xolani Nzuza, a winch operator at Karee mine, was in his mid-20s at the time. He recalled in his witness statement to the Marikana Commission of Inquiry:

> I joined the strike for the first time at about 10h00 on Saturday 11 August 2012. While I was walking on my own to the meeting venue near Wonderkop stadium I met up with groups of workers moving westwards of the stadium. Upon enquiry, I was told that these workers were fleeing from an armed attack by NUM officials and I also learnt [sic] that a decision had been taken to henceforth meet at the nearby koppie so as to avoid further attacks by NUM.[14]

At this stage the strike had not stopped the mine from operating entirely, and many workers were still going underground. Although there had been earlier informal committees (including the one that had been initiated by Mofokeng and others in Karee) which approached management in small numbers, Thomas (from the Eastern mine) concluded:

> We had no special committee that time [prior to 11 August]. Anyone that can talk and listen [had been part of the earlier committee] .... Then after NUM [showed that it did] not care about the workers ... [we elected] a special committee. [We decided] you and you are the leader today on this mountain ... we must make [a] plan to promote.[15]

The committee elected on 12 August included five men from Eastern, five from Western, and five from Karee. Thomas (who was elected a member) called it the 'mountain committee'. He described its members' role as 'marshals' who were intended to keep unity among the workers. Marshals have a long history of violent 'enforcement' of strikes and solidarity in the mining industry, and at times violence was obviously employed during the 2012 Lonmin strike. However, Thomas also pointed out that his job was 'to avoid violence .... If I am going to . . . [the] shaft, I don't want anyone to break the motor car or ... [to hurt] someone .... If I go to Wonderkop, just go smartly.'[16]

One worker explained the logic behind electing people to represent all the different shafts:

> People from here in Western knew who their leadership was and who is the leader in Karee and then that is when they choose their leaders, when we met they all knew who their leaders were. And [because] we knew people from Karee [we could be sure that] they will stand there [and be disciplined] .... We wanted to make sure that there was order ... because people from Karee don't know people from Western and a person from Western does not know a person from Bob mine and a person from Eastern does not know the other one ... and we said that a person that should be there should be a person that will be able to know these people, you see?[17]

Mgcineni 'Mambush' Noki, who later became known as 'the man in the green blanket', was among the physically strongest of the men elected to help lead on the mountain. His loud voice made him a good choice to communicate between the police and workers – and later with the thousands of workers on the mountain. He became the workers' spokesperson. A keen soccer player who had helped organise games in Marikana, his nickname came from a Sundowns soccer player named Mambush Mudau. His colleagues described him as a 'born leader', and his family at Mqanduli, in the Eastern Cape, recalled that he always resolved conflicts when they arose in the household and that he feared unnecessary violence and destruction.

On the following days, Mambush was among the workers who initiated a further plan to extend the reach of their strike. As one striker who was involved at the time put it:

> we talked about the people who were still going to work and we said that they [those not striking] also wanted that money and maybe if we all did not go underground then the employer will hear us fast enough ... the employer will respond to us quickly. And we really did stop people from going to work.[18]

One of their strategies involved engaging the bus drivers that take people to their shafts. The same worker recalled that 'we told the bus drivers that they should also go and park the buses at the depot because no bus was going to come back and take people anywhere'.[19]

On 12 August, the workers attempted to march again to the NUM offices, but they did not get far:

The employer was not able to come and talk to us. And the mine security just pointed their guns at us and we asked them if they might be able to call the employer for us. And [we said] that if they called the employer, they [the employer] will understand better and it happened that they did not call the employer for us. And then came a general worker from the employer's office and he said that he has heard about our complaint. And he asked us to wait, and at that time we have not said what our grievances were [so we were surprised that he knew them] and these men stopped us 10 metres from the employers' offices. And then the men from NUM came and said that the employer will not answer us. And then the mine security said they were giving us one minute, and if we were still standing there then they will do what they want. And then we agreed that we should be going back.[20]

Thereafter, workers were shot at and bloodshed ensued. According to Alexander and colleagues, 'Two security men were dragged from their cars and killed with pangas or spears. Their cars were later set ablaze.'[21] On the following day, workers proceeded to Karee mine to convince other workers to down tools. They were part of an armed battalion of about 100. Mambush was arguably the key leader at this time and he acted as their spokesperson when the police demanded that the men give up their weapons as they were returning from Karee, and they refused to do so. One participant summarised:

We cannot give them our weapons because we have been beaten by the union, NUM. And it will become difficult if we do not have our weapons .... The police wanted [to take] our weapons by force and told us that the law does not allow us to go back to the mountain where we are staying. They [the police] wanted to go there and we told them that we are not fighting with anyone, and we have the weapons that we have, but we want to go back to the mountain, and we want the employer.[22]

Refusing to leave their weapons behind, the workers were attacked by the police as they left the area and there was further violence, in which two security guards, two police officers and four workers were killed. The workers had initially sought refuge on the mountain because they saw it as a vantage point from which they could see anyone coming to attack them. Later they effectively drew a battle line at the foot of the mountain and placed a 'wage negotiating table' there. They were not prepared to enter the company's offices, and instead demanded that the employers come directly to meet them on their own ground.

FAILED NEGOTIATIONS AND THE MARIKANA MASSACRE

Each day, more and more employees came together at the meeting place on the mountain. One worker, for example (I shall call him Ntandazo), had heard about the strike earlier, but only decided to join it on 13 August. Born in Qumbu in 1987, he explained why he initially came to Lonmin in 2009 during his early 20s: 'I dropped out of school early because of financial problems. I dropped out in standard 9 because I didn't have anyone to support me financially and to pay for my school fees. I was forced to look for a job and I got hired here.' From his perspective, the NUM had already betrayed him and the workers at Karee mine in May 2011 when they fired Steve as branch chairperson. Nevertheless, more than a year later, when he heard about the mass meeting of RDOs on 9 August, he decided to stay at home. He recalled that on 13 August:

> The reason why I decided to join the other workers is because as a worker you cannot be alone. You need to be informed what is happening with issues relating to work … we were informed that we were [all] going on a strike. So I wanted to be informed … whether or not we were returning to work, I felt I needed to be among other workers.[23]

On that particular day, he explained, 'there was hope that we might get answers so I wanted to hear the answers for myself'.[24]

Siviwe Sobopha, 26 years old at the time, explained that on 13 August he became part of the worker committee because 'everyone started excusing themselves'. He was called in front of the workers and they were asked if anyone opposed his being their leader. They did not. Having been a worker at Lonmin for a mere three years, he was part of the younger generation. Sobopha joined the NUM when he first arrived only to come to believe that they betrayed the workers. He explained that being a mineworker at Lonmin has been difficult since 'every dream in South Africa is realised if only you have money'. He further reflected:

> I used to be a captain for a soccer team, so I always had a way of controlling and understanding workers. Because firstly before you become a leader you need to understand people's needs and listen to what they say. And you must be polite and you need to be proactive and able to resolve complex problems …. People depend on you for solutions, not problems.[25]

Luke Sinwell (author and researcher) finalises some details for this book with Siviwe Sobopha, whom he had known for nearly three years when this picture was taken. Sobopha was on the mountain when the workers were massacred on 16 August 2012. Behind us is the corrugated iron shack in which Sobopha lives. It has no running water or electricity. (Picture taken by Siphiwe Mbatha).

Others were elected onto the committee on 9 August, but he believed 'most of them dragged their feet'. He understood that 'they were scared':

> because we are all aware that after a strike, leaders are marked as the ones who fuelled the strike. I am well aware that when I get back to the shaft fingers are going to be pointed at me. I am going to be the person who is going to be blamed for continuing the strike, so when people started excluding themselves someone had to step in to represent the people.[26]

On 14 and 15 August police and union officials attempted to negotiate with the workers, but the workers insisted that they wanted to speak to the employers only. Thomas summarised:

> the NUM failed to convince workers by coming to ask what the problem was and why they were sitting at the mountain. That's when I saw that the NUM could not protect me. They did not even come to find out what the problem was from us at the mountain. On TV and on radio the NUM's Zokwana said he had no members on the mountain. [He said] 'They were all AMCU.' That made us angry because he did not ask us why we were on the mountain. It showed he did not care about the people.[27]

While on the mountain, the workers and their leaders carried out fundraising to ensure that they at least had some food to eat. On 16 August, in the afternoon, Mambush handed Sobopha R1,600 to buy food for the workers. Sobopha was getting ready to leave but then AMCU president Joseph Mathunjwa arrived and the leader decided that he should stay and listen. He recalls that the police 'started putting up the razor wires, then they started shooting'.[28]

Mathunjwa had received information that AMCU and the workers were being betrayed, and this indicated to him that the workers were going to be killed. As he prayed that bloodshed would not prevail on that fateful late hour in the afternoon, he literally begged the workers to leave the mountain:

> I told the workers that there was no one to whom I could give a report of what the workers wanted. I pleaded with them. I said to them that if they did not leave the koppie, the police were going to kill them. I said that AMCU did not want people to be killed, but rather that their demands be addressed. I knelt down, I pleaded with them. I was on my knees holding

the microphone. I said, 'Comrades, it has already been decided, please leave this place.'[29]

Workers also took the microphone and explained that they had done nothing wrong. From their perspective, it was they who had been attacked by the NUM officials, and now they wanted employers' representatives to speak to them, but they would not come. They said to each other courageously that the police must go to them and kill them if that was their destiny. Mathunjwa responded that being killed was not necessary, and 'please leave the koppie'. He told them further that 'the life of a black worker was cheap, that they would be replaced and that their demands would not have been realised'. 'The workers,' he recollected, 'again asked me to leave.'[30]

Mathunjwa and his team nevertheless hesitated to leave, but as he and other AMCU officials drove away, one of them asked, 'If we are all killed, who is going to tell the story?' Soon thereafter, they were informed by Steve that the police were killing the workers.[31] From that moment on, Mathunjwa would never be the same again. As we shall see later in this book, his belief that he had been planted on earth as a messenger from God to serve oppressed black people would solidify in the weeks, months and years to come. Almost exactly two years later he would pronounce that 'I learned about the brutality of the capitalist system on that day.'[32]

Bishop Jo Seoka was also present on 16 August 2012 just before the workers were brutally slaughtered. He could have watched passively and from a distance and been informed later of what transpired, like virtually everyone else, but he decided to act. A few words about his background and involvement are necessary since he engaged directly from 16 August and then throughout the strike, when a new worker committee was established at Lonmin. Ordained in 1974, he described his first decade of pastoral work as taking place 'at the height of the township political violence which engulfed the country in the 1980s'. He was no stranger to the need for peaceful conflict resolution.[33]

Arriving at about 1 pm with the general secretary of the South African Council of Churches, he later declared that 'from my instincts and experience, I advised that, in order to gain the trust of the protestors and to establish our independence upfront (both of which are key ingredients in such situations), it was imperative that we approach the workers/protesters without any police escort or assistance'.[34] The two men

introduced themselves to the workers, who told them what had transpired with the NUM days earlier, and asked them to bring a representative
of the employer directly to the mountain so that he could address the
workers there. The workers also asked for food and water. Seoka then
passed this information on to the South African Police Service (SAPS),
but they informed him that the employer was unavailable.

He was then told by representative of Lonmin management, Mr
Mokwena, '*Bishop, you can no longer return to the koppie. The place has
been cordoned off and is now a security risk zone.*'[35] Seoka believed that
the trust he and his team had forged with the workers would be broken
if they did not go back to update them. Hesitantly, his men entered
their cars and drove away. Approximately 15 minutes later, he received
a phone call. The person speaking in isiXhosa sounded to him like
Mambush. 'Bishop,' he asked, 'where are you? The police are killing us.'
He then heard the sound of guns firing and the phone call ended. When
Seoka tried to call back, no one answered. Mambush and 33 other mineworkers were never to utter another word. Seoka later indicated that he
is 'still haunted by that brief telephone call'.[36]

A middle-aged woman was in her shack in Wonderkop at the time
of the massacre, watching television. She had been a keen member of
the ANC branch in the area. In an attempt to represent the community as a whole and to press the local government councillor to deliver,
she became the local secretary of the South African National Civics
Organisation (SANCO) on 26 June 2011. At approximately 1 pm on
16 August 2012 she began to sense imminent danger:

> I saw some men ... on the screen of the TV. It was said that the
> police are ready to act. So that thing it was [a] surprise [to] me and I
> screamed, walk out, ran out and called some people outside. *Makhelwane*
> [neighbour], 'Did you see the TV?' ... and after some few hours I see the
> razor wire at the screen again at the mountain and I cried. I wonder[ed]
> what they are going to do now about the razor wire.[37]

She saw a man passing by who had left the mountain. He explained to
her, 'Eish, I am afraid, I see the wire there, they want to surrounding
[sic] us by the wire, by the razor wire and so I am running now.' She
found a whistle and began to call the women of Marikana. She devised
a plan: 'Let's go to the stadium near the mountain and go straight to the
management to ask him to stop that thing because now our sons, our

fathers are gonna die there.' But they were too late. She received a call from another woman whom she didn't recognise asking, 'Where are you? The people are dying here in the mountain.' She looked over and saw:

> the ambulances, the police, so we go straight there and then when going straight there ... we didn't exactly reach the mountain because it was over. The ambulances were taking the people. So we were afraid just to go straight there exactly, but we are near the mountain and we are crying ... they [women] are fainting and the police were standing there.[38]

A man I shall call Cebisile was one of the workers on the mountain between 11 and 16 August, so his testimony is particularly valuable. He touched on negotiations with the police, the NUM and the AMCU, who had all come to see the workers on the mountain. As the three-minute-long massacre itself began to unfold, Cebisile was targeted by police, who hunted him down in a helicopter hovering over the mountain. As he literally ran for his life, he saw a man wearing a yellow T-shirt who was hit by one of the bullets and fell to the ground immediately. Another young man gave him the T-shirt from his back, saying to him, 'If you don't want to die take off your jersey and wear mine instead.' He took off his shirt and put on the other man's. He managed to survive by running for cover to a nearby shack.[39]

Others, like Thomas who was on the mountain committee, escaped narrowly 'through the Kraal because I had been scratched by the [razor] fence. I had ducked bullets under the fence.' Thinking back on those few moments, he explained that 'it was like a horror movie or an action-packed film. I can't watch movies with guns any more since then, due to the trauma ... it reminds me of the 16th of August. So I switch off the TV if there is a movie on.' Like many other workers, he went home and attempted to rest.[40]

AFTERMATH OF A MASSACRE: FROM ORDINARY WORKERS TO WORKING-CLASS HEROES

Others did not sleep on the night of 16 August, nor did they run away from the perpetrators in fear or outright shock. A few hours after the massacre they began to consolidate their power. The Lonmin worker committees did not fall back in response to the murders, but stood up, organised, and made themselves a stronger force, intensifying the strike in the two days that followed.

At around 7 pm that evening about 10 to 20 workers held an ad hoc emergency meeting in the dark below the mountain where the bodies of their slain colleagues still lay. They 'wanted to know what their [the police's] intentions were and whether they will kill us also since they had killed our fellow brothers'.[41] The meeting was not chaired by anyone and it was not called by a central committee or individual.

Workers had come back to the mountain to find out what had happened and to discuss the way forward. Mofokeng explained that:

> I was there. On the 16th later ... not on the mountain ... at the shacks there. At Nkaneng there [inside]. We met but it was so scared [sic] that people cannot even go there ... that is why I say it was ten, I don't know how many people there ... twenty, ten ... they were talking about how they continue with this thing as people died ... there were some of the people, those who were talking, [asking] 'how could we do gents?' They said we could meet tomorrow, but we could not go to there at the mountain again. We will go [elsewhere]. We will look somewhere to sit here at Nkaneng. Then tomorrow they found a place to sit, they didn't go back again [to the mountain] ... there were many there on the following day the 17th ... we went outside the shacks there.[42]

Cebisile was also at this meeting and he corroborated: 'We decided to meet at the bottom of the mountain and [we] took a decision that we were not going back [to work] until we got what we were asking for [R12,500]. We decided to come back tomorrow morning [17 August] so that we could find out for sure who was arrested, killed and in hospital.'

The workers came to a consensus about two key issues: the strike had to go on and workers would stop carrying weapons. They were adamant that 'we [the workers] were not going to be intimidated by the death of our fellow brothers. We were going back [to continue the strike] in memory of those who died.' Most went back to their homes, but Cebisile and others stayed there the whole night to observe the police.[43]

At 7 am the following day (17 August), thousands of workers met below the mountain 'to nominate a group of people who will go and check the names of all the people who were killed, arrested. Some went to hospital to check the names of those people who were in hospital.'

One of the worker committee members, who became responsible for organising the funerals of those who were killed on 16 August, vividly captured workers' feelings on 17 August:

> that is when our pain showed because … we wanted to go and see if our brother or my friend or someone I was working with [had died] as we knew each other as people. And then we were asking ourselves if so-and-so survived or what and the people [who] you had phone numbers of, you called and found out if they had survived and they would say, 'No, I survived.' Phones were going up and down on the 16th, on the 17th, and you were yearning to see each other's faces just to make sure they survived, especially those [who] we did not know their numbers …. But we did not know who survived because everyone was running to save his life, but when the reports came and we even heard from the radio also … how many people died then and then … when they tell you who died and you find that you know that person, and that started to give us so much pain. We had pain also on the 16th but it was more painful … on the 17th while we were reporting to each other who was left there … [some workers] did not come back and we did not know if he had died or what and we were worried the whole time …. On the 17th we were still asking each other if they had seen so-and-so and then one would say 'No I have not seen him.' And then that is when we started to look in hospitals and in jails and then what they did was give people a list from jail and even in hospital to find out who was where … you see? And then after we were given that thing we knew who was where and who was in jail and then we saw that now there is something that makes us happy because now we see the one we thought had died was alive, he is [actually] in jail you see? And still because people were in jail, we did not see why they were arrested, so what happened was very hurtful.[44]

Prior to 17 August the committee had served as the interface between the mass of workers and visitors such as police or management. Thereafter, their roles changed slightly. Cebisile explains that:

> we heard rumours that the police were targeting those of us who were elected into the first committee, so we decided to elect new people into the committee. People who [the police] would not recognise. So that these people would be able to go to hospital and say they are friends and family members looking for their brothers or relatives instead of saying they are workers.[45]

Furthermore, he recalls that the employers wanted to speak to the leaders in the strike committee and the committee decided to choose different people:

> because we were afraid that they will arrest us if we were to go ourselves. We chose new people who will go and talk with them but then they will come back and report to us and then we would be the ones to report to the workers.[46]

Those who became involved after 16 August identified a shift in the approach taken by the committee, particularly from 17 August, the day after the massacre. A man I shall call Thobile became part of the committee after leaders were killed on 16 August. Thobile believed he was chosen because he was 'very outspoken and honest' and that all the members of the committee were chosen because of 'our good manners and integrity'. He resolved that 'The workers wanted rational people who could do a good job in representing the needs of the workers.'[47]

He remembered thinking 'it was a difficult task indeed, but someone had to do it'. After three days of contemplating, he accepted a leadership position. 'All I wanted', he recalled, 'was peace between the workers and the police.' He explained that after he had become part of the committee, 'there has been nothing but peace ... workers even put down the weapons. There has been no shooting or fighting with the police. When the police come looking for weapons, I give them weapons.' Indeed, after 16 August the workers stopped carrying machetes and spears, but turned to whips and knobkerries because 'we wanted people to know that we are not fighting'.[48]

Another worker, whom I shall call Andile, became part of the worker committee on 18 August, was not present on the mountain during the massacre. He was identified as a leader since he had been captain of a soccer team, and this meant that 'you are able to talk for other people, you know what to do'. He claimed his leadership abilities were also keen because he kept sober: 'As I am not drinking, I can see a person when they come to me drunk... I will ask him about what he was saying and they will say, "No, I was drunk, sorry and I will never repeat that again."' At Geya Secondary School in the Eastern Cape, he was on the school committee from standard 4 to 7. When the children nominated him, at first he refused. But when the elders from the school called him, Andile agreed because 'I do not want to disappoint old people, and I always like to listen to them.' He recalled that the elders told him that he was a good listener and also that he treated his parents with respect.[49]

After attending meetings on 7 and 8 August in the various shafts and again on 9 August, he headed home to deal with a family issue. Andile arrived back in Marikana on 15 August, and on 16 August he went to the mountain, but he received a call from his brother who asked him 'to see me about things back home'. He took a taxi home and then 'got a call that I should stay where I am because things were now bad there [at the mountain]'. On the morning of 17 August he went back to Lonmin's Eastern shaft and held a private meeting with two other shaft leaders. Reflecting on the events of the evening before he told them, 'No man,' our people are dead.' He remembers asking them if they could make a plan together. Seeing an immediate need to lead the workers and respond to the crisis, they:

> went around Eastern collecting people in Eastern and stop[ping] them [from going to work] because we were afraid of what happened ... because our brothers and our friends and our fathers are dead, our neighbours are dead here. And then the men agreed and we called a meeting in the ground on the 17th and 18th.[50]

Andile and five other workers from the Eastern shaft were chosen at the meeting on 18 August to form a renewed worker's committee. The six went to Vunzi (below the mountain) and were told that six was too many to represent one shaft, so they selected three, including Andile, to be on the committee. He noted, 'we had to have one committee. Even if you come from Karee or Western, but the committee had to be one.'[51]

Bongani, one of the elder members of the worker committee, was another of the three chosen. He was born in 1960 in the village of Ngquthu in Idutywa, Eastern Cape. He began working at a mine in Swaziland in 1979, and then from 1982 to 1997 he worked in Carletonville. He was hired by Lonmin in 1999, and between 2001 and 2010 he was a NUM shop steward. He became a steward because 'I saw that people were suffering and someone from NUM had to represent them, and [someone] who will be able to fight for their rights.'[52] He explained that he had volunteered to be on the newly formed worker committee because 'we heard that there were people who were working when we were striking ... and then we thought that if we want to win and get everything that we wanted ... then we thought that it was best that I come and tell the workers what was supposed to happen here in Eastern.'

In addition, Bongani explained, he 'saw that people were in danger and I wanted to prevent that danger'. He called a meeting in the grounds at Eastern on Sunday 19 August. The following day they held another meeting, and they continued to meet in Eastern every day at 7 am. When they finished their separate meeting they joined the rest of the workers from the shafts below the mountain.[53] According to Bongani, the purpose of having small representative committees in each shaft (Karee, Eastern and Western) was to create 'a link with the workers and the information in the mountain where we were based as a committee'.[54] As before, the representatives of each shaft took the mandate they received from the workers to the wider worker committee for discussion, and also to keep each area informed. Bongani affirmed the democratic nature of the committee in terms which were reiterated by many others:

> we [the elected leadership] went to the workers to hear about their views on the matter and then hear what they have decided. We do not make decisions on their behalf. We hear first what the workers have to say, they give us their mandate and then we take that mandate to the employer.[55]

LEFT-WING FORCES INTERVENE

The events of 16 August 2012 brought a number of left-wing organisations to Rustenburg. They sought to offer solidarity with the rising tide of working-class activity. Two socialist organisations, the Democratic Socialist Movement (DSM) and the Democratic Left Front (DLF), provided support for mineworkers' struggles while simultaneously seeking to build an anti-capitalist alternative rooted in the rank and file of both workers and communities. Both sought to tap into pre-existing networks of worker leaders in the platinum belt.

These organisations were from the start seen as a threat by both the ANC and the NUM. In an apparent reference to the involvement of these so-called external agents, NUM general secretary Frans Baleni described the people behind the strikes in the platinum belt as 'those dark forces who can mislead our members, make them to believe that they have got extra power to make their life to be different overnight'.[56] This statement totally overlooks the already existing organic capacity of the mine-workers themselves, which our research makes manifest.

Notwithstanding the potential difficulties of entering into a virtual state of emergency, the emergence of independent worker committees had opened up new opportunities for engagement, and prompted a shift in the political trajectory of the DLF and DSM. Each was central in creating new organisations in the aftermath of the Marikana massacre.

I shall discuss the DSM first since it had already begun organising on the platinum belt prior to the 2012 strike wave. According to its website, it is:

> A revolutionary socialist organisation which takes part in the struggles of workers, youth, students and working class communities. While we fight to take the struggle for decent jobs, education and public services as far as possible based on maximum unity in mass action [sic]. We also work towards the overthrow of the capitalist system which has got South Africa, and the world, cornered in a dead-end.[57]

Its first significant intervention in the Rustenburg platinum belt was in 2009 at the Aquarius mine run by Murray & Roberts. Mametlwe Sebei, then media campaigns management and co-ordinator for the Metal and Electrical Workers Union of South Africa (MEWUSA), was also an outspoken member of the DSM. MEWUSA, which was part of the National Council of Trade Unions (NACTU), had about 100,000 members. Mametlwe was at the forefront after 4,500 workers at Aquarius were dismissed for going on strike in August 2009. He explained that a new committee was created when the NUM reneged on its decision to go on strike:

> NUM ... had applied and issued a notice on the intention to strike [for higher wages] and management made a last minute meeting and made an offer. And NUM, without a mandate, made an agreement in principle with the management, but it was subject to workers' agreeing. They [NUM] had a meeting on the 24th [August] ... to check with the workers if they approved. The workers unanimously rejected the deal and the NUM still went ahead to sign that deal ... the workers [then] elected a strike committee.[58]

The DSM worked closely with workers in an attempt to develop a cadre. Among those involved was Kemela Ernest Mokgalagadi, who became the branch secretary of the DSM in Kroondaal, Rustenburg. When he died, Mametlwe said in his obituary that:

> When I first met Comrade Ernest, he had just been released from jail, together with about 30 other workers. They had been charged with attempted murder amongst other serious charges, after they had occupied the mine underground for days and wired the mine with explosives in response to police threats to shoot them underground.[59]

The DSM was thus no stranger to militant labour struggles which challenged the NUM.

Mametlwe and others acted on behalf of both MEWUSA and DSM by opening a labour court case against the employers. In early December 2009 he wrote a letter maintaining that 'seeing a more militant leadership and also the opportunity to remain connected to other workers, the workers [at Murray & Roberts] renounced their NUM membership and the entire branch joined MEWUSA en bloc.'[60] He further pointed out that 'it was out of those comrades [from the strike committee] that we set up the first DSM branch [in Rustenburg].'[61]

Mametlwe noted that the DSM's:

> emphasis is on cadre development and we work with unions. So it becomes less a question of numbers but more of quality ... if you have 2,000 shop stewards and you put one Marxist in their midst – in terms of ideas, methodology and programme – that one can provide the most mortal threat to capitalism. Marxism is the memory of working-class struggle so the starting point moving forward is what not to repeat.[62]

By the time the 2012 strike wave began, the DSM had members who had worked closely with workers in the platinum mines. Importantly, it also considered itself an affiliate of the DLF, founded in January 2011 at Witwatersrand University. The DSM attempted to prompt the DLF to intervene as an organisation in the platinum belt, but it was not until after the Marikana massacre that the DLF became embedded in the politics there. However, the DLF (as will be highlighted later) arguably managed more sustained and powerful interventions specifically at Amplats and Lonmin, and to a lesser extent Impala.

In the run-up to the Lonmin strike, the DLF's strategic focus was primarily to work with a cadre of community-based leaders in an attempt to build an anti-capitalist movement. On 17 August 2012, the day after the massacre, the DLF had its first intervention in Marikana and the Rustenburg region more broadly. At that very moment, Bheki Buthelezi, a socialist activist based in Umlazi township in Kwa-Zulu Natal (KZN), was present at a DLF political school in Magaliesberg with community-based organisations from around the country.

Born in 1976, he essentially became a full-time DLF organiser in the platinum belt in 2012 (and remains so at the time of writing), and he has a degree of insider knowledge of mineworkers' organisational forms which is arguably unmatched. He has never worked in the mines nor was he formally a member of any union, and yet he became a respected worker leader at both Lonmin and Amplats. As he put it in a DLF national meeting, 'I was never a mineworker, but now I am a mineworker.' On several occasions he was selected to act as a representative of the workers when speaking directly to management and other authorities.

In at least two instances – one at Amplats and another at Lonmin – his physical well-being was put in danger by workers in volatile situations before he was recognised by others who knew his stature as an organiser and sympathiser in the mines. In his own words, he said, 'I left my family and risked my life to become part of the struggles here.'[63] Members of the DLF – who assigned him to Rustenburg following the Marikana massacre – have raised grave concern about his protection. They have even considered raising funds to build a 'safe room' – with a panic button – at his place of residence in case of attempted assassination.

In early 2012 Bheki had heard that strikes had begun at Impala and later that they were spreading to Rustenburg more generally. At that time, he recalled:

> I was involved down in Durban in my own organisation UPM [Unemployed People's Movement]. It was a struggle ... [in] communities. So seeing that the workers were on strike in Rustenburg too, you can see that there was a link between our struggles as a community and workers. [We are all] complaining about the injustice in our society. We see that we have got no houses, we live in an informal settlement, we have got no water, no electricity. And the same workers that were struggling [in Rustenburg] are complaining about the same conditions that [my people in KZN] are living under.[64]

While Bheki and the UPM were occupying the councillors' office in

Durban, they had no idea of the organising that was bubbling beneath the surface at both Amplats and Lonmin. Bheki could not have known about the relationships he would later build with some of these workers, and also the sustained, and seemingly uncompromised, solidarity he would bring to their struggles.

Another activist, Siphiwe Mbatha from the Thembelihle Crisis Committee (TCC) in Lenasia, was present at the meeting of a community organisation in Magaliesburg when the massacre happened. He remembered that:

> We just saw this gruesome killing and it was shocking in South Africa because we are under a democracy. We couldn't believe that this was happening in our country. So we wanted to see, is this really happening? [At that time] we were in the political school at Magaliesburg with the Democratic Left Front so they just elected us to go and see the situation.[65]

Their responsibility was to report back to those who remained behind in Magaliesburg and then collectively they would decide a way forward. Bheki was also elected at the meeting. He explains the difficulty they faced when attempting to build relationships with the people in Marikana:

> it was after [the] massacre... it was not easy to communicate with anyone because the workers were angry even [with] the journalists. They were angry at everyone who is [an] outsider. They were not even able to give their names to anyone because everything was confusing at that time. So we went to [the] informal settlement [Nkaneng] trying to get house to house ... we were even pushed out of the informal settlement by the same workers [we were trying to assist] because they regarded us as a spy ... so there was no trust between us and them, especially from the side of the workers.[66]

On 18 August a mass meeting was held with 10,000 workers. Julius Malema, then an expelled ANC Youth League (ANCYL) leader, asked the police to keep a distance, and gave a captivating speech. He had offered solidarity in the platinum belt since at least as far back as the Impala strike in early 2012. The massacre alongside the growing tide of resentment against both the ANC and the NUM, helped pave the way for eventual success of the Economic Freedom Fighters (EFF) in Marikana and the platinum belt more generally in the national election in 2014 (see detail on Malema and the EFF in the prelims). One worker reflected the general attitude of the workers to Malema following his speech:

> the politicians. What they did was, the first person to come was Julius Malema. If I remember correctly, no someone else came ... but the first person to come to us was Julius Malema. And when he came he was very sympathetic to us with what has happened. And we told him that we have members in jail and he tried to bring his lawyers, and the lawyers helped us to help our people in jail.[67]

Within a day of the massacre, Professor Peter Alexander, who holds the University of Johannesburg's South African Research Chair in Social Change, sought to extend a quick-response approach to researching hot-spot areas by mobilising a team of researchers including scholar-activist Trevor Ngwane. Together with film-maker Rehad Desai and others, they began a process of organising an independent inquiry into the Marikana massacre.[68]

On 20 August, led by what was then provisionally called the 'Justice Now for the Marikana Strikers and Communities (ad hoc support group)', a picket took place at the Gauteng South African Police Service (SAPS) Regional Command which focused on police brutality and the 34 killings. Two days later, on 22 August, a public meeting bringing together about 150 worker and community leaders from Marikana as well as community-based organisations (mostly affiliated to the DLF) took place at the University of Johannesburg Bunting Road campus in the School of Hospitality and Tourism. The Marikana Solidarity Campaign (MSC), as it was then called, which was initiated by members of the DLF, was launched. It was, however, later decided that they did not have enough capacity, nor was it necessarily the most strategic move, to undertake an independent commission. The MSC would focus instead on the Marikana Commission of Inquiry itself. Rehad Desai, who became the spokesperson for the MSC, described a process whereby:

> some people on our Facebook [pages], we set up a group and we realised a lot of people were also very angry about the shooting, very shocked .... We decided to launch the campaign. We then went to organisations like Amnesty International, Lawyers for Human Rights, Legal Resource Centre, Centre for Applied Studies ... the list goes on. Slowly but surely we built up a support base of people who were prepared to endorse the campaign .... It's really a single-issue campaign and the issue is justice for

the Marikana miners, for those that were killed. Justice for their families so they can get some compensation from the police, from the government. Prosecution for the police and dropping of charges for the 270 miners that were injured and arrested.[69]

Other prominent members of the campaign included the lawyer Jim Nichol, film maker Anita Khanna, Trevor Ngwane and Noor Nieftagodien.

On 29 August Bheki went back to the workers in Marikana. The MSC produced 2,500 posters with the new name of the organisation, 'Marikana Solidarity Campaign'. The organisation acted quickly and decisively, and the posters included the names of the 34 mineworkers who had been killed less than two weeks earlier. However, the workers did not approve but rather became angry with the face of the campaign. They told Bheki to 'go back with these posters and change the name solidarity, instead put "support" because the [name] "solidarity" is in line with the name of another union … so now if you hand over these things you are breaking up the relationship that we wanted to build with you'.[70] Hence, the name was eventually changed to 'Marikana Support Campaign'. The workers, along with the MSC, further resolved that the T-shirts should not be the colour of either the AMCU (which is green) or the NUM (red) because it would politicise the support being given to the community, when in fact members of both unions died on 16 August 2012. The T-shirts worn by the MSC, both inside and outside the community of Marikana, are therefore black. They read, 'REMEMBER THE SLAIN OF MARIKANA'.

Bheki explained the way in which he was posted to the belt:

> After the massacre in Marikana, there was a resolution taken by the DLF that I must be posted here [in Rustenburg] so I came here … and met with the worker committee of Anglo because it was the only mine that was still on strike. We met with them in the park. We normally come to the meetings as, it was me, comrade Solomon Makhanya and Mxolisi Dada.[71]

Bheki's and the DLF's involvement would become an important feature in the 2012 strike at Amplats (see Chapter 4) and the 2014 strike (see Chapter 6). As Chapter 4 will show, the DSM played an important role by seeking to unite various striking committees under a common platform. Neither organisation, however, played a significant role in the ongoing negotiations that the Lonmin worker committee was involved in during the 2012 unprotected strike.

THE SWEET SORROW OF A PARTIAL VICTORY

While left-wing organisations were providing solidarity and seeking to develop a stronghold in the platinum belt, the strike at Lonmin remained internally independent and unabated. The period following the immediate aftermath of the massacre can be characterised as a dual one of mourning and also consolidating the immediate strength of the mineworkers for a face-off against their employer. While 23 August 2012 was declared a national day of mourning for the people who had been killed, the people of Marikana were slowly recovering from the outright trauma of the brutality and horror that was inflicted onto their community. When asked about what happened to the strike during the period following the massacre, one leader who slept near the mountain on the evening of 16 August said bluntly that 'the thing is, we were in mourning for the people who died'.[72] But this did not prevent them from meeting and remaining united.

A task team was delegated to deal with journalists and other groups of people who arrived to meet with the workers. Critically, a sub-committee arranged funerals in the far-off places of Lesotho and the Eastern Cape from where most of the deceased mineworkers originated. A mineworker whom I shall call Molefi was part of this organising committee. He offered an account of what this aspect of the committee involved did from mid to late August 2012:

> we said everyone who had a loved one dead, they should come and register in the committee here in the mountain. And then people would come and say, 'I am here to register so and so and he is from a certain place'. So they registered ... and so we decided on which dates they would have their funerals. And the dates that were many [funerals which took place] was the 1st [of September] ... we [the committee] met with the municipality in the area[s]. And then we told them that what we wanted from them was transport going to the funeral ... so the municipality in the area organised some buses for us so that we were able to go to our siblings and our brothers.[73]

On 31 August, the Friday before the weekend when most funerals were to take place, 'we woke up around 1 at night because we wanted to wait for the bodies of our brothers [who were killed] here in the mountain, those who have left us [for another world], so [that] we could talk to them'. 'We took their boxes out of the funeral car and then spoke to them.' As part of this remarkable ad hoc ceremony, they told the souls of their slain colleagues that 'what we wanted, we have not received ... we ask you to go in peace'. They pledged to the dead that, 'we are not going to turn on what you died for, on what we wanted ... men, we are not going to turn. We are going forward.' On that specific trip there were more than 50 taxis (each holding about 15 people) and 20 buses, so 'no one was left behind'.[74] 'When we go there [on Saturday 1 September], we showed them [the families] that we were in pain. The pain we felt in our hearts for our brothers.'

The funeral itself proceeded and, Molefi recalled:

> we saw the pain in the people's faces when we told them our history, and our story of how the whole thing happened. And that is when the people saw [what really had happened] because radios and TVs don't show the whole thing. They shorten everything and they show certain things only ... they were happy to hear [from us] because we told the story the way it happened.[75]

As the workers returned to the tumultuous striking environment in Marikana, Molefi was amongst those stalwarts who reflected that 'we have always been strong. But we lost it a bit. What caused us to lose it was because we wanted to go to people's funerals first ... so when we come back [to Marikana] we would see what the situation is like then.'[76] Attending funerals in large numbers meant that many workers would not be in Marikana to monitor, and perhaps where necessary direct, the strike.

In the meantime, negotiations with Lonmin were under way. On 5 September the workers marched to the management's offices, according to reporter Thapelo Lekgowa, 'for the first time after the massacre. There was no permission granted for the march.'[77] They were escorted to the management's office by the police as they sang 'Kebomang bareng bat-shaba Zokwana, rona raya' [Who are those who say they fear Zokwana? We are going].[78]

It will come as no surprise that the company refused to provide the living wage of R12,500. Lonmin reported that the offer they had put on the table for the striking mineworkers had been rejected by the small delegation who was sent to represent the workers, and that they were disappointed that workers would not moderate what they saw as an impossible and irresponsible demand. The company concluded that 'a peaceful settlement was only possible if all parties negotiated in good faith'.[79]

The company and other stakeholders had also hoped that all parties including 'the delegation of the striking employees' would sign the Lonmin Marikana Peace Accord. Its main objective was to 'restore social harmony and peace'. It maintained that the claim for R12,500 would be negotiated by a range of parties including the unions, the company, the workers themselves and (would be facilitated by) the CCMA. In the meantime, the accord indicated that if workers returned to work by 10 September 2012, Lonmin would pay its employees at the mine, 'a once off payment equal to five (5) days … normal basic pay within fourteen (14) working days'.[80]

However, from the workers' perspective it was the company that was not negotiating in good faith. Had company representatives come to the mountain to engage with them, the strike would have ended peacefully: they would not have needed to attend funerals in their villages. What the company was now putting on the table was considered by the workers to be meagre, if not insulting. Molefi highlighted his frustration about the way in which the Peace Accord was delaying the real issue at hand:

> they sent us to the CCMA in Rustenburg and when we got the report they gave us [it] did not show us still where we were going. Because what they first rushed to do was want us to sign a peace agreement and so now we saw that what they want to start with is that last thing [that we need], because what they were supposed to start with is the . . R12,500 issue … and then they said, 'Men, let's make peace.'[81]

The accord was signed by minority unions Solidarity and UASA as well as the NUM, Lonmin, the South African Council of Churches (led by Jo Seoka) and the Department of Labour. The delegation of striking mineworkers refused to sign, as did the AMCU. In an article in the *Daily Maverick* Sipho Hlongwane argued that the stakeholders who signed the accord were not taking the striking mineworkers seriously given the fact that it was a distraction from their core concerns. He also suggested that the fundamental reason AMCU did not sign the deal was because it wanted more members to compete with the NUM:

> AMCU's reason for rejecting the document was that it was never party

to the violence in the first place. But that's not all – the union knows NUM is effectively finished in Lonmin, and if not, it is well on its way to that. At many of the mines where the two unions have battled it out, the newer AMCU has been able to expand rapidly by recruiting unrepresented workers. With so many choosing to forgo union membership altogether, NUM already had a big problem before Marikana happened. There is absolutely no reason for AMCU to cooperate with a deal that might strengthen NUM's hand. It just has to keep disassociating itself with NUM and Lonmin and take the easy pickings of what's left over when the dust finally settles.[82]

Another interpretation of AMCU's refusal to sign is that it was not entirely opportunistic, but rather – like the left-wing counterparts described in the earlier section – that the AMCU was offering its solidarity to what it believed to be a legitimate struggle. Describing the AMCU as a selfless union responding to the needs of workers, Joseph Mathunjwa explained much later how it became involved:

> at the 2012 strike the strike committee came to AMCU to inform us that they had lost comrades killed by the police and they don't have transport to take the dead back to their rural homes for burial. And even though we had no members there, AMCU intervened and hired buses so that comrades could go bury their fellow comrades. AMCU also advised the striking committees as to what they can do to get their jobs back since they had been fired and they took the advice [which] was coming from the leadership of AMCU.[83]

On 10 September 2012, the great general of the workers for those few long days on the mountain, Mambush, was buried at his rural home in Mqanduli near Mthatha. As he was being laid to rest, men sang 'Ingwenyama ise khaya' (the lion is now home). Moaning and grunts could be heard as mineworkers explained to those in attendance what had happened in the events leading up to the police killings of him and his colleagues.[84]

The day after this funeral, on 11 September, another life was taken in Marikana (in a different context), highlighting the ongoing spate of violence during this period. This time it was 51-year-old NUM shop steward, Dumisani Mthinti. It is not clear why he was killed, although his body was found to have been slashed by a sharp, heavy object.

Of key concern throughout the strike was the fate of future

generations – that is, of the mineworkers' children. On 12 September an RDO who was on the mountain at the time of the massacre told researcher Botsang Mmope that:

> we cannot get loans at the bank because our salary is very low. I can't even get a 20,000 [rand] loan to pay for my children's education. I have been working here for nine years but still [I am] getting the same amount of money. It is not good what they are doing to us. Now we heard Ramaphosa has shares in this mine. If this is the South Africa we fought for, then we have no hope. It means our children are going to grow up and suffer the same fate, also work[ing] here in the mines. Because the rich and wealthy want to get on top on their own [and they] forget about the poor.[85]

He therefore resolved that 'we will not leave that [area below the] mountain until we get what we want or else [they should] give us our packages so that we can look for jobs elsewhere'.[86]

Lonmin's mantra, that unprotected strikes were putting the business in a position where it was losing profits, threatening black mineworkers' employment, continued to be the order of the day. The CEO at the time, Simon Scott, commented:

> Our view is that negotiations are the best way to achieve a sustainable return to work. Clearly however, there will be consequences to jobs if there is a continuing delay in returning to production. The situation is delicate but we have limited options in terms of managing the trade-off between lost production, higher wages and business rationalisation, including a significant reduction in jobs. There are already jobs that are at risk because of the current economic climate. The unprotected strike has already added pressure to some of our higher-cost shafts. A prolonged delay in production will only force further difficult management decisions.[87]

The strike seemed to be at a deadlock between workers' determination and bosses' stubbornness. The weekend of 15 and 16 September marked yet another turning point in the strike, however. This time police repression was effective in obtaining the workers' quiescence at least in the short to medium term. Critically, the Amplats strike (discussed in detail in Chapter 4) had finally erupted on 12 September, leading the security arm of the state to respond to what they viewed as a virtual state of emergency in the platinum belt more generally. From the perspective of the ruling party, something needed to be done to put an end to anarchy. After a cabinet meeting on Friday 14 September, the minister of justice and constitutional development, Jeff Radebe, publicly noted, 'Government recognises that if the current situation continues unabated it will make it even harder to overcome our challenges of slow economic growth, high unemployment, poverty and inequality .... Government has put measures in place to ensure that the current situation is brought under control.' He added, perhaps in an attempt to put investors at ease, that 'this is not a statement of emergency'.[88] The following morning, police along with 1,000 SADF soldiers were brought into the area.

They intervened perhaps most vehemently in the Nkaneng hotspot. According to Sipho Hlongwane, 'the police had descended into the settlement, some firing teargas and rubber bullets into the shacks. The official word was that they were looking for weapons, but as an intimidation tactic, the raid certainly was effective.'[89] In a way, residents were re-experiencing the trauma of the massacre itself. An ANC councillor and women's leader in Marikana, Paulina Masutlho, was shot by a rubber bullet, as were four other women, and she died a few days later. Before her death she explained:

> We were just standing by the shop on our way to the community office. We saw the Nyala [large armoured police vehicle] coming and we thought they will not shoot women. But one policeman opened the door and started shooting. We were not armed. We were not even singing. We were just standing in the street. People scattered. There were children around. They started shooting randomly at people and their shacks. Next thing I saw there was blood flowing down my leg.[90]

Primrose Sonti, who was best friends with Paulina, was understandably outraged. At a gathering of women she told those attending that 'it wasn't enough that they killed our sons, our husbands, our brothers, who were only asking for a living wage. The police drag us out of our shacks. What have we done? We want these police out. Our children are traumatised. When they see the police they run.'[91] Another resident reported, 'My child is sick. She breathed in the tear gas yesterday. The police were firing tear gas and rubber bullets just anywhere. It didn't matter that there were women and children in the shacks. Many children got the gas.'[92]

A mass meeting of workers had been planned on Sunday in the regular spot in the grass below the mountain next to Nkaneng, but it was cancelled. Jo Seoka, who had been part of the delegation of strikers which was negotiating with management, was quoted by the *Taipei Times*:

> '[The] government must be crazy believing that, what to me resembles an apartheid-era crackdown, can succeed,' Seoka said. 'We must not forget that such crackdowns in the past led to more resistance and government can ill afford to be seen as the enemy of the people that they put in power ... The problem will not go away even if this crackdown wins the present battle' .... 'The "war" between workers who do not receive just remuneration against the enormous amounts of money paid to executives will continue to fester.'[93]

As noted earlier, Seoka had signed the Peace Accord despite the fact that workers would not do so. Fearful of further bloodshed which could be inflicted onto the community, he began to argue for ensuring peace by ending the strike. One worker commented:

> The reason why we went back to work was that there was a pastor [Seoka] we used to go with [to management] who said to us, what was going to happen now was that we are going to be fired one by one and our photos are with the police and they also have them in the shafts underground as members of the strike. And then he asked us to go back to work and take that 22 per cent that they are giving us and that we should know that come June next year, then we [would] have the right to go back on strike again.[94]

Several Nyalas (large armoured police vehicles) were parked outside the stadium where workers were holding a mass meeting on Tuesday 18 September. The situation remained tense, and my research team was threatened by a few workers standing outside who told us not to go in and interfere with their deliberations. The workers concluded the strike on that day, settling for a rise of 22 per cent. One worker who was dispersing from a long line of cheering workers told us he was unhappy: 'This is peanuts compared to what we were asking for.'[95] The vast majority, however, seemed satisfied. 'I am happy – and forward with the struggle,' Sithembile Sohati told Reuters.[96] Worker committee leader Zolisa Bodlani confirmed, 'It's a huge achievement. No union has achieved a 22 percent increase before.'[97]

As we shall see, Marikana was to have a symbolic significance that extended well beyond one concluded wage deal. The great strike at Lonmin was over, but at nearby Amplats another strike which had been brewing beneath the surface had by then been under way for approximately five days. Amplats workers were to carry the torch of Lonmin's unprotected strike for a further ten weeks, with equal determination in a stoppage that lasted longer than its predecessor.

4

Amplats Carries the Torch

[I]it was just a moment in waiting, that who is going to blow the whistle and say, 'No, let's rally behind this.' So in Amplats it was very easy, people were waiting for that time, for that action. But we cannot take away from those courageous leaders who have stood in front and said, 'No we need to do it ourselves.'[1]

The strike at Amplats began on 11 September 2012 and lasted until 18 November 2012 – an impressive ten weeks in total, longer than the unprecedented strikes at either Lonmin or Impala. Responding in part to the suggestion that the strike at Amplats was directly linked to the massacre on 16 August 2012, one strike leader told the *Mail and Guardian* on 20 September, 'Our issue started on May 31 [2012]. Marikana at that time didn't have anything .... It took our action time to build up. Lonmin doesn't have anything to do with it.'[2] As is demonstrated below, the origins of the ad hoc independent worker committee at Amplats can be traced back to two individuals – an old stern man named Zukile Christopher Mbobo (whom I shall call Chris) and a composed young man named S. K. Makhanya – who worked the night shift together as winch drivers in the Khuseleka mine. They clearly proved an exceptional pair of organisers. Much as others questioned them throughout, this did not prevent them from continuing their quest to put Amplats on the path towards worker-led wage improvements.

I shall discuss Chris's background first since he was a long-standing leader in the mines with vast experience, the quintessential insider, who laid the groundwork for a new, younger generation of leaders to emerge at Amplats. Born on 26 June 1961 in Springfontein, near Bloemfontein in the Free State, he considers his home to be in the Eastern Province in a town called Sterkspruit in Ndofela village in Kwambhobho. His first

Siphiwe Mbatha (researcher) sits with Zukile Christopher Mbobo (referred to here as Chris) in Freedom Park. This was one among many meetings that we had with Chris because of the central role he played in the contemporary mineworkers' movement and his historic involvement at the mines, which dates back to 1978. He was 17 years old when he first arrived at the mines to work. Siphiwe spent virtually all of 2013 (and parts of 2012, 2014 and 2015) in the Rustenburg platinum belt undertaking research. He knows the mining communities in Rustenburg like the back of his hand. (Photo by Luke Sinwell.)

language is isiXhosa but, as with many from the old Herschel district, he also speaks fluent seSotho. As we sat in Chris's RDP house in Freedom Park – which houses mostly workers from Impala and their families – he clarified that he wanted us to record and write about his story so that his children could know about and learn from his struggles at the mines.

He told Siphiwe and me that his first job was as a contract worker in the construction industry. His first 'stable job', however, was at Goldfields in a mine called West Driefontein, where he began in November 1978 at the age of 17.[3] He was employed as a winch driver at the mine for four years, leaving in 1982. 'I worked for the mine', Chris recalled, 'because I was not educated and it was the available job. At that time the money paid was better than at the construction contract jobs. But I worked for R3 a day in 1982 ... that's why the unions were formed.'[4] He explained that he had never attended school in any meaningful way and had achieved no standard. His education was rather far more practical, and took place underground during working hours and above ground after he clocked off. It does not seem an exaggeration to conclude that his entire adult life has been centred on working, surviving and organising at the mines.

In 1982 Chris met James Motlatsi, then recently elected president of the NUM, at Western Deep Levels. The NUM had struggled for a decade at the Goldfields mines, becoming a formal structure only after many failed campaigns. Chris was thus an informal organiser:

> it was in September [1982]. We held meetings outside in the bushes, out of the mine premises.... [My role was as] an organiser, a recruiter, because there was not yet any proper organisation at that time. But we used to speak to fellow workers privately, on the side, about the union. People would ask us questions like, what is it? Who leads it etc.?[5]

In 1983 Chris moved from West Driefontein to Buffelsfontein mine in Klerksdorp (now called Matlosana). Buffelsfontein was a Gencor mine. Gencor was as anti-union as Goldfields. Chris, however, disliked Buffelsfontein for other reasons. It was too hot, he said, and as a result he suffered from all sorts of ailments. In October 1984 he took leave and then deliberately overstayed his time, sacrificing his re-engagement bonus in order to be removed from the mine. When he re-engaged through TEBA, the Chamber of Mines recruitment agency, he was sent to another Gencor gold mine, Bracken, on the far East Rand, near Secunda.

On 2 July 1986, right at the end of Gencor's most repressive period (a new executive, Derek Keys, changed the company in the middle of 1986 to a much more liberal labour relations regime), Chris and his friends who were trying to get the union going at Bracken were subject to brutal 'disciplinary' action by the local mine management. Chris was staying at a hostel with another man who he believes sold him out. He was working the night shift and when he arrived back at the hostel, exhausted from a full night's work, he lay down on his bed to rest. He was awakened by a brutal assault. 'I got the shock of my life when I was being beaten by the police at around 4 am,' he recalled. 'They did not even wake me up properly to say "Hey man, wake up.""[6] He was hit over the head with the butt of a gun. His crime? He had been handing out NUM forms. Chris got dressed and the police ordered him to enter a hippo.[7] Then he got the shock of his lifetime. 'Can you see how I look? I have no teeth. It is not as a result of falling off a horse or bicycle. I was being beaten. Serious beating!' He found three other comrades he knew in the hippo. When they arrived at their destination (probably the mine prison cells, called *sokisi* by the workers) he was put into a room alone:

> They told me that they had been longing to get me for a long time. It was a very small dark room with no window, it was also airtight. So they threw me in and threw a tear gas canister after me and quickly shut the door on me. As soon as they did that I took off my jacket and grabbed the tear gas and covered it and I sat there bleeding. I could not cry or do anything – I was all alone. Who could have consoled me? There was no one to console me.[8]

When we interviewed him he kept referring to this incident as the price he paid for bringing the NUM to the mines. Time passed and Chris could now see some light from the early morning sun. His eyes were swollen. He was given a bit of food by nearby security guards and he slept part of the next night in that same room. However, Chris recalled:

> It was not even an enjoyable moment because they started beating me again and then took me to the whites. But I saw my manager there, compound manager. I saw him and some policemen .... They then asked me if I was the one who had brought NUM to the hostel and [if] I am the one who is recruiting NUM. What are my intentions? [One police exclaimed] 'Fine, you have achieved your goals, there is a strike in the mine now.'

'Since there is now a strike,' he was asked, 'what do you say about that?'[9] Chris was venting a story which seemed to present him with both pain and strength simultaneously. He was reportedly told 'Today for the last time, your life is coming to an end.' He did not whimper or sit fearfully in silence, but instead replied with conviction, 'Perhaps if you kill me it will be better because the arrogance will finish you, but if you do not kill me, nothing will change in me without first getting what I was demanding – better pay. Without that nothing will change.' He recalled, 'They beat the hell out of me for daring to reply in that way.' They asked him, 'Where is Mandela?' to which he responded that he did not know, but all he wanted was money. He was finally released into a local game reserve with the others. When, after dealing with the lions, they arrived back at the compound, he began singing one of his favourite songs, 'Hey Winnie Mandela'. Workers raised him into the air, thankful that he had survived.[10]

In 1989 he was fired, and later that year he found a job at Lonrho. When he arrived there was much work to do with regard to union organising: 'There was no union ... nothing much was happening, it was weak, they were afraid – the organisers and recruiters were fearful because they never said anything about the union to us'. At first, he was 'just observing the situation'. In 1990 Chris recalled that he 'started to ask people about the union ... you know if something is in your blood and a part of you, you can't stop it'. Within the next year, he began to obtain forms and actively recruit people to the NUM. In 1992 there was a strike at the mine and his life came under threat, so he was forced to go home.[11]

Another year passed and yet again he began working, this time at Johannesburg Consolidated Investment (JCI) in 1993. When Amplats was unbundled from JCI, workers' provident funds were under threat but the NUM did not assist. A new union called Mouth Peace was formed in 1997 by a group calling themselves the five *madoda*. Chris joined Mouth Peace since in his view it represented the needs and interests of the workers.

As the years continued to go by he realised that the same union he fought for had turned against him. An organisation that had helped liberate him and his fellow workers, for which he sacrificed even his front teeth and risked his life, now was viewed as the opposite: an oppressor. 'We are afraid of our baboon which is NUM, yeah our own baboon,' he exclaimed. Reflecting subconsciously on his own experiences and that of his co-workers, he added that 'there is nothing that we are afraid [of], even the lion we are not afraid of it. What we are afraid of is the NUM only because we have seen their work that [they are] targeting us.'[12]

Chris worked night shift with another winch driver, S. K. Makhanya, in the Khuseleka shaft at Amplats during the late 2000s. Makhanya was a young, committed and talented organiser with a seemingly natural skill of sensing the emotional disposition of those he was leading, while Chris was a disciplined, hard-nosed and vastly experienced working-class warrior who had been through it all. Makhanya had something in mind, something which would transform into a call for justice and freedom at the mines, and in the months and years that followed, capture the imagination of the entire workforce at Amplats and beyond. Like the strikers at Lonmin, some of whom 'died for a living wage', Makhanya remains until this day fully committed to the workers' struggle.

Makhanya was born in 1979 in a mountainous town called Ingwavuma in KZN, which is 400 kilometres from Durban and just outside the border of Swaziland. His mother died in 1981 when he was two years old, and he went to Qoshama school, where he finished his matric in 1999. At the time of writing, he has a wife, six children (four boys and two girls), two brothers and a sister – most of whom he assists financially. The first job he had was as a truck driver at Goldfields in Carletonville from 2003 until 2009. However, this did not last long because 'my body wasn't allowing me to drive the trucks. At that time we were doing double clutch, you can even see my leg, it has been hurt. I had pulled my muscle so I am wearing a knee cap ... I left within a year.'[13]

Makhanya became politically active between 2005 and 2009 when he acted as a local government councillor of the Inkatha Freedom Party (IFP) in Carletonville (in Mogale City). However, he did not enjoy it because:

> all the wards in Gauteng, all the wards in Mogale City, were won by ANC and two were won by DA. You can't produce anything, you can't say anything because you are the minority. So there was no delivery in the community which I think was a priority. As they have elected you, they are expecting you to do something ... so they [the community] were losing their morale because of what was happening.[14]

Makhanya had voted for the ANC in 1994, but he soon saw that the government failed to deliver basic services to communities. 'Emotionally,' he exclaimed, 'I hated the ANC.' 'I liked [the IFP] for no reason. I like it because I hate ANC. It's not because I saw that their policies are better than the ANC's policies. But I thought maybe they can do better than the ANC.'[15]

He arrived at Amplats in January 2010. He was never a member of a union until he and his fellow workers decided to join the AMCU in 2012 – a decision that will be revisited throughout this book. Makhanya could see that the NUM had 'failed us at Goldfields' in Carletonville. He remembered that by the time he came to work in Rustenburg, 'I was fed up with the NUM. I was fed up with the way they treated the workers.' When asked about how people began to identify him as a leader, he said they could see his strength at mass meetings, and the fact that he did not drink or smoke contributed to his positive reputation as a respected leader.[16]

The NUM had lost virtually all worker support at Impala, leaving a gaping wound to fester, a factor which would remain critical in terms of the transformation of labour relations and the opening-up of new possibilities for workers' independent collective action in the months and years to follow. When the company fired the 17,200 workers who went on an unprotected strike at the Impala mine in January 2012, the NUM did not defend them. An additional 11,000 employees who were former NUM members at Impala resigned from the union on 30 March 2012. Since Chris was living in Freedom Park, a neighbourhood full of Impala employees, he was acutely aware of these developments. As he stated, 'I was so close with the comrades at Impala.'[17] When he went to work at Khuseleka, he told his fellow workers about what was happening at Impala.

At 56, Chris was 22 years older than Makhanya. Makhanya initially approached Chris because of his vast experience:

> He was the one that would have better information on Anglo and why we get small salaries. And why there are different salaries while we do the same jobs. Because you can get 7,000 and I get 5,000. So I approached an old man to get clarity on these divisions in terms of salaries.[18]

Reflecting on their relationship, Makhanya stated that 'he can't be my friend … about the issues that were happening in the mine, I took him as my father'.[19] Chris explained to Makhanya, 'even at Impala, there are people that have a new organising [platform] because NUM is taking us nowhere'.[20] They agreed that they should take AMCU stop orders[21] to Khuseleka.

Makhanya further clarified the context in which their engagement took place in April:

> Mbobo [Chris] was working night shift and we were just talking about the strike at Impala and we said that 'Here at Anglo the strike will come.' People heard [what we were saying] and they joked about it and the following day they came with stop orders of AMCU. The first [stop

orders] of AMCU is [the] stop of Mbobo. And we take this stop order and gave it to people and the mine police come and search our places trying to get these stop orders.[22]

Chris knew an unemployed woman in Freedom Park who was an informal organiser for the AMCU. 'I ask[ed] for the forms,' he remembered.[23] She brought a stack of them to the Jabula Hostel by Khuseleka. Pointing to a seated man wearing a green AMCU T-shirt, he elaborated that there 'were T-shirts like this one. We did try to get new members who were joining.' Soon he was able to obtain over 300 signed forms. The NUM did not take this lightly but understandably wished to preserve its own authority at the mine:

> Those comrades of NUM. Those who were ... our leaders, heard about [the fact] that I'm recruiting and they called police ... [to get] me. Luckily police came when the stop orders were finished and I had taken them to Impala, we were taking them to Impala at [that] time.[24]

Makhanya recalled that at 'the time we met, there was already an issue at Impala, a strike. So we started realising that the reason why Impala has gone on strike is because of these same kind of issues. That's how we started to engage each other.' They agreed that the workers needed to decide for themselves the way forward. They discussed issues: 'Like it seems as if the company is robbing us here and there. The [risk] allowance we won't get it when we are working at night shift, but it is the same as if you are working during the day... the area that you are working at, it's risky.'[25]

More specifically, they each began to hold meetings with other workers in their zones:

> What we have done is that each and every day when we go underground we had meetings. So in our workplace we started explaining to our crews, we were working with different crews, me and Mbobo [Chris]. I was working the other section, so I had a meeting with people I'm working with, trying to address this issue from Impala about how things should go [here at Amplats]. And then before we go underground now [for meetings], after we realise we have more than 20 people, we had a meeting on the surface so other people can come. We addressed these issues and [then] we would go check the development until June [came].[26]

77

One of the earliest workers involved, whom I shall call Tumelo, was another non-unionised worker who would soon establish himself as a key figure in the platinum belt. Born in 1983, he grew up on the West Rand of Johannesburg. He started his formal education there, but later went to a secondary school and finished his matric in Soweto. He then undertook piece jobs to raise money for future schooling. In 2004 he began studying mining at a college in Carletonville, where he met Makhanya. Thereafter, Tumelo began working at Goldfields in Westonaria as a contractor earning a meagre R1,400 per month. He changed jobs, looking for something better, and worked at First Uranium which mined uranium and gold, but resigned in 2012. Tumelo decided to go to Anglo Platinum, Rustenburg in January 2011 after being recruited by TEBA on 22 December 2010. He elaborated that his:

> friendship, or relationship with Makhanya [then] became very close because at first we weren't that close. But just by seeing the environment around and the company [united us]. Because the reason why we decided to work here at Anglo, it was the last hope, because this was known as the biggest company. So we thought in order for us to prosper in life, we would rather work for, at least a big company so that you can be developed and be somebody one day.[27]

At the gold mine, Tumelo was a member of the NUM and he could see that it was doing something to improve people's lives and build their capacity. However, when he arrived at Amplats, the NUM rejected him outright:

> The first thing that I did [when I arrived in Rustenburg to work] was to go to an NUM office. And say, 'I came to join.' But instead they ask us questions. 'How did you get recruited? Where are you coming from?' We told them, 'We are coming from Carletonville.' They said, 'No, you must go back because we don't want you here. We only want Rustenburg guys here.' And that's when we started to hate NUM .... So we were ready to fight them.[28]

March and April 2012 was the focal time for the emergence of a small group of organisers at Amplats in the Khuseleka mine. A few workers, including Tumelo, Makhanya and Chris, began organising. Their ad hoc group which was uniting workers, could not yet be called a worker committee as such.

At first it was difficult as some of the workers believed they would be fired. Others, though, thought they should engage with management around wage demands. The numbers began to increase to around 10 or 20. Tumelo remembered that:

> Other union members such as NUM and UASA, they were usually laughing at us, telling us that we won't get what we want because there has been NUM since 30 years so there is nothing that we can get. [They said that] the only thing that we will receive from what we were doing, we will get fired... but we go forward [as workers regardless].[29]

During April and May they had simultaneously begun a process of re-cruiting for the new union and organising independently from unions. In June, when the number became large enough, about 20, they began meeting above ground with the day shift and other occupations. Tumelo recalled that:

> Most of the employees were interested in what we usually talked about
> .... Every day, every night we could discuss, what can we make so that we put our demands in front of the company that all of us, all of the classes underground, we want not only RDOs or winch operators, but all of us, we want at least our salaries to be adjusted.[30]

Chris and Makhanya decided that in order to expand their organising efforts, they needed to draft a memorandum. It included a basic salary of R10,000, slightly more than that was being demanded at Impala. When they included a range of allowances the total came to R16,070. The two workers met together: 'We draft this sitting in the changing room ... when we went to the mass of plus or minus 50 people to 100, we were on the surface now.' It was concluded that 'it was simpler because everyone understood it ... they adopted it and said it is good, it makes sense when we demand safety allowance, bonuses, basic, and I think it's six or seven demands to make it 16,070.' While they were having meetings outside the Jabula hostel, other more established organisations – in particular the NUM – were gathering inside. Makhanya remembered being told that in those meetings workers were advised, 'Don't stress about these meetings outside the hostels. It doesn't make any sense.'[31] Tumelo explained that they met outside the hostel 'so that everybody who is interested can come'.[32]

In June, workers became aware that RDOs had been given an increase of R750 per month and then promised an additional R250. In March 2012 RDO meetings began to take place, as had also happened since the late 1980s at least at Frank shaft at Amplats.[33] Tumelo explained that:

> the RDO[s] wanted some increase. And then the company heard that the RDO[s] want money. So to prevent the strike, the unions gathered with the company promising to give them an extra 1,000 rand ... but at first they put 750, later on in the stage they promised to give them 250 ... [to] be activated January 2013.[34]

Winch drivers were then asking themselves, 'Why [did] the company decide to increase the salary of the RDOs only and not us as the winch operators and other levels such as stop tillers and so forth? All of us [should] ... get an increase.' Tumelo added, 'That's where everything started.'[35]

During a speech at a much later stage, Makhanya used the conditions for mineworkers to justify the pay they were demanding:

> I am working 1 km down underground ... it is on the height of 1.2 metre[s] – that is the maximum place that you can work [in] ... it is supposed to be eight hours [shift per day], but you can't complete this shift in eight hours. So we stay here almost 12 to 14 hours without getting food. Sometimes without getting water ... you can lift maybe [as little] of [sic] 25 kg, but you can lift even the things of 80 kg alone.[36]

In an attempt to dispel the myth that some job occupations are better or more difficult than others, he contended that 'There is no better job than others. When you are RDO, whether you are scraper winch driver.' He argued that, regardless of their official occupation title, mineworkers were expected to 'work each and every job'. Multiskilling was in vogue: 'When my brother is not at work, I am becoming [an] RDO today. Tomorrow I am the winch driver. Tomorrow I am the stop timber, supposed to support the ground underground.' Regardless of the occupation, he painted a picture in which there is no 'flexibility' for workers to make conscious decisions regarding their safety:

> we work under the pressure of the bosses ... he is my boss, I must do whatever he says no matter the condition or how it [underground]

looks like. I am forced to do this work. When the place is not safe, it is a matter of must to enter the place. Because if you don't then they say you are refusing instruction and then you can get charged or you can get suspended.[37]

Underground, workers encountered extreme anxiety and the daily fear of death. In addition, certain jobs carry with them specific risks. Makhanya highlighted the process through which winch drivers follow up on the work done by RDOs when he explained the health problems that result:

I am the scraper winch driver. I am working on the night shift ... so when we were looking there, after a blast, the morning shift ... is almost working with the drillers which is RDOs. After they drill, they will blast. After they blast, I must come and take the rocks from the place for surface. So during these works, we get [contact] with the smokes. Because after blast we are using a chemical called Amphlax .... So after the blast, the platinum is too soft ... there is a silica dust where we are working ... so we get affected by this dust ... [most] workers in the mine, when they get sick, it's because of this dust ... it can enter your skin in the wound. So it can make a deformity of water in the lungs.[38]

The dust causes silicosis, and Makhanya noted that he has himself been affected by it. When workers go to the mine hospital however, the staff mistakenly said, "'No, it is the TB" and then they chase them away from the company', leading to a situation where sufferers go untreated at times.[39]

In June 2012, following the realisation that RDOs were being provided with a salary increase, Makhanya approached Chris and said to him in the changing rooms after work:

Hey old man, it's been a while [that] you are working here. How [did] it become that the RDOs are being paid this money and then we do not get that money? If you are imagining, the RDOs that are boring a square, they are five of them, but I was a winch driver, I was opening the square alone, it means it's five against one .... So if they say the RDOs are given the R1,000 allowance ... because they say they are working very hard, more than who? Because we are all working hard.[40]

The two discussed this issue in addition to the other issues that they were using to prompt workers to join them. Chris said, 'We must sell this to the workers.'[41] At one shaft, Khuseleka, the process of organising was beginning to gain traction. The ad hoc group of organisers tried to approach the NUM several times, but to no avail. As one of the strike leaders later stated, 'We can look out for our own interests. Even AMCU is not part of this action because we do not need unions to represent us.'[42] 'As we go forward', according to Tumelo:

> Our group became large, about 30, 40, 50. And as everyone was seeing that we are serious, uh, it was around July ... where we decided that we are not talking unions here. We are talking salary adjustment. So each and every employee that feels that we are getting a little, let's come together, we draft a memorandum and then we go and submit to management. So we went on the 12th of July to submit the memorandum of 16,070 rand. ... the whole of Khuseleka mine, known as Jabula, was there to support us. And that's where we were chosen by the workers [they said], 'Since you are in the front line, you might as well lead us for the meanwhile.' Because it might happen that if the management refuse then we choose to go on strike. And if we go on strike, when we come back we need to have new leaders because the current leaders [in NUM], they [are] failing us.[43]

Makhanya and Chris met with management on at least three occasions between June and July. Makhanya described a situation in which 'the company nominate[d] me and Mbobo ... I was [also] leading them [workers] on the other end.' He concluded that he was essentially a 'middleman' between the workers and company. The company took the contact details of the two workers and told them, 'as from today, if there are any grievances from the workers ... we know you, we will negotiate with you.'[44] Makhanya kept a diary of their meetings, explaining that 'we were following all these processes in order that if the company wants to fire us, we show them [the records] that we have followed the proper procedures.'[45] The numbers attending the mass meetings outside Jabula hostel swelled, and virtually all the workers at the shaft were now committed to the common memorandum.

The few informal leaders had thought that it was time to go on strike some time in August, but 'the workers stop us and say don't. [They said] "Let's follow the procedures."'[46] Neither the unions nor the management would respond to the workers' grievances, so they decided to take the case to the CCMA:

> On the 25th August it was the first submission of the case, which we

want to go on strike. Around 1 September, we went to CCMA to get feedback and they told us that, 'No, we can't sit now, we will sit on the 25th September.' And then we came back as leadership and said, 'No, let's have a mass meeting and tell the people what the CCMA had said', and have a one-day agreement on when we will strike. So when we come from the CCMA it seems like a conniving company [to the workers since the company is delaying]. So we agree that from the 8th to the 11th we go on strike, all of us. During these three days we use to drive all the operations of Anglo trying to make sure that the strike starts on the same day.[47]

THE FIRST AMPLATS STRIKE: SEPTEMBER 2012

As the Lonmin strike was coming to a close, workers at the largest platinum mining company in the world began to down tools. What appeared as a major victory at Lonmin (a 22 per cent wage increase) prompted other employees in various workplaces over the next two months to engage in unprotected strike action, including in the gold, diamond and coal industries, and spreading eventually to automobile and truck manufacturing and the public sector. Although the organisation had been under way for a good while under the leadership of Chris and Makhanya before the Marikana massacre, this nevertheless provided significant impetus for the unfolding events at Amplats. The uprising, however, was not spontaneous. Someone needed to 'blow the whistle' and initiate a plan of action which could unite the workplace in collective action. What began at Khuseleka spread widely through existing informal networks to the other shafts at the Rustenburg mine: Siphumelele, Bathopele, Thembelani and Khomanani. Each of these shafts had issues regarding salaries and existing unions which were bubbling beneath the surface.

As at Lonmin, Amplats workers were strengthened not only by the inadequacy of the NUM, but also by other existing formal channels which failed to address their concerns. Unlike the Lonmin strike, which was a response to management feedback, at Amplats the dilatory response of the CCMA enabled them to successfully unite the entire workforce.[48] At first, they formed a more formalised committee at their own shaft. However, the police and management did not stand still, but were busy strategising how to contain the workers' new-found insurgency. There were ongoing attempts to destroy the workers' independent power by making threats and pressuring them to go back to work. These attempts largely backfired, strengthening worker consciousness. While the state was cracking down on what they deemed an 'illegal strike', left-wing forces (the DSM and the DLF) were supporting the initiative of the Amplats employees by implementing programmes to extend their reach and to reaffirm their existing power.

According to Lazarus Khoza, who was an important leader in Khuseleka, the Marikana massacre resulted in the general conclusion that 'No, enough is enough, we have seen our brothers have been killed and the thing is they are fighting for a decent wages … we were inspired by the workers at Lonmin and we said like, "We would also like to join the struggle of the miners."'[49] He further maintained that the massacre 'made them brave yes … nothing made them to become angrier'. In addition he thought that because Lonmin is a comparatively small company, workers should be demanding more at Amplats.[50]

At the end of August, when the CCMA told the leaders at Khuseleka that they were dealing with their case but that they should come back in 30 days to make a further arrangement regarding the matter, the workers' mood swung. They decided they would wait no longer and rejected the offer. The informal leadership went back to the mass meeting and discussed with the workers:

> that's where they get angry, that's [when they ask] 'How is it that the case of so many people is going to be responded [to] after 30 [long] days?' You see? It's where they [the mass of workers said], 'Fuck, let's go on strike!' And when they say 'You have to go on strike', we agree.[51]

During the course of the next week a mass meeting of about 6,000 workers was held outside the Jabula hostel. From there the workers intended to submit a memorandum to the management. Makhanya had made copies of the memorandum: 'I had like five [extra] pages, those were the copies of the memorandum. Five copies. So I have said, I will ask five members who will take these copies to the management, it mustn't only be me and Mbobo [as it was before] because it is us who called the meeting.' A top seven was chosen at this meeting, and these individuals remained at the helm of the forerunner Khuseleka shaft in the events that followed.

Makhanya explained the process that unfolded:

Voluntarily … [Tumelo] had come. He came and take the memorandum in my hand. I have chosen another leaders, who is Tebogo [a
woman whom he knew], I said Tebogo take this memorandum. And
then I said, 'It won't be men only', so I give it to her. The memorandum.
And then there was … [Daniel], they pointed to him to say he must
take the memorandum. So whoever I gave a memorandum to, he just
take[s] it.[52]

Daniel (a pseudonym) was among those who were selected on that day.
He recalled that at school he was frequently reprimanded by his teachers
for his stubbornness, something which he brought with him when he
established himself as a leader in the mines. As an individual who was
uncompromising when it came to money, he was later chosen to be the
treasurer of the worker committee:

While we were still on strike people would come and give us money and
I was the one who was handling it. And that was not easy to get people
to give me that money. And when I wanted that money, I wanted it. And
I got it by force and I was not playing … and then they saw that I would
be the best person for that role.[53]

According to Daniel 'the committee was elected by the workers':

[Chris] Mbobo told people to choose seven people who will take the
memorandum forward because we went there as a mass and we were
singing while going … but we were only seven when we took the
memorandum inside and I have been part of the top seven until now.[54]

The intention of the 'top seven', according to Daniel, was 'to see the
workers' lives improve for the better and [to see] that their rights are
met and that the workers are safe while at work'. From his perspective
as someone who would become the treasurer, they were also involved
in ensuring that 'the workers do not go to the cash loans and take on
more debt [leading to a situation in which] at the end of the month the
workers are not happy'.[55]

When this team met with management that day, they were told, 'You
are the ones who we are going to communicate with if the workers have
issues, because we can't allow all the workers to come into the office.'
When they reported back, the mass of workers also endorsed their representative authority: 'Yes, you are the ones that are going to lead us all

the way.'[56] At this stage, it was only workers from the Khuseleka shaft who had accepted the memorandum and decided to strike.

Mametlwe (introduced in Chapter 3) and Liv Shange were both from the DSM and had been building their relationship with the independent organisers at Khuseleka. During this time Makhanya and Mametlwe took the opportunity, as Amplats representatives, to offer to join forces with the strikers at Lonmin. According to Makhanya, 'We said let's combine the strike now because we [are] going to a strike very soon as Anglo.' The leaders at Lonmin responded, however, that it was too late since people had been killed as a result of their industrial action. 'They said they cannot combine with any company, so that's where we take a stand and say "OK as Anglo, we [are] going on strike alone."'[57]

Bheki judged that the CCMA's delay regarding the demands at Khuseleka provided the workers with 'the weapon' they needed to unite with other shafts at Amplats. In his version of events, the company could afford to brush off Khuseleka, since their numbers were relatively small: 'At the time it was only 6,500 workforce at Khuseleka. While the company is claiming that we do have 48,000 workforce. So we cannot entertain your issue... your wish [for R16,070] is broad. It's affecting the whole operation at Anglo.'[58]

Tumelo recalls that the top seven told the people at Jabula, 'We can't make it alone. Let's rather go to other operations at Anglo... to give the memorandum to them.'[59] At first it was difficult for other workers to join as they were afraid of being fired as a result, but within the next few days, they were able to identify leaders in various shafts who bought into their programme. Makhanya explained:

> we move[d] with them group by group to the shafts .... We make it simple that you here in other shafts [besides Khuseleka] will have to elect leaders here that will lead you. Because we cannot afford to come and hold the meeting here and go back to Jabula [the hostel near Khuseleka] on a daily basis.[60]

A mass meeting was then held at 1 pm on 8 September 2012 at Jabula Playgrounds for 'all employees'. The organisers printed a pamphlet calling workers to 'please join us in matters that affect us all concerning salary improvement'. The purpose of the meeting was to discuss 'feedback from the CCMA', and it was further noted, in a democratic fashion, that 'your views and imputs [sic] are valuable and very much appreciated'.[61]

Jonathan, a staunch worker leader turned NUM dissident and then underground AMCU organiser, was present at the meeting. Although AMCU did not have a stronghold in any of the shafts at Amplats in Rustenburg by this time, it had gained members perhaps largely through Steve and Chris. Steve went to Amplats to recruit disaffected NUM leaders including Jonathan, who was involved in worker-related struggles (although he was not an office-bearing member of any union). Jonathan was suspended by the NUM in 2011 while working at Khomanani in Amplats, and later fired, since he reflected workers' concerns underground and was therefore considered to be a challenge to the union leaders' authority.[62]

Born in January 1977, Jonathan left school in the Eastern Cape in 1994 having completed standard 8. Like many of the others, he and his family did not have money for school fees. He migrated to Rustenburg, becoming an RDO at Impala in 2002 and joining the NUM because he thought the union could help if he had a problem at the mines. But he eventually concluded that the subscriptions he paid each month were going to waste. In February 2011 at Khomanani the antagonistic relationship between rank and file members of the NUM and the leadership at the branch level was coming to a head. Jonathan was at the epicentre of this conflict. On the one hand, Jonathan was an active member of the NUM and an ordinary worker underground. On the other, he had become a vocal and outstanding leader, committed to the interests of the workers and with no specific title. When Jonathan attended NUM mass meetings, it was apparent to him that the branch leaders decided the agenda and outcome of the meeting from the top down without consulting workers. 'The leadership of NUM,' he explained, 'was implementing propaganda because when we give him eh, the issues saying [to them], "OK go tell management we want one and two"', the leadership would ignore them. He remembered telling the NUM officials at Khomanani:

> no comrade. No I don't know if you are still the shop steward of the workers or [if] you are a lawyer of the mining [company] because now you give the workers the wrong information. So I am not going to allow it as [I am] a member of the NUM [for] you to use [workers]. Management [is] using you to betray the workers.[63]

He concluded that if the NUM did 'not want to work with us now, then you [NUM leaders] must be fired'. However, the NUM was left relatively unaffected and it was in fact Jonathan who was suspended from the mine in February 2011. He attended three disciplinary hearings and in August 2012 he was fired. He recalled that in August 2012, 'Steve come[s] to me as he know[s] I'm so vocal.' Steve said to him, 'I know you are fired with the NUM. Even me I'm fired as the former chairperson of Lonmin so now I [have] got plan B. Take this form, give the workers to join [AMCU] … we are going to survive with you.'[64]

Jonathan thought about it and when Steve called him the next day to ask about his decision, he took the AMCU forms. He termed the nature of his organising at the time as an 'underground movement' because he did not want the NUM to know what he was doing. He described a situation in which 'You are not going to call the mass. You must give someone something [an AMCU membership form] to give someone 'til you have got the 20 members. Then when you are 20, you are ready to organise the media.' Alongside at least a handful of other workers at Amplats, Jonathan was thus involved with recruiting for AMCU during its embryonic stage in the Rustenburg platinum belt.[65]

Although he was not employed at the mine at the time of the pending strike in September 2012, he nevertheless became part of the worker committee. RDOs, stop timbers and other job holders were volunteering at the mass meeting, and the purpose of the committee was to 'sit with management when the people go to the strike':

> people were saying, 'OK comrade, if you are going to be the volunteer for this illegal strike, we go [together] because you [are] going to fight with NUM.' Because NUM didn't want [the] illegal strike … we didn't say we nominate who[ever we want] … you volunteer, you come forward then we write your name down.[66]

Jonathan further explained that the strike was led by the workers independently: 'it was separate from AMCU because AMCU didn't take part and parcel at that time because we are not members in good standing because AMCU was not recognised'. However, in his view, 'we push that agenda as worker committee because we didn't have a union [which represented us properly or fully], but plan B was AMCU'.[67]

Other long-time members of the NUM, including one shop steward

I shall call Desmond, did not become leaders of the worker committees but nevertheless joined the strike action. Desmond had attempted,
through thick and thin, to engage within the NUM over a sustained period
of time. He came to Amplats in 2008 as a chisa – a mineworker who fills
with explosive the holes that are opened by the RDOS. Echoing the sen-
timents of other workers cited in this book, he remembered that when
he arrived at the mine he was 'coerced to join NUM ... You are made to
believe that it will be easier, that you will be protected under NUM.' But in
reality he recalled that 'people were fired like normal'. There was also a
strong sense that the union was not doing anything to build the capacity
of ordinary workers. Three years later, he was thoroughly disenchanted.
Nevertheless, he still believed that if the NUM could harness its power
properly, particularly given its majority status and its relationship to the
ANC, it could make real changes in people's lives at the mines. Rather
than merely complain about the union, he decided to become actively
involved in the NUM as a shop steward in early 2011. He remembered
thinking that 'it doesn't help for me to criticize this whole grouping
from outside. If I feel like we need change, let me be the change that is
required. I decided to be the change in person, then I joined them.'[68]

He went to the NUM leadership and said, 'Let's take stock'. He further
asked, 'What have we done ever since we were in office?' The question,
according to Desmond, 'was perceived as very rude and provocative
because the actual response would have been, "basically we have done
nothing for the workers"'. His inner convictions steered him towards the
ultimate objective of genuinely representing workers. Desmond soon
came to the realisation that power squabbles in the NUM undermined
the ability of shaft and branch organisers to have any significant influence over the conditions of employment in the mine. Around the end
of 2011, he resigned from his job as shop steward – he also ceased to be
an active NUM member – although his subscription still reflected that
he was a member. He had friends who were leading the unprotected
strike, but he decided, for personal reasons, to join the strike but not to
lead it.[69]

In tune with the leadership of the dominant union at the time, and
also seeking to advance the interests of the rank and file, he was in a
somewhat unique position to analyse what was transpiring during
his time at the mines. His experiences led him to capture the process
through which the NUM historically served and empowered the masses,

then betrayed and was subsequently buried by the masses. Since its formation in 1982:

> the union bore the identity of the emancipation of the black oppressed. And it was aligned to the ANC, which was perceived as the messiah of the majority of oppressed workers in the mining industry. But then as it went on, it became a perception of the workers to say the relationship between NUM and management in the mines is too close. And they were becoming cosy at the expense of the majority of the workers.[70]

He further contended that the NUM staff were using workers' subscriptions to advance their own interests: 'it was more like a self-enrichment scheme. And their closeness with the management became too comfortable for the masses.' Referring to former NUM heavyweights such as Cyril Ramaphosa and Gwede Mantashe, he described a situation in which they 'suffered under the mining industry' but failed to uplift their followers. 'They instead cashed in on the miseries of the masses.'[71] When Khuseleka sought to unite under a common non-union-affiliated plan for strike action, it made sense to Desmond and a vast number of other workers from across Amplats.

KHUSELEKA UNITES WITH OTHER SHAFTS AT AMPLATS

Tumelo elaborated on what had transpired at the initial mass meeting on 8 September. The small ad hoc committee which had been formed by employees at Khuseleka in previous deliberations told the workers, 'No, guys, here is the feedback from CCMA .... What do you think we should do now? Now that we have failed, CCMA have failed. We have tried the legal way but there is nothing we can do.'[72] The crowd responded 'that guys, there is no [other] way that we can do. Let's form another union.' But others were displeased with this conclusion. The committee came together in a further attempt to reconcile the opposing views among the workers, and chart the next course of action. 'We convinced them', according to Tumelo, 'that, no, let's leave this issue of unions. Since our demands have [already] been forwarded. Let's go for the money first ... for the living wage, and forget about the unions.' They resolved that 'we are going on strike, but not using any union's name here, just workers. We are going forward and after we have come back [from the strike] we will discuss that [issue of unions].'[73] As another worker put it, 'when we went on strike we did not say that we did not want a union. We asked the unions to wait a little bit and we will take it up ourselves [for now].[74]

The idea of the strike began to spread overwhelmingly to other units. On 9 September Brian Ashley and Martin Legassick, who were then both on the National Committee of the DLF, joined with Bheki Buthelezi, Solomon Makhanya and Mxolisi Dada to meet with the worker committee at Amplats for the first time. Among the shafts represented were Khuseleka (by Makhanya and Tumelo), Thembelani (by Thebe Maswabi) and Khomanani (by Gaddafi Mdoda).

Let me briefly describe Gaddafi, who soon became a forerunner of the workers at Khomanani and at Amplats more broadly. While doing his matric, he had gained some leadership experience as the deputy president of the Students' Representative Council (SRC). He began looking for work in 2010 and finally obtained a job at Amplats in February 2011. Gaddafi explained that he was 'exposed' to the weaknesses of the NUM early on, as well as to the difficulties faced by mineworkers who wanted to change their working conditions:

> my uncle was working in the mining industry at Anglo American in the shaft of Khuseleka. Long time ago he used to tell me stories while I was still in school .... he also tell [sic] me how they wanted to be involved in strikes and how things didn't go well ... but I didn't think that one day I would be part of the situation until I came personally to ... Anglo American .... I've heard the older guys, older men that are working for Anglo American complaining about the system and the situation of which some of the guys on our generation didn't notice that there is an oppression because they never experience anything concerning the way of working in the mining industry.[75]

The dismissals that resulted from the strike of 1996 scarred the older generation and, as some have explained, has made them wary of being involved in a large-scale strike action again. The younger generation, which included Gaddafi and others in their late 20s and early 30s, came in fresh without this baggage, and began organising boldly and relatively quickly. Gaddafi recalled that when Tumelo and Makhanya 'blew the whistle' he 'started with them but in a very secretive way so that no one can know we are engaging and we are discussing the uprising or the revolution until the 12th of September where the shaft[s] of Anglo American Rustenburg section just stopped operating at the same time'.[76]

Reflecting on what had taken place in the meeting on 9 September, Bheki understood the workers at Khuseleka to have concluded that:

> the company is agreeing about the grievances that were submitted by Khuseleka shaft, but the only problem is that the company represent[s] [all] the Anglo shaft[s] which is 13 shafts including Amandelbult ... Northam side. So well it was the workers' duty to say that they must mobilise all the other shaft[s] so their grievance must be in one [collective voice].[77]

Individuals from the informal committees at Amplats were forging relationships with the DLF, some of which would fall by the wayside, while others would be long-lasting. The mission of the DLF was to engage with workers in a conversation and to provide solidarity at this critical moment just before the strike. It was in effect following the insurgency of the working class by engaging with pre-existing informal networks through the core leaders of the imminent strike. The DLF activists maintained that:

> we are here to support you no matter what you want. We want you to invite us to the meetings, so that we can advise when it's possible .... [we told them that] we need to form a worker committee or a striking committee that will raise some funds for the expense because if you are talking about mobilising farther to Northam, you will be needing money to transport you to that side.[78]

They were upfront and honest about their capacity when they communicated to the workers, 'it's not that we have money, but we do have some friends, we do have some comrades who can contribute towards it'.

The team further elaborated on the need for the workers to self-finance:

> even yourself ... you must have that mind of contributing towards your struggling because this thing now means you are independent, you are doing it on your own. There is no union who's funding you, there is no one who is funding you, but as comrades who come from the left we are willing to fund the struggle of the people that we want to persuade.[79]

Leaders from Siphumelele and Bathopele (a significantly smaller operation) had not yet been identified by those seeking to unite under the banner of R16,070. The DLF activists told the workers that day, 'we will assist to write some pamphlets to notify that there will be such meetings taking place'. They began after the meeting at Siphumelele shafts 1 and 2:

> We called those two shafts together in one place at Ntabeni hostels and informal settlement. People came in numbers. It was more than 8,000 workforce. So the four comrades [Tumelo, Makhanya, Gaddafi and Thebe] need to address the meeting. They address the meeting. At the same meeting, people have come out and [were] volunteering to be leaders.[80]

Bheki recalled that at these meetings a great deal of the time was spent explaining the breakdown of the demand for R16,070.

The Thembelani, Siphumelele, Bathopele and Khomanani shafts each had already been organising separately, signifying that there were sparks underground, and Khuseleka would become the fuel that ignited them under a common banner. Their concerns and demands had also been consistently ignored by the branches of the NUM in their shafts, making the idea of a general strike very attractive. Gift, born in the Eastern Cape in February 1978, was among those who organised workers outside of the formal structures of the NUM. He arrived at Amplats in 2003 under a temporary contract until 2007, and in 2008 he became a permanent employee. 'I had no choice [regarding employment] because I am not educated and I have no qualifications. That's why I come to work at the mine because here you can work even if you don't have [a] matric certificate.' He recalled that he joined the NUM in 2008 because:

> NUM was the only union for the people. There are threshold and working-class levels so NUM is the union for the working class. Then for officials, captains, shift boss[es] and management it was UASA. So those were the only two unions. So obviously, if you are permanently employed in the mines then you have to join NUM. It's not like you decide that you are going to join NUM, you already know it if you are in the position I was in at the time … we believed that NUM was the union for the people.[81]

By 2010, workers in his shaft – Siphumelele – were fed up with the way salaries were determined through benchmarking. The NUM branch held mass meetings every month or two, and when they were questioned by the workers about salaries, the branch officials responded that levels of pay were set during negotiations with management. Every three years, the negotiations would come to a rise of 9.5 to 10 per cent, which barely kept up with inflation. Gift began to see that the NUM was failing them dismally. He remembers saying to workers:

> Even a country's constitution can be changed. So why isn't this bench-marking changed? Who signed for it? Because this thing was signed in 2005 and how long has it been now? Now Lonmin and Impala are better than Anglo but during the 1980s Anglo was the best. Now people leave from Anglo to Impala and Lonmin because Anglo is not paying any more.[82]

In June 2012, a similar process to that which had unfolded in Khuseleka started in Siphumelele. Hand-made pamphlets were pasted on the walls to invite people to meetings. Leaders of the NUM could see that their power was being challenged, and they began to remove the pamphlets and write alternatives, threatening those who organised meetings without their or management's approval. The meetings started with a small number and when they became large enough, five men were elected as representatives. Gift was one of those elected. He referred to what was taking place as an 'underground movement' because:

> it was not public ... even those meetings we have to have them outside the company's premises. We were not allowed to have such a gathering ... but we were forcing so that at least we can have 20 minutes, we meet and we go back, so that when the security arrived we were already done with the meeting.[83]

Workers also began organising independently in July 2012 in Thembelani. Among those leading there at that time was Elias, then a winch driver, who was born in late 1969 in Limpopo at Mahlaba village. He completed his matric in 1989 and then worked in Secunda at Leslie Gold Mine until 1992, when he was made redundant. He then went back home to obtain further education, but eventually ran out of money to continue, so he went again to the mines, where he was injured in a cage accident in the mid-1990s. Elias eventually found work in Rustenburg on 5 August 2005. During this time he was a member of NUM because 'there was only one union for us to join.'[84] Initially, he had good experiences with the NUM and believed that it was very strong. That is why, he explained, 'I was very surprised when they disappointed us.' He began to see that the NUM was disrespecting the workers: 'I never even go to the office of NUM. Because of their [negative] actions ... when you go to the office, when you reach the door they say, "What do you want?" You see, in harsh words. So what kind of people, what kind of union is that?'[85]

Furthermore, he deduced that the NUM was involved in business at the mine. This meant, from his perspective, that there was a contradiction: 'you can't help the workers ... so if the employee says that maybe they need 10 per cent for [an] increase, no you [the NUM] are going to refuse meanwhile you are a union. Because what you are seeing is your business within the company.'[86]

As a Shangaan with a deep voice he was also discriminated against: 'if they know you are a Tsonga [and that] you are coming from Limpopo ... they undermine the people'. Elias also concluded that the workers were being exploited:

> underground it's a desert place and then at the end of the month you earn peanuts ... like a CEO, he doesn't go underground but they earn a lot of money ... what we are doing is what we are not going to allow because we have seen that they are playing some games. Underground is very, very dangerous ... you can't allow [us] to earn 5,000, 6,000 per month. You understand? You can't allow [us] to earn that and then others, you see, aren't [at risk and they get paid more] when you are underground but you never even get a cent of risk allowance.[87]

When the CEO of Amplats, Cynthia Carroll, came to Royal Bafokeng Stadium after the 2010 FIFA World Cup, workers arrived on buses to listen to her address. According to Elias, she asked them 'Why you didn't [sic] come with you cars because at Anglo American Platinum ... [there is] no one who is earning less than R10,000?' Elias and other workers were astonished that she could come to this conclusion given that the majority of workers were earning just over half that. They began to investigate. 2011 passed, and in 2012 'things started'. He recalled that in 2012, the NUM announced a 10 per cent increase in wages for all categories and that RDOs would get an additional R750. 'So other workers again [were] surprised [and asked], "why we don't get it [R750] all of us because we are all employees?" Like say when you [have] got [a] child, myself I [have] got four children, you see? When I buy something, I buy it for [my entire family]'.[88]

The workers at Thembelani met regularly under a tree in July 2012.

All categories of workers as well as RDOS were meeting with Elias and others: 'The RDOS were ignoring it [us] you see? Because they were having money ... in their pocket, that R750. But it turns [out] that they have seen that ... the union, NUM, are playing seriously with the management so [eventually] they also come.' At first there were only two or three people, but the numbers grew until there was a large mass of workers: 'they understand what language [the kind of issues] you are saying so when they go there tomorrow they will tell somebody [else] .... They will [also] like that [what we are discussing] until everybody come[s] to the tree.' Elias remembered that the NUM shop stewards did not join in because they were 'afraid ... they [workers] were no longer trusting them'. They acted as if this group of workers 'were playing'. When the insurgency gained traction, however, they partnered with management in an attempt to spoil the endeavour. Eventually, however, 'the whole shaft [of Thembelani] came there'.[89]

Godfrey Lindani soon formed part of the worker committee structure at Khomanani. He was born in Rustenburg on 19 May 1982. He attended Luthula High School in Rustenburg and finished grade 11 in 2000. He also drove taxis and ran a small business for nearly a decade selling fish and chips and fruit (including bananas), and obtaining the nickname 'Mabanana', by which he is still largely known. In 2009 he became a winch driver at Amplats. He explained that 'I wanted to empower myself.' He joined the NUM because it was the majority union. He worked at Bleskop (Khuseleka) and the School of Mines until 2010 or 2011, when he was transferred to Khomanani shaft.[90]

He was also a member of the local ANC Youth League (ANCYL) branch, and was secretary until the end of the 2000s. He worked with young people while the NUM continued to ignore the issues raised by ordinary workers: 'You know something, it starts as a smaller thing. It grows it grows but guys most of the times we are telling you [NUM] to help us with things, you don't do that. But each and every month there is something that you [NUM] get from us.'

Just prior to the strike at Amplats (at some time between 9 and 12 September), a mass meeting organised by workers was held at Khomanani. Mabanana recalled that:

> The workers they just came in a mass meeting and spoke to us that now we need to choose. That's when they start to call the names. I never

thought they would call me by then ... and my name was there. I said, 'No I am a leader I can lead these people, if I am a leader then I must do it.'[91]

Others from the shaft, including Gaddafi (who had already begun organising) were also officially selected as leaders of the shaft at this meeting.

Workers from Bathopele, which was regarded as a 'middle-class' operation by some of the mineworkers because of its application of mechanised mining and the larger amount that workers earned there, joined the mobilisations from 11 September 2012. It was a smaller operation with only about 1,500 workers, a few of whom took the lead, including an articulate man I shall call Edwin. Born in 1972, he started school in the Eastern Cape where he grew up, but left in standard 1 to go to Rustenburg. Edwin completed his matric at Batleng High School in 1992. He began a small security company which had five guards, but it was not very profitable or rewarding, and in 2001 he joined Amplats as a mechanised mining roof bolt operator. This involved being responsible for 'the installation of the roof bolts' which prevent material from falling on people while they are underground.[92]

He joined the NUM in 2003, became a full-time shop steward and studied labour law for six months. He served as a steward until 2009 when there was an internal squabble within the NUM structures at Bathopele. Edwin recalled that 'a few guys wanted that position I was in so they were busy fighting behind my back creating many impossible stories for me [so] to have peace of mind I just resigned'. From November 2010 and throughout 2011, he was non-unionised. As other workers trusted him, he maintained that they followed his lead en masse and that 'we were the first to derecognise NUM'.[93]

The ground was fertile at Bathopele when leaders arrived there in an attempt to get them to join the strike. Edwin remembered that a small group, or what he referred to as the '"executive committee" ... had a caucus and decided to go to the [mass of] workers and hear their views of how we can overcome the problem of earning little money whereas we work very hard.'[94]

Lazarus, who was a member of the top seven, summarised the process. Khuseleka was able to identify the leaders of these shafts who responded positively. He explained that Khuseleka was 'coming with something that we already wanted'.[95] The workers asked leaders of Khuseleka to 'please come to our shafts and talk to our employees about how far you are or what do you want and tell them this is what we also want to do. And so, how can we strengthen ourselves in order to make sure that [we win]?'[96] The final mass meeting was held at Jabula Playgrounds with representatives from all the shafts. The agenda had only one issue: the way forward, which it was agreed was to go on a collective unprotected strike uniting all shafts around the R16,070 demand.

THE STRIKE BEGINS AT AMPLATS

On 12 September about 6,000 mineworkers at Amplats went on strike.[97] Hundreds of protesters gathered at the Thembelani mine and marched to the Waterval smelter plant to demand that it shut down. One leader asserted that the current unions were unable to meet their needs when he put the question of the company's ability to afford a living wage at centre stage:

> At present we are all getting paid a basic salary of about R5,900, which is nothing after deductions. We know very well that Anglo can afford to pay the workers what we are demanding and we know we will not get what we deserve if we continue being represented by these unions .... We can look out for our own interests. Even AMCU is not part of this action because we do not need unions to represent us.[98]

The company indicated that the workers' demands were illegitimate, and CEO Chris Griffith challenged the idea that a mass of employees were on strike, suggesting instead that there were a few troublemakers who were intimidating other workers.[99] After the labour-related violence at Lonmin the previous month, management at Amplats claimed that they would halt operations until they could ensure the safety of their employees. Therefore Amplats in Rustenburg shut down its operations at key shafts including Thembelani, Khomanani, Siphumelele and Khusuleka, leading Mabanana to ask why. The answer was obvious to him: 'because we have downed our tools and more workers will do so'.[100]

The DSM, which had called for a general strike the day after the massacre, launched the Rustenburg Joint Strike Coordinating Committee on 11 September (obviously coinciding with the start of the Amplats strike) in an attempt to unite all the platinum mines in the region under one banner. Not coincidentally, Jacob Zuma told Parliament on 13 September that the government had initiated a plan to deal with 'instigators of the mine violence'. Furthermore, he argued, 'The illegal strikes, the incitement and intimidation will not assist workers. Instead it will make them and the country worse off'.[101]

The next day mineworkers gathered at Bleskop Stadium to continue pressing for their demands – stating that NUM had not responded to them, and that management knew about their demands. The workers indicated that they 'committed themselves to a peaceful strike'.[102] By Saturday 15 September, seven striking workers at Amplats were arrested for 'illegal gatherings' and some of the leaders went into hiding. Gaddafi told the press on the phone that 'we are fearing for our lives, we are somewhere in a secretive place. Cops are looking for us'.[103] As the then justice minister Jeff Radebe made clear, 'our [ANC] government will not tolerate these [unlawful] acts any further'.[104]

The committee held mass meetings on a daily basis to inform workers of ongoing developments and to hear their views. Because they were organising independently and on an ad hoc basis, they had no formal meeting venue and were forced to shift their gathering points from one place to another depending upon the response of the police and the strength of the workers:

> We are holding meetings at the park here in Rustenburg next to [the Rustenburg] Civic Centre. There is a small park next to [the] Shell garage. When we start the strike, we found that when we hold the meeting, it will only last for 30 minutes, then we will move when the police arrive. We move. Maybe we are going to hold it in another place [or close it completely until the following day] or we move to where we book the hall [at the hostel]. Sometimes we go out and hold our meeting at the community hall. Sometimes, we hold it at the church place. At that time, they wanted to arrest us. You see? Things [workers in different operations] were not combined. But after like all the shafts were on strike, normally we would go to the civic centre without any problem. Even though anyone comes, they understand what is happening. That was our meeting.[105]

On Sunday 16 and Monday 17 August the police intervened following the government's decision to crack down harder on strikes in the platinum belt. The army was deployed as well, reportedly to 'help restore order'.[106] Mametlwe of the DSM attempted to unify workers from various companies under a common socialist political platform in a general strike. Acting as a spokesperson of the workers, he directly challenged the police and government, making himself a potential target and saying, 'We will not be intimidated. They can deploy the army, they can be shooting people, shooting old men in their shacks, tear gassing young kids ... but there will be repercussions.'[107]

Amplats representatives, who had become accustomed over the years to engaging with workers through the formal bargaining structures of the NUM, were pushed back on their heels. According to Anglo-American CEO Cynthia Carroll, they were hoping to find a quick solution to the impasse: 'We are in touch with the authorities at the highest level to identify how we can work together with our tripartite partners – government and the recognised labour unions – to achieve a swift and peaceful resolution to these illegal actions.'[108] But with the emergence of independent worker committees and the subsequent antagonistic response by the NUM (including the unions' involvement in the events leading up to the massacre at Lonmin), the tripartite mediators had now become, in practice, largely a thing of the past. Once a key tool by which to manage labour relations and class compromise, they were no longer legitimate in the eyes of workers. Nevertheless, workers continued to have NUM on their stop orders (that is, to pay their dues to the union) and therefore had not officially left the union.

The NUM itself maintained and perhaps even believed that it still had a stronghold in the mines, and its spokesperson, Lesiba Seshoka, agreed with Amplats' decision to close Rustenburg operations. Reflecting company discourse, he claimed that the strikers were a minority since 'many of our [NUM] members are in danger of attack and this [suspending of operations] will help in cooling the situation down.'[109] On the other end of the spectrum, Mametlwe of the DSM continued to support the workers while simultaneously laying unequivocally into the alliance: 'We have taken the National Union of Mineworkers out of its offices at this mine and we will take government out as well – the government that sends police to kill us.' He further stated that President Jacob Zuma had 'failed and lied to the people.'[110]

The primary cry of the workers themselves, however, remained higher wages: 'You know R12,500 is nothing to do our work ... they can't say they don't have money. Look how much profit stakeholders get and the whites at the mine are earning well.'[111] In the words of another worker, 'The NUM can fuck off. They do nothing but steal our money and don't help our situation.'[112] In response to political parties and chiefs seeking to intervene in the strike, the workers were steadfast that it was only about the relationship between 'us [workers] and management. [Even] if Zuma comes here, we won't give him a chance [to speak].'[113]

WORKERS RESPOND TO MANAGEMENT'S ULTIMATUM BY GOING ON THE OFFENSIVE

By the end of September the strike had grown to 80 per cent of the workforce. Moreover, as *The Citizen* reported, nearly 100,000 unprotected and protected employees were on strike nationwide.[114] The bosses at Amplats turned to intimidation. The CEO of Amplats issued an ultimatum stating that if workers did not go back to work, the company would be forced to dismiss about 21,000 workers: 'Despite repeatedly urging our employees to come back to work, attendance at our Rustenburg operations remains low. We have been left with no choice but to initiate disciplinary action which could lead to dismissals.'[115] By 5 October the threat became a reality when Amplats announced that it would dismiss 12,000 workers who did not attend the hearings to which the company called them.[116] These threats ironically empowered the strikers:

> He [Griffith] gave an announcement that 12,000 people are dismissed for going on an unprotected strike .... those words gave us courage and we became very strong .... we are going forward because we are already fired, so there is nothing [else] that we can do. We will stay on strike until they give us our money.[117]

Makhanya corroborated, 'That made us move to Limpopo [Northam] because we saw that we are already fired .... So those announcements and SMSs [sent by the company] that say that we are fired are the ones that made our strike to be solid.' He also indicated that the workers had concluded that 'we don't want to go back to work until our demands are met'. They had witnessed the fact that 'Impala went on strike and they came back with something' and asked themselves, 'how come we can go [back] to work empty-handed?'[118]

There was no time to lose. Makhanya concluded that the strike was at a critical turning point and that solidarity from other mines was needed. He explained that 'I moved fast to Limpopo [Northam] in Amandelbult section'.[119] He went with Thebe, the key leader at Thembelani mine at that time, in his car for the hour-long drive. This visit was successful as they found the workers already having their own meeting:

> we went on the ground and we talk to them. We told them that, 'at Rustenburg [section] we are engaging with the company. We are having this kind of problem, but you are not on strike, you are working. We want [you] to get the reality that if the company puts the money for us, it mustn't put money for you. Because you are not on strike.' So everyone understood that they must join the strike.[120]

Thebe and Makhanya then requested that the Limpopo workers select leaders of their shaft to represent them. By the beginning of the second week of October, both Amandelbult and Swartklip were on strike.[121]

Makhanya's stature as a key strategist in the labour movement was solidifying. Reflecting on his experience with this strike, he later spoke about the way in which the state's actions were sharply biased against the workers during industrial conflict:

> Tomorrow, I am going to open wage negotiations. We will talk. The government will not interfere .... But the time when there is disagreement, and then when you say, 'We as workers, we won't go underground' ... then the government will intervene. Because the company realised that we are going on strike ... [for example] on the 14th, the company [and not only the workers] will start its strike. Then that means the company has [gone on] strike [in order not] to pay the workers. So when the workers say we are striking with our labour, the government intervene[s]. So that is the problem that we have. The time when the company does wrong things, the government doesn't intervene .... So today we don't fight with anyone, we just stay with our labour at home. We don't work, we don't take anyone's money. The government will try to force us to go back to work.[122]

In the midst of the state's backlash against the striking mineworkers, the DSM saw an opportunity to unite independent worker organisations. On 13 October 2012 it launched a National Strike Committee (NSC) with Mametlwe acting as the spokesperson. The DSM boasted that the committee would be extended beyond Rustenburg, since it now involved 125 mineworker representatives from provinces such as Limpopo and Gauteng. Among other proposals, it called for a national march on 3 November to take place at the government's centre in Pretoria, the Union Buildings. Wearing a 'Remember the Slain of Marikana' T-shirt during the press conference at which the NSC was launched in Rustenburg, Mametlwe boldly told the media that:

> all the workers in all the workplaces must elect the strike committees and those strike committees must confederate into coordinating committees around regional lines which should together come for a national meeting … [at which] we elect a representative national strike committee on a day that is going to be announced very soon. We are also calling here, together with the representatives of communities, solidarity committees to be formed in each and every community in all the regions across the country. Because it is very clear that the bosses and the government … the entire … tripartite alliance, are uniting in order to make sure that they crush the strike committees, they crush these people on strike. The government has, beginning with the strike here at Lonmin, made its intentions very clear: that they are prepared to drown the strike of the workers, with blood if it need be. These workers are saying that no amount of threats or of killings and arrests and any other attack by the bosses and of course their government is going to deter them.[123]

The situation on the ground remained tense, as workers maintained the strike in spite of the management's intimidation. As one man put it, 'Tell them [management] we are waiting for them to fire us. Tell those people they are the ones who'll leave this place. They can fire us but then we'll close the mine down … no one will come here [in our place].'[124] With the company's threats, it was no longer strictly a matter of a wage increase; livelihoods were now in jeopardy. The mood shifted as employees became desperate. In early October, people were reportedly stripped naked as they returned to work and their clothes were burned. Stores were set alight and looted, and cars were torched allegedly by striking mineworkers. According to one anonymous mineworker, 'some of the people wanted to go and tell management they can't come to work because of intimidation, but they were stoned by striking workers'.[125]

The stakes were now getting higher and the heat was on. When persuasion did not work, intimidation was the name of the game. Tumelo, who was at the forefront of the strike at the time, recalled that when employees attempted to clock in, teams of workers would prevent them from doing so. First they would reprimand them by communicating that 'What you are doing is unfair. Because we are on strike here, which means we are mad [angry]. If you are earning a lot of money here then don't disturb us. Stay home.' Tumelo concluded that 'they [teams of workers] were guarding those kind[s] of things so nobody could come to work'.[126]

One rank and file worker was perhaps more frank when he painted a gruesome picture for those who sought to work during the strike:

> We had to kill the traitors if we got them ... we [would put] him [the traitor] in the middle and ask him, 'When we will [sic] get our R16,000?' Since he is going to work [we thought] he must have already received it. And if he could not respond, we had to kill him.

The worker further elaborated that they were becoming desperate and ill-tempered: 'We were hungry in October and angry so we started looting etc. If you were selling stuff, we just grabbed it and ate it. We burned cars, especially those that went to work while we were on strike. We beat them up and burned their cars.' He and others resolved that 'they were traitors because they too would have benefitted from the increase'.[127]

One female mineworker, who looked as if she was in her mid-30s, painted a bleak picture of the strike at Amplats. As the breadwinner of her family, she needed to make money to put food on the table, but the strike prevented her from doing so. This worker and others took alternative routes to get to work because teams of workers were hiding in the bushes waiting for 'traitors'. She recounted, 'if they caught you with a clock card they would kill you'. She became traumatised because 'people were dying, they cut off someone's hands and ears .... I was scared. They [workers] told me ... that they were going to come here and burn this house because we are going to work. But because of prayer, and my mother was also praying, so nothing happened [to us]'.[128]

The worker committee was also under extreme pressure, particularly in October as people's pockets became empty and hunger set in. Furthermore, the leadership had only begun building tight relationships with each other in a short space of time, and it was not clear who people could trust. During that month, intra-committee violence nearly ensued when members of the committee developed a strategy of engaging inside the formal structures of the NUM as a means to access management directly. As Makhanya explained, 'We went to the office of NUM ... always when we go to the meeting, NUM was opposing that we sit [with management] ... always the company is starting to reject us and we said, "No, we need to sit with NUM, secure the issues with NUM.'"[129] NUMSA had also been working with members of the committee, and according to Makhanya they 'encouraged us ... that we need to wear these NUM T-shirts sometimes so that we can use them for temporal [temporary] time ... we used to engage with them so that we can be approved to sit with the company'.

Makhanya nominated four men to speak to NUM officials in their offices, and they had a discussion. The delegation told the union, 'Comrades, we can't fight now, being on strike. Let's address these issues. After that we will come and sit [and see] as to what we can do together.' The comrades from the NUM agreed. However, when certain members of the committee learned of this, Makhanya and others were deemed to have sold out. They were seen to be traitors who were now joining the NUM. Seven workers arrived in two cars and threatened to shoot the leader. Others came to his defence, however, and he was left unscathed.[130]

Resembling the character of workers in Lonmin who, after being mowed down by the police continued fighting for a living wage, the majority of Amplats workers remained undeterred despite the daunting circumstances. One worker reflected on the reality of the workers' desperation:

> we are working underground and it is hard and when we look at other people, they are doing better than us and they are not working underground. And so when we try to get [a] decent salary... [government] keep[s] forcing us to go back to work .... That is what made us feel so strongly about going on strike and that the work we are doing is difficult ... working underground is like a police man pointing a gun at you because where we are working ... you are faced with death every time and we know that death here on the surface is better than death underground and now the police are trying to kill us ... we thought it better that we die in front of him.[131]

Negotiations were ongoing, as the company and all interested parties attempted to find a solution to the impasse. According to a document entitled 'Anglo American Platinum offer return to work by 30 October 2012', management held a meeting with the NUM, UASA, NUMSA and 'the Workers Committee' (capitalisation in original) on 26 October 2012.[132]

The company had hoped that workers would return by 30 October (which was a Tuesday), and extended an offer which was valid until 6 November 2012. The one-time offer was called, 'The Safe Start-up Programme'. It consisted of several components:

1 The dismissed employees from the Rustenburg Mining operations would be reinstated on return to work. The employees would retain the same terms and conditions of employment.
2 The striking employees at Union, Tumela and Dishaba Mines would also be allowed to return to work on 30 October 2012 on the same terms and conditions of employment.
3 The employees who participated in the illegal strike would be paid a once-off 'hardship' allowance of R2,000 net (after deductions) in order to assist those in financial difficulties arising out of the 'No Work, No Pay' principle. Employees would have an option of taking a cash voucher equivalent to the value of R 2,000 hardship allowance, subject to practicalities.
4 The employees who did not participate in the illegal strike would be paid a one-off 'loyalty allowance' of R2,000 net (after deductions).[133]

The fifth component consisted of a loan of R2,500 to offset the debt people might have accumulated while on strike. The sixth element of the offer insisted that 'striking employees will also be required to sign a letter of undertaking prohibiting participation and/or incitement of illegal strikes and work stoppages in future'. Number 7, which stated that those who participated in the ongoing strike would be 'subjected to normal disciplinary action as per the company policy, where the outcome will be short of dismissal', was deleted almost undoubtedly as a concession to the worker committee. The offer nevertheless concluded that those who did not return to work by the time stated would indeed face disciplinary action and would be ineligible for any of the benefits outlined.[134] Nothing was mentioned about the demand for R16,070. The committee thus refused the offer, and the vast majority of employees remained on strike.

The tripartite alliance did not sit back quietly as their power seemed to be crumbling. Rather, they sought to salvage it. One central intervention led by Zwelinzima Vavi was a COSATU rally held on 27 October. Workers who were involved in strike action at Amplats debated whether they should take part. Bheki summarised:

It was a big issue there ... big debate [with] the workers and we [DLF] advised them not to go to that rally since it was initiated by COSATU and because it's going to be dangerous for them because they want to oppose the people who are saying they are reclaiming Rustenburg because the slogan of COSATU on the march was that they are 'reclaiming Rustenburg'.[135]

The DLF communicated to the workers that COSATU had 'organised extensively within their affiliates. It was not only NUM.'[136] The argument was therefore that the Amplats strikers would be targeted as people who were anti-NUM. However, the workers thought otherwise and responded:

we are going to that rally because we are still members of NUM. And as members of NUM, we are bound to be part of that rally because it's being called for us. And maybe it's an opportunity for us to come face to face with the top office bearers of COSATU and tell them directly why we are against NUM.[137]

Bheki, alongside Rehad Desai, was not entirely persuaded, but because they respected the workers' right to decide, they joined them.

On 27 October, Zwelinzima Vavi, Frans Baleni, Sdumo Dlamini and Blade Nzimande appeared to be jovial when they marched through Rustenburg with about 1,000 unionists.[138] However, they were very late and did not anticipate what was to come. Early in the morning, the stadium was full with 'anti-NUM' workers. Prior to the start of the rally at 9 am, 'NUM people came to issue T-shirts to workers in the stadium not knowing that these people [whom they were distributing to] were actually against [the] NUM.' The plan was to wear the NUM T-shirts and then later to show 'the true colours of the workers', and at 9 am these individuals burned NUM flags and T-shirts. 'The other people that were in support of the rally from other affiliates', Bheki recounted, 'ran away from the stadium because they were surprised [at] what's happening.'[139] In the midst of the turmoil, NUM spokesperson Lesiba Seshoka fled to safety. Along the way, the *Daily Maverick* noted that 'three COSATU loyalists had been assaulted'.[140]

Five people were elected from Amplats to speak to the organisers of the march. They included Vavi. Rehad found himself in the middle of the COSATU supporters and Amplats workers. According to Bheki's version of events:

When he [Rehad] approached to talk to Vavi that the five people wanted to come and address him, members of COSATU stripped him off [of his clothes] and that's when the clash started. And even the crowd that had been peacefully removed from the stadium with the decision that five people would be chosen to speak to Vavi, reacted .... the police shot directly at the people [targeting those] that were anti-COSATU ... with rubber bullets and dogs and horses and [they] disbanded them. They shot several people that were hospitalised on the day so we came back to do the 'post-mortem' in our own house.[141]

Rehad was taken away by the police to jail, and Jim Nichol came to his rescue and bailed him out.

Mabanana from the worker committee felt that the message they sent to Vavi at the rally was 'Don't say you [COSATU] will reclaim Rustenburg. You don't own Rustenburg. We own Rustenburg.'[142] The workers from Amplats, alongside Bheki and Rehad, reflected on what had happened, including what it meant for the balance of forces. It was apparent to them that 'the power was lying with the worker committee because they had organised many people to oppose the rally itself'.[143] It was decided that in order to solidify their strength, 'workers must have their own rally'.[144] This became the DLF's single most important intervention in the platinum belt. At Lonmin, the organisation did not arrive until after the strike had started, and making matters more difficult, the DLF made its presence felt immediately following a massacre, when people were traumatised and levels of distrust were extreme. The workers at Lonmin, seeing that their colleagues had been killed, were hesitant to unite with political organisations or even strikers from other mines.

At Amplats, DLF personnel had made themselves available prior to the strike and had nurtured their relationship with key leaders for nearly two months. The DLF raised R80,000 in a period of a few days, primarily from individuals who supported the co-organising of a rally with Amplats workers at Olympia Stadium. This was intended to surpass the previous rally organised by the powerhouse COSATU, in both symbolic presence and the sheer number attending (estimated to be several thousand). This intervention helped sustain the workers' resolve as they vowed at that time to strike until Christmas or even January if necessary, stating specifically that it would be 'a black Christmas'.[145]

Trevor Ngwane, who had become a key figure in the DLF, spoke on behalf of the organisation when he told the energetic crowd in the stadium that they supported the demands of the mineworkers. He maintained that the Marikana massacre 'will always be a crime against the working class as a whole… [and a] spark for a new South Africa that works for, affirms and advances the interests of the workers and poor'. From his perspective, the capitalist system was the culprit for mass inequalities between rich bosses and low-paid workers:

> The lowest minimum wage in 2012 was R996 per month in the South African economy. Half of CEOs of companies earn 762 times more than the lowest minimum wage. Generally in mining the lowest minimum wage is just over R4,000. Yet 75 CEOs of the 80 largest listed corporations took home jointly over R1.5 billion in 2011. One individual alone took home R39 million in one year. This has to end now![146]

Trevor had long been an advocate for the unity of the working class as a whole. He therefore called for the assemblies of mineworkers from different companies who had met to demand a living wage to invite the unemployed segments of the population to join them. 'The demands of the striking mineworkers', he claimed, 'are shared by the unemployed.'[147]

The strikers left the rally with more confidence that they would emerge victorious in their battle for a living wage. Earlier, Chris Griffith of Amplats had given a deadline that there must be an agreement by Monday 12 November. Now, COSATU general secretary Vavi had an alternative plan. Seeing the strength exhibited by the workers at the rally, he told Safm that 'the deadline would be extended from today [12 November] to Wednesday [14 November], to give a new initiative a chance …. This afternoon, late, we will be meeting with the strike committee.'[148]

Indeed, they did meet. Among those present were members of Contralesa traditional authorities who had an interest in the workers since many of them came from the Eastern Cape where Contralesa is based. Seven members of COSATU were also present. Others attending included prominent leaders Zwelinzima Vavi and Sdumo Dlamini.[149] Twelve worker representatives from Amplats attended, including Bheki, who recalled that 'the workers insisted I must be part of the meeting and attend the meeting as a worker'.[150]

Mabanana saw the meeting as a sign of respect being given to the worker committee by COSATU. Vavi shook their hands when they came into the room, and in an attempt to make amends communicated that

'I can see that you are strong here ... young boys, even if they called you names like "wild cats", "strike committee" etc. ... . you are good leaders.'[151] Bheki corroborated:

> Vavi and Sdumo were withdrawing their statements submitted on the 27th October rally because Vavi had said these people are thugs, they are not members of NUM and were being used by a 'third force' being funded by the European and US people ... and what they are demanding is [too] huge ... and they must be regarded as such as people who disrespect their organisation and are being used and cannot think for themselves.[152]

The workers present asked the two to withdraw their statements publicly. Seeking to potentially revive COSATU's strongest union, Vavi requested that the new-found leaders 'must fight within NUM so that they could assume positions within NUM'.[153] The workers responded that 'if Vavi could go and negotiate with Anglo on their behalf ... [they would agree] that there can be a settlement that can be reached'.[154] With few exceptions, management had refused to meet with the strikers. Workers therefore agreed to let Vavi speak to management on their behalf. The following day, Vavi spoke with management without the committee.

The strike was not as powerful as it had been previously: some operations were dropping out and workers were getting tired. On 18 November, four days later, the strike ended. According to Makhanya, the worker committee was told the negotiations for salaries would begin in January 2013, and they then reported this to the workers.[155] They were then presented by management with two options: to receive an allowance of R600 or a salary adjustment of R400. The workers chose the latter:

> workers look at it and said, 'Salary adjustment, it will benefit us in a lot of ways. Like to say your overtime [salary] will increase, provident fund will also increase, so everything that you do will increase [the amount of money you eventually receive]. But if it's allowance, allowance will remain R600 until you die, and your child will come again and they will die, and still it will be R600, it won't change.' So we decided to take R400. With the understanding that early January they will open the wage negotiations.[156]

The R400 increase was seen as a victory by the workers, although it was a drop in the ocean compared with the R16,070 increase they had been demanding. Daniel, the treasurer of the committee, explained the logic behind this perception: 'The worker committee came with R400 in two months and then NUM comes with R400 in 12 months.'[157] Moreover, no workers were fired.

The next chapter discusses what happened in 2013, including re-trenchments (that is, redundancies) at Amplats which followed and the ongoing state harassment (and even torture) which was being inflicted on workers at Lonmin. It also details the rocky transition between the worker committees and the new union at both of the mines. The rise of working-class power through an independent organisation which sustained the militant unprotected strikes of 2012, it seemed, was to be tamed and institutionalised by the AMCU.

5

The Rise of the AMCU and the Demise of Worker Committees

It was the only strike [workers'] committee ... that could face the unions [head on] and do what they believe in. So, I would say, he [Mathunjwa] is right to dislike the idea of the worker committee.[1]

During and subsequent to the 2012 unprotected strikes, the NUM's subscriptions at each of the three major platinum mines were in a sharp decline and its reputation was, to say the least, tarnished. While the union had already lost legitimacy among many as a potential ally which could serve the interests of workers, it was now in crisis, as was the alliance more generally (at least on the western limb of the platinum belt). As one AMCU shop steward summarised in mid-2013:

We do not want NUM to represent us. So NUM, the chances of [its] revival [are virtually non-existent] considering the Marikana massacre, the arrogance of the ANC, the arrogance of SACP calling AMCU a vigilante union ... you know things like this, they keep the tripartite alliance, the ANC in hostile view [to the workers].[2]

In Lonmin, the workers at the mountain who had been fired on by NUM officials on 11 August 2012 had promptly become vehemently opposed to the NUM. Such opposition spread rapidly to the Lonmin workforce more generally. One worker later reflected his understanding of the relationship between the tripartite alliance and their former union: 'The ANC is COSATU. COSATU is NUM. All those people, they have got a hand in the killing of those people who died at the mountain. Because they are the ones who called government and said we must be killed.'[3]

The competition, the AMCU, which had a firm membership in Karee mine prior to the massacre, grew at an exponential rate throughout 2012 and 2013, initially at Impala, but also at Lonmin after the police killings at Marikana. This was in part because the president of the AMCU, Joseph Mathunjwa, had come to the mountain sympathetically to listen to the workers as an equal, whereas the president of the NUM appeared to side with the management, opposing the workers' decision to go on strike. Mathunjwa's reputation became entrenched not only in Lonmin but across the platinum belt, and he was generally perceived as a leader who could potentially represent insurgent workers.

By the end of 2012, however, the AMCU had yet to gain a strong hold at Amplats, and management needed a structure with which to negotiate and also to maintain order. The committee at Amplats already had legitimacy in the eyes of both the employer and the workers. The latter eventually chose the AMCU as their union, and elected virtually the entire worker committee into office-bearing positions in early 2013. The situation at Lonmin was much more complicated, however.

This chapter discusses the rocky and incomplete transition from worker committees to AMCU at both Lonmin and Amplats. When the leaders of the worker committees, and the rank and file themselves, were incorporated into the new union, this raised questions regarding the extent to which the militant working-class politics of the committees remained, or would be side-swiped by the AMCU's top structure. How things worked themselves out in that regard is part of the story to be told in this chapter of this book, and will be continued in Chapter 6. First, however, we need to address the complicated events that occasioned the rise of the AMCU in both Lonmin and Amplats.

The first half of 2013 involved a struggle for recognition by rank and file AMCU members and the organisation more generally. First, I deal with the specific case of Amplats. Following the Amplats strike of 2012, retrenchments (redundancies) were announced by the company in January, and became a key feature of workers' organising, which distracted from wage negotiations throughout 2013. The second part of the chapter hones in on this period in order to investigate what was happening at Lonmin, where the mine and its surrounding area (Marikana) continued to be marked by intimidation and violence. Finally, I return to the difficult question of the relationship between the AMCU leadership and the erstwhile worker committees, especially at Amplats where the worker committees had been most deeply entrenched.

FROM INTERIM COMMITTEE TO RECOGNITION AT AMPLATS

On 18 November 2012 the strike at Amplats finally ended. According to a reliable source, every worker at Amplats was given a staggering bonus of R24,000 on their return to work.[4] Management at Amplats needed a structure with which to engage that was legitimate in the eyes of the workers, or – in their view – risk anarchy. The company therefore issued 'interim access' to what they called the 'interim committee', made up of worker committee members.[5] The agreement presented to the worker committee stated that 'the granting of the interim access to the Interim Committee as set out in these guidelines was a precondition to the return to work by the supporters of the Interim Committee'. Management made clear, however, that they were not granting organisational rights, but merely providing access to 'office facilities and basic amenities'. The agreement concluded by insisting that the committee would 'have to be registered as a trade union in accordance with the provisions of the Labour Relations Act of 1995 ("the LRA") prior to it being eligible for recognition at the operations of Rustenburg Platinum Mines'.[6]

All Rustenburg Amplats units (mine shafts) were granted up to three part-time representatives and one full-time representative. This also included the Northam units, the Amandelbult and Swartklip. The purpose of these representatives, from the perspective of management, was to resolve conflicts in the workplace in order to ensure productivity. The interim access was to end on 31 December 2012.[7]

Based on his own direct observation of the events at the time, Bheki described a situation in which:

> Those offices were run by the worker committee …. Worker committees were afforded transport. If they wanted to meet, they would just request to the relevant department to say we want to go to a meeting … so the comrades from Rustenburg [from different shafts within the committee] all of them they would get a 22-seater [a large minibus] to transport them. They were given that right to go and meet because management understood that these are the committees who represent the workers [and] that keep them [workers] productive. [They] represented the workers without any unions.[8]

Both management and the committees were aware that eventually the workers would need to join a union. Desmond, a worker committee representative in Khuseleka, summarised management's communication to the workers' committee prior to the transition to AMCU:

> We [management] want to talk to you [the worker committee]. We want to engage with you gentlemen. We must agree that you have made your point. We agree. We are losing ounces, we are losing credibility with the markets .... Let's sit down and chat, but we can't talk to you if we don't know who you guys are. We want to talk to NUMSA, we need to talk to SATAWU. A recognised structure.[9]

At this stage workers were debating which union to join collectively. One thing they knew was that they were not going back to the NUM. The leaders of the worker committee engaged with each other and the rank and file about the way forward.

Chris further elucidated what had transpired at the end of the 2012 strike prior to the transition to the new union:

> If we agree to go back to work there must be some conditions that we have and that will allow us to go back to work. We must not show that we are defeated. And we are not defeated by going back to work. We were thinking for [with] the masses that are at our back and secondly we saw the difficulties of fighting the employer while you're outside [of the formal bargaining structures]. Because when you fight the employer while you are outside, you are calling the police. We saw that at Marikana. Their people were killed so now in order to prevent what happened at Marikana, so we decided to go back ... so that when we are inside [we can then approach management under the auspices of a union].[10]

The worker committees, operating on their own terms without engaging an institutional structure, had limitations at both mines. It was clear that they had done an impressive job, but the committees believed they needed to be inside a formal institution in order to continue to press for changes. One worker, whom in this book I call Ishmael, became a shop steward of the AMCU, joining the union after the strike. He expressed a sharp contrast between the approaches of the AMCU and the NUM, of which he had been a member:

> I had no organisation [during and directly after the strike] and I was in the

field. And we were just there as workers only and NUM was not there. And when we came back from the field, then AMCU promised us that they will do what we wanted. And he [Mathunjwa] also said that the money that we want, he will not say [to us later] that it is too much ... but he will go to the employer and talk to them about it and he will try to get me that money exactly. And NUM will tell you that the money that you want is too much before even going to the employer. And then AMCU came and told us, 'No, I will take your mandate as it is and take it to the employer without changing it.' And [now] they [AMCU] are using our mandate as workers.[11]

The AMCU had not only emerged as a result of the insurgency of the committees, it had also promised, to a certain extent, to engage with rank and file workers before making decisions in wage negotiations.

Another mineworker offered a more structural explanation, suggesting that particular interests of the NUM caused it to identify with management:

I trust AMCU more .... AMCU has no shares in the mines. The main challenge with NUM is that it had shares in the mines, which was a conflict of interest. It cannot represent the workers well because it thinks of protecting its shares. So it agrees with anything the management comes with. You can't bite the hand that feeds. But I trust AMCU because Mathunjwa comes to speak to the workers in person as a president which NUM did not do. He consults with us before signing an agreement. He hears our views, so that's the difference. That thing of unions having shares in mines is killing us because they cannot be trusted.[12]

Lazarus, now an AMCU branch leader at Khuseleka, remembered that they needed a 'union that is going to hear us, the union that is going to take our mandate. We don't want a union that is mixing now with NUM. And so we were searching, searching only to find that, no, this [AMCU] is the right union that we can take.' The committee itself began systematically to recruit members for AMCU during the last months of 2012. According to Lazarus, 'We called AMCU head office and we said, "No guys, come. We want you to come and work as a recognised union from our side." And that is where now we took it from shaft to shaft and also to the corporation of Anglo [American Platinum].'[13]

RETRENCHMENTS UNDERMINE WAGE NEGOTIATIONS

In January 2013, however, Amplats announced that it would make 14,000 workers redundant. Arguably, this was in order to tame the workers in the most militant shaft, where the 2012 strike had emerged – Khuseleka. Worker leaders had expected to begin wage negotiations that month, but this did not happen. According to Makhanya:

> it wasn't that maybe we were retreating [by going back to work]. So it was an agreement that .... Now it's November [2012]. Let's agree that let's go back to work. And then January is nearby and then we [will] sit down and negotiate concerning our demand ... everyone has signed [the agreement]. So that's when they played the dynamics of politics, they hit us with retrenchments.[14]

Throughout 2013, the struggle for a living wage was therefore put on hold as the workers became involved in a defensive battle against redundancies. Furthermore, as we have seen, the committee was in the midst of transitioning into the AMCU and seeking to put it into power as the majority union.

During this time Mabanana had become disgruntled because he and other former committee members no longer had the power they had once had. He believed that the decision to join the AMCU undermined workers' potential to enter wage negotiations, and put them in a position where the company was threatening to lay off workers:

> Now that we are recognised the management is taking advantage saying, 'These guys are recognised so they won't go on an illegal strike.' Now they win because we can't go on an illegal strike. Being recognised is killing us. It's killing our morale and has divided us because if you remember well they never used to say we will retrench people. Even last year [2012] when we got back to work we had a written agreement ... [in which] management agreed that early January [2013] we are going on wage negotiations, but even up to today we have had no wage negotiations. All they are talking about is job cuts.[15]

In his view, 'What is happening now is nothing much compared with that [which was happening in 2012]'.[16]

Prior to gaining official recognition, the AMCU NEC was already holding meetings with the worker committee and other leaders of Amplats in order to collectively plot a way forward. As early as February 2013, Gaddafi Mdoda, who was a leader of the committee and would soon become an AMCU branch member at the Khomanani shaft, could sense the way in which the victories of the worker committee could be undermined when they became part of the AMCU. During a meeting on 24 February with AMCU representatives and the various leaders at Amplats, he asked Mathunjwa what could be done in order to keep the worker committee alive. The president's response was evidently straight and to the point. He stated that he was 'not interested on [the] worker committee and their issues. They [the workers and AMCU] are here in the name of AMCU. They [the AMCU] are not going to discuss anything concerning the worker committee.'[17]

For Mathunjwa, it seemed clear that the committees at Amplats had been temporary and were no longer necessary. We might suspect he was aware that an independent organisation could potentially challenge the authority of his established union. Instead of viewing the committee as a complementary force, Mathunjwa is likely to have considered the worker committees as a threat and therefore aimed to destroy them. On the one hand, this made a great deal of sense since the AMCU needed to build its own politics, and as a union, its success was based on its ability to maintain and extend its membership. On the other hand, for Gaddafi this was devastating since the worker committee at Amplats was 'the strongest structure that I have ever seen'.[18] He began to anticipate, 'Now that power, they are going to lose it. AMCU is going to take it. [The AMCU] is going use them as their steward[s]. Some of them are going to the region and some of them are going to the national level of AMCU.' He lamented:

> There are some agreements that the worker committee have forced the management to sign [the return to work agreement]. Now just because they [the worker committee] are getting to AMCU, they [the agreements] are lapsing .... There are [also] some things that the bosses, the mine bosses, can't be forced to do by AMCU. It's only [the] worker committee [that can do it]... now [the] worker committee is facing too much challenges and actually I'm not sure whether...[the] worker committee and AMCU are going to go [on] a long road together ... because the worker committee is used to make sure that if something is dissatisfying them, they put an end on it.[19]

It soon became apparent to other leaders as well that the AMCU was now in the drivers' seat. Former leaders of an autonomous organisation that did not need to report to anyone but their mass-based worker constituency were now partially controlled by a union structure. According to Tumelo:

Mathunjwa ... doesn't like the idea of the worker committee, but the bad thing here is that AMCU is where it is right now, [in] all of the [platinum] companies, because of the worker committees. So I understand, the worker committees are a threat to the unions, all of the unions, because we don't take nonsense. We [move] forward with what the workers want. So I would agree, even if I was to be a union owner, or a top union leader, I would also hate the idea of a worker committee, because I would know that if I make a mistake, somebody is there to grab me, or to be there as a threat. Because this strike committee, it was the only strike committee in the world that could face the unions and do what they believe in. So, I would say, he [Mathunjwa] is right to dislike the idea of the worker committee.[20]

As late as mid-August the relationship between the two forces was still being ironed out. 'Basically, it is difficult now', Tumelo explained, 'some of the comrades since we have joined AMCU, uh, they don't like an idea of the worker committee any more.' He elaborated that those who were meeting as an independent committee were called 'the anti-AMCU guys .... Because they [head office] are saying if there is going to be a meeting, then AMCU must know about the meeting. If there is a meeting that AMCU doesn't know about, it means that meeting is a very dangerous [one].' He summed up the somewhat obvious situation that the committee was faced with: 'We have chosen AMCU as we love it as a union. But some of the things we are not happy about.'[21]

In contrast to other new AMCU branch leaders, Daniel's point of view was that there was a relatively smooth transition from the workers' committees to the AMCU:

The difference is that now we are no longer worker committee, we are AMCU. Even the management, when they call us they no longer address us as the worker committee .... They say they want the secretary from the branch or chairperson for the branch [of AMCU] and we know who they want, that is the only difference.[22]

Others continued to see the need for a committee that was autonomous from the AMCU and which was therefore able to represent the interests of the workers outside of the union's 'official' structures. Lazarus, for example, concluded in mid-2013 that 'once now we fall under AMCU this means that now the worker committee is no longer there ... but at the moment we are discussing as a worker's committee ... [how] to do things on our own.'[23]

Makhanya reflected that although the committee no longer continued to meet officially, the branch members were well respected as worker committee leaders in their shafts, and they therefore had a responsibility to act as watchdogs:

> So this is the reason of [the] worker committee that after working hours let's go and meet and observe AMCU [to ensure] that it's doing what we want. Because another thing we said, we took almost like 30 years to form a worker committee. We can note that when NUM started operating there was no [prominent] worker committee. So we sat and said from the history of 30 years, we can't just kill it in one day. Because it doesn't mean that we trust AMCU [to act in the interest of the workers].[24]

Offering a balanced account of the transition to the formalised union, he said that some leaders 'took their heart completely and gave it to AMCU'. He estimated that of the 47 people who were part of the committee during the strike of 2012 (which included workers from Swartklip and Amandelbult), by mid-2013 two or three people from each shaft (about 15 in total) remained. They met about every two weeks depending on the circumstances. Makhanya maintained that this was 'the strongest leadership that can influence everything', contending that despite the diminished size of the committee it was still representative and could actually make decisions more quickly.[25]

Trevor Ngwane carried with him an activist Marxist lens through which to understand the fact that former independent worker committee leaders had become part and parcel of the branch structures of a union – the AMCU. He had been advising platinum mineworkers about the Labour Relations Act (LRA) at the time, and concluded that there were two opposing viewpoints among the new leaders within the AMCU:

> Currently, workers at Amplats [leaders] are divided. Some want to be shop stewards and coordinators with the attendant perks, while others want to remain as militant as they were when they broke through the NUM bureaucracy and called strikes; when they were saying even the LRA can't stop us.[26]

The decision to go on strike without a union was not illegal but rather required a certain degree of independence from both established unions and the company – something that, from Trevor's perspective, was likely to assist workers in getting their demands met.

During this critical transition, the DSM sought to engage with the new AMCU branch leaders. As discussed in Chapter 4, several individuals had built a firm relationship during the 2012 strike. The ground workers of the DSM, Liv and Mametlwe (among others) contacted individuals including Tumelo and Gaddafi, and they held an informal meeting around a picnic table at a mall in Rustenburg on 23 February 2013.[27] Again, the DSM sought to tap into the existing context and ongoing struggle faced by workers at Amplats. Mametlwe raised the question of the 'seriousness of retrenchments', which in his view were 'inevitable'. He showed concern when he questioned the leaders of Amplats who were present: 'Are comrades studying the seriousness?' It appeared evident that:

> They know you are going to have to strike. The state will have armed bodies of men to protect [the interests of the employer]. There will be massive military intervention to ensure retrenchments [occur]. If Anglo is defeated, Implats, Anglogold, and farmers will not be able to go ahead. Anglo alone cannot win.

His conclusion was that 'solid organised support' was imperative and there was a further need to 'revive the national strike committee and prepare for a general strike'.[28]

However, when the former committee was asked about the way forward in this regard, the question of redundancies was put on the back burner. 'What I think you must first worry about is AMCU', Gaddafi stated, '[because] the policies are binding us.'[29] Tumelo explained to them that 'we need a union that can fight for us, against NUM [and the] AMCU can do that'. Referring to the ongoing attempt for the AMCU to gain legitimacy, he further stated that 'if AMCU is not recognised by the company, there is nothing we can do'.[30] The idea of an independent committee was becoming outdated in the new context in which they found themselves, at least for some former leaders who had jettisoned it. Others, in particular Gaddafi, continued to maintain the idea that the worker committee needed to be revived. 'AMCU is not fit to fight [even] a small battle. [but] I made them [the workers] join AMCU and now it's hard to say this is not the place to go. They [AMCU NEC] say I am talking too much. If I come with an issue opposing their strategies, maybe I will be expelled.' As Gaddafi signed the LRA and began to experience the ways in which being part of a formalised structure was hampering the potential for workers to hold their employer accountable, he conceded that workers needed unions while simultaneously questioning whether it was possible to 'create a situation whereby we do not need unions any more.'[31]

The DSM and its representatives in the platinum belt, for their part, had never been opposed to the AMCU as such, although they have been accused of being so. In this instance, Mametlwe responded to Gaddafi and the others when he argued that 'We need AMCU. But we need to retain the worker committee [so we can] operate outside of collective bargaining structures so we can fight effectively.' Reflecting in part on the experience of the 2012 unprotected strikes, he pointed out that 'worker committees ... can appeal to all unions.'[32] Liv added that 'AMCU is nothing without our members.' Seeking to shift the terrain of the trade union space at Amplats, Liv concluded that the branch leadership seemed 'demoralised'. In a sense, from the perspective of the DSM leaders in Rustenburg that day, 'strike [workers'] committees are [now] recognised and work full time in the offices'. What was need at that point, she argued, was 'unity and clarity .... AMCU offices should be war rooms.'[33]

On 3 March 2013, Amplats officially signed a recognition agreement with the AMCU. The spokesperson for Amplats, Mpumi Sithole, stated at a press conference that 40 per cent of the 60,000 workers at Amplats were members of the AMCU.[34] Mathunjwa concluded, 'We have full organisation rights and will now be able to implement formal structures and appoint shop stewards at Amplats.'[35] In an ongoing bid to preserve the reputation of the NUM, its spokesperson, Lesiba Seshoka, told the press conference that workers would eventually rejoin his union. Clearly, however, this was not going to happen any time soon.

THE BITTER STRUGGLE FOR RECOGNITION AND THE BLOODY AFTERMATH OF MARIKANA

While the worker committee at Amplats was concluding its strike and working with management to take over the former NUM offices, 271 workers at Lonmin, including former committee members, were up on murder charges through the apartheid 'common purpose' clause. De

Vos, who was scathing of the ANC government's move in an article called 'No common purpose to commit suicide', noted:

> News that the National Prosecuting Authority (NPA) has decided to charge 259 arrested Marikana miners with the murder of their 34 colleagues who were shot dead by the police, is bizarre and shocking and represents a flagrant abuse of the criminal justice system, most probably in an effort to protect the police and/or politicians like Jacob Zuma and Nathi Mthethwa .... The Apartheid state often used this provision to secure a criminal conviction against one or more of the leaders of a protest march, or against leaders of struggle organisations like the ANC (and later the UDF) whose members (on the instructions of the leader or leaders), had taken part in sabotage activities or the assault or killing of representatives of the Apartheid state. Even where that leader had not taken part in the sabotage or killing, he or she would be convicted of inciting the assault or the killing.[36]

Those older workers who survived might have felt they were reliving their experiences under the old authoritarian regime. At least two committee members had been killed by the police on 16 August, Andries Motlapula Mtshenyeho and Mgcineni 'Mambush' Noki. The Marikana Commission of Inquiry was launched by President Jacob Zuma and first sat on 1 October 2012. No families or workers were present, and this seemed to signal the way in which the commission would be whitewashed in favour of Lonmin, NUM, ANC and the police, all of whom were blaming the AMCU and the workers more generally for the events which unfolded on 16 August 2012.

During the course of the Lonmin strike and following its aftermath through until the end of 2012 and early 2013, the state was hitting hard against the striking mineworkers. Thomas (discussed in Chapter 3) stated that in September 2012, the police went to his home. He was sitting down in a chair at the time when, he alleges, the police shot at him and took him to jail.[37] 'The police started looking for us as leaders who were leading the strike', Rasta recalled. They were arrested and taken to jail. He remembered, 'We were beaten [and we were] asked, "Who killed the police? Who killed NUM members? Where are the gun[s]?" All sorts of questions.' He responded, 'I know nothing about the guns, yes I was a leader, but what you are asking about, I know nothing about it.'[38]

Bhele (see Chapters 2 and 3), was among those who experienced some of the most inhumane torture at the hands of the police, most likely because he could be seen so clearly at the forefront of the workers in the early days of the strike. Early in the morning on 25 October 2012, 'five plainclothes policemen broke down his door and stormed into his one-roomed shack in Wonderkop village, Marikana.'[39] They then suffocated him in his shack, holding a plastic bag tightly around his head and mouth. They took him to two police stations, including Phokeng, and continued to torture him, asking the whereabouts of the leader of the strike. His voice remained weak and for three days he did not eat. Another 26-year-old man was tortured to the extent that his bowels loosened, wetting his pants which he had to wash in the prison basin. He waited naked until the clothes dried.[40]

While the commission proceeded, workers continued to suffer at the hands of the state. Bhele reflected about the situation more broadly:

> You never know who to trust. Even the people we regarded as our union [the NUM] to represent us betrayed us, the police were even worse. We live in fear now because we do not trust anyone any more. Even if a person calls you to ask where you are, you are scared to tell them because you do not know if they are genuine or not. So we are still living in these conditions because we need money so that we can send the money back home to our children and families. If there were jobs back home we would go back but we have to be here because we need the money. Even when you walk down the street, you constantly have to look over your shoulders because you never know when your enemy can strike.[41]

On 5 March, 6,000 employees at Lonmin went on an unprotected strike demanding that the NUM 'offices be shut down' on the grounds that the AMCU had a majority of members in various shafts. According to *The Star*, the NUM responded that 'we have co-existed with other unions before and we don't see why they [the AMCU] find it difficult'.[42] For AMCU members, however it was clear: the NUM was the enemy which had shot at them on 11 August and subsequently come to the mountain to tell them to head back to work. Tensions were high, and we were told on more than one occasion that wearing a red T-shirt at the mine could get you beaten up or killed. NUM representatives had argued that in order to avoid violence the 50 plus one policy should be jettisoned, and despite the fact that NUM was losing members, it should nevertheless be involved in negotiations and also have office space. Mathunjwa questioned this approach. He maintained that management 'are trying to accommodate the NUM at any cost ... the NUM has been in bed with these companies for many years. Filing the divorce papers is hard for them.'[43]

Mawethu Joseph Steven, a forerunner of the AMCU in the platinum belt from 2011 and then regional organiser (see Chapter 2), was gunned down on 12 May 2013 as he was approaching his turn to testify at the commission. This paved the way for further inter-union rivalry. Some believed that he was behind the 2012 strike, and accompanying violence, in the platinum belt. In a bid to counter the false accusation that the AMCU was a vigilante union, Mathunjwa responded, 'We condemn these senseless killings of our members in the strongest terms possible. We hope this time that our police will find the killers and that justice will be served in the same way it would, were it not an AMCU member.'[44] He went further to urge his members not to retaliate. Two NUM members, who were brothers, were however killed in what seemed like a retaliation.

The following Tuesday, 14 May, AMCU members went on an un-protected strike demanding that the NUM offices be closed. The next day, Mathunjwa addressed a mass meeting of workers at Wonderkop Stadium, where he sought to convince employees to return to work. AMCU branch leader Jack Khoba, however, publicly refused to return since NUM members were carrying guns: 'The carrying of weapons at work is very scary ... some workers are afraid to go underground, which is making life difficult for us. There is a company policy with regards to weapons on the mine premises.'[45] Lonmin representatives responded by increasing the number of random searches of offices and employees.

The AMCU and the NUM blamed each other for the violence that was being inflicted in the platinum belt. On the one hand, Mathunjwa argued that 'they [the tripartite alliance] have been telling their people that they need to reclaim the platinum belt back for NUM'. He asked, 'Is this why we are being attacked and killed by NUM?'[46] On the other hand, NUM spokesperson Lesiba Seshoka claimed the opposite was the case: 'NUM leaders live in fear on a daily basis because of the violence from AMCU. Why are they demanding that we close our offices when they should be concentrating on their union work instead of focusing on NUM?'[47]

In light of the ongoing spate of killings, ANC President Jacob Zuma called for a series of 'peace talks'. According to Tau, this was in order to assure 'investors that his government was intervening to restore stability in mining to boost the country's economy'.[48] On 3 June 2013 a meeting was held between representatives of the AMCU, its federation (NACTU), the NUM and its umbrella, COSATU. Labour minister Mildred Oliphant was also present. She commented that 'If we [need] to deploy a peace-keeping force then we'll do it. We can't take chance[s]'.[49] Attempting to appear non-partisan she confirmed, 'We've agreed that if AMCU Is the majority, let it be so.'[50] However, NACTU president Joseph Maqhekeni was not as optimistic about the meeting, claiming that 'the NUM and COSATU attacked us (making statements) suggesting that AMCU were killers and we challenged them to give us proof'.[51]

In the midst of the ongoing turmoil, AMCU members held a mass meeting of 3,000 workers at Wonderkop Stadium in a bid to take a decisive move that would grant the union a recognition agreement with the company. Mathunjwa (who was accompanied by two bodyguards) put the matter in the workers' hands when he asked them to decide the way forward. The workers decided to strike. However, Mathunjwa requested they give the company a final opportunity: 'If Tuesday [the following week] ends and they still sing the same tune, then we will give them a notice on Wednesday and the strike should resume from Saturday [15 June].'[52] The Labour Court had also issued an interdict which stated that the NUM needed to leave the offices by 16 June.[53]

The Lonmin mine executive had also become involved in an attempt to ensure that the violence came to a halt. The executive vice-president responsible for dealing with division and sustainability, Natascha Viljoen, reflected, 'We saw murder and violence last year and we have a duty to ensure this doesn't happen again.'[54] The company sought to increase the police presence at the mine and for leaders from the unions to stop antagonising each other.

As the commission was dragging on and the AMCU continued to battle for recognition at the mine, there was also a perceived need to commemorate the Marikana massacre. The union's NEC, including Mathunjwa, was initially not forthcoming about this process. Members of the MSC, including Rehad Desai, Trevor Ngwane, Anita Khanna and Bheki Buthelezi, provided the impetus for the 16 August 2013 one-year commemoration of the massacre. Not coincidentally, they are core members of the DLF. The president of the AMCU, Advocate Dali Mpofu, and Bishop Jo Seoka, among others, eventually joined them in planning the event's logistics. On 8 August 2013, alongside a number of former worker committee members, they had a small meeting in a church in Pretoria to discuss how to proceed, and it was determined that the focus of the day (16 August) should be commemorating those who were killed while simultaneously continuing to demand a living wage of R12,500. There was also broad agreement among those present that the government should recognise that day as a public holiday.[55]

When asked about his relationship to Bantu Holomisa's United Democratic Movement (UDM) at the meeting, Mathunjwa spat back, 'Don't frame me! We [the AMCU] don't sleep with any political party and we will never, that must be clear.'[56] About two days later, on 10 August, a similar meeting was held at St Albans Cathedral in Pretoria. During the discussion, which was chaired by Mpofu, Mathunjwa mentioned that he was against workers going on unprotected strikes as this threatened their jobs. The outspoken Trevor Ngwane responded that he was concerned about this since 'that is the only way workers can win. That's what they did in Marikana and they won.' He added, 'Bosses don't move unless we do something militant. The idea of a protected strike comes from the bosses to keep the working class weak.'[57]

Pamphlets were passed out with the DLF's name on them in support of the 'AMCU commemoration'. Mathunjwa, apparently unaware that the organisation was present in the room all around him, told the meeting, 'I am worried about the DLF, they are creating problems for us left and right.'[58] The others sat quiet and Bheki responded, 'The DLF is clear, we follow the lead of the workers.'[59] As the meeting went on, one of the workers announced the disdain they had for the ruling party, saying that 'there are parties that have been historically helpful. Those should be accommodated. But no ANC.'[60]

On the actual day of the commemoration, indeed, the ANC was not present officially as an organisation. Approximately 10,000 workers congregated below the mountain to commemorate the massacre. Malema was amongst the most prominent of those who gave speeches. Seeing the opportunity to win a constituency in the platinum belt generally, he had gone to Impala to add fire to the flame during the Impala strike in early 2012. He was present with a team of expelled ANCYL members in Marikana on 18 August 2012 (see Chapter 3) a mere two days after the massacre. Now on the 16 August 2013 anniversary commemoration of the massacre, he was poised to form a new political party, the Economic Freedom Fighters (EFF). Along similar lines to the AMCU, which offered a radical critique of the NUM's relationship to the ANC, the EFF laid hard into the ANC.

Malema did not organise the commemoration but nevertheless took centre stage on the day. The DSM was present with a large banner in the middle of the field below the workers. In an informal conversation I had with Mametlwe that day he noted with disappointment, 'Malema is taking, in one fell swoop, advantage of all the hard work we did here.'[61] Indeed, Malema's electrifying six-minute speech spoke directly to the emotions of the workers at Lonmin, who appeared in awe as they could be seen smiling throughout. As one who had himself been dismissed from the ANC, he claimed to identify with the experiences of the workers at Lonmin. The speech began by saluting the EFF, AMCU, and in particular Joseph Mathunjwa. He then proceeded to chant down Jacob Zuma and the ANC government: 'Phansi [down] Jacob Zuma! Phansi! Phansi the government ANC, Phansi! Phansi Zuma!' As is the South African tradition, the crowd repeated, 'Phansi!'[62]

Aspects of his speech are worth quoting at length since it helps us to understand the strategic discourse that the EFF employed, which paved its way to prominence in the Rustenburg platinum belt in the subsequent 2014 national elections:

> The CEO of Lonmin, those who are so telling you [that he is on your side], they are misleading you. Lonmin together with the ANC government has killed our people. And you must be reminded of that [crowd cheers] so that you don't forget and commit a similar mistake. You've [Lonmin have] got blood on your hands. And blood of innocent people! And that's why we're here today. If you [the CEO] and Lonmin had agreed to meet these workers we were not going to have blood! You refused to meet them. Today in the name of 'peace', you come here and say nothing! And [you] tell them [workers] we will still talk about R12,500, when you promised 12,500 [crowd cheers]. You can't say to us, we must come here, commemorate this day and not talk politics, I am a politician![63]

In parallel to the workers, he blamed Lonmin for not giving them the money which they demanded. He even took a more radical step in order to blame Lonmin for being responsible, not only for their wages, but for the people who died in the massacre. At the climax of his speech, he was clear about whose side he and the EFF are on:

> Lonmin, you will only be our friend, the day these people have got R12,500 in their pocket [cheer]. You remain the enemy of our people. You have butchered our people! Our people were protected by nature

when they were on their knees! This mountain protected them from murderous police! ... this soul [in the mountain] will never rest in peace. We are here to say to the soul we will never betray you. We will never want to be friends of a murderous [ANC] government .... Today we are told we are here to talk peace, [but we must ask ourselves] peace with who? Because no one has accepted responsibility .... They say to us let's forget, let's forgive, let's be peaceful. With who? .... all of them today, they still have their positions. They are still in government. Phiyega is still commissioner. Nathi Mthethwa is still minister. President Zuma is still president. Yet, yet, our brothers are dead. Only in South Africa where 34 people can be killed and no one takes responsibility.... They killed them. Zuma sent police here. When you, when you workers, you were here, when you were here. Zuma passed you and went to meet *mulungu* [a white person] in the factory.[64]

Malema's disdain of the ANC was shared by ordinary mineworkers at Lonmin and elsewhere. Rasta's position on the matter epitomised the attitudes of mineworkers in Marikana when he reflected that 'To be honest I will not vote for the ANC. It has not delivered, the bucket system is still there in Cape Town, [and] people got killed in Marikana.' 'Yet', he concluded:

it is in government because of [us] the mineworkers .... A mineworker that votes for the ANC knows nothing totally. Our government does not feel for us and they forget that they get a lot of money from us we dig out the platinum and pay taxes and we only work for R4,200 .... If anyone was at the strike last year they would not vote for the ANC.[65]

Following the launch of the EFF in Marikana later that year, he had been somewhat undecided about which party he would vote for given its newness, but he nevertheless maintained, 'Malema tried to come to the mines but was blocked by the government. Yet [ANC President] Zuma did not come to stop the killing at the mine. The government is killing us. Malema is better than Zuma and it seems he walks with us, the miners. We would rather vote for EFF than the ANC.'[66]

New political organisations, including the Workers and Socialist Party (WASP) and the EFF, had sought primarily to build electoral support for the 2014 elections. However, they were relatively disconnected from rank and file organising. Two days prior to the commemoration, the AMCU was finally in the driver's seat as it had gained full organisational rights at Lonmin. While the workers were on the mountain risking their lives seeking a living wage of R12,500 in 2012, branch leaders of the NUM had long since attained this goal. Now, the new branches of the AMCU were also ahead of the rest of the workers in terms of their financial standing. There was concern that the AMCU, like its predecessor the NUM, would betray its members. The Greater Lonmin Workers' Council (GLWC) emerged to advise AMCU in this context.

THE RISE AND DEMISE OF THE GREATER LONMIN WORKERS' COUNCIL

While the committees at Amplats remained relatively constant, with individuals becoming branch committee office bearers of the AMCU once the new union became recognised, there was more than one core committee at Lonmin. Thus far, I have discussed the initial organisers who approached management on 21 June 2012; the committee of RDOs which represented the shafts at the beginning of the strike on 9 August; the Mountain Committee that emerged following the attacks by NUM; and then the multi-pronged committee which was transformed following the Marikana massacre. With the AMCU being awarded a recognition agreement which was accompanied by violence, few were likely to create an alternative structure. Despite its significance, many (perhaps most) of the community of Marikana and Lonmin mine had probably not heard of the last committee at Lonmin discussed in this book, the GLWC.[67] It appeared to offer an extension of the Mountain Committee, and to hold the possibility of maintaining the priority of mass workers' control over decision-making processes in the AMCU, in the wake of the strike at Lonmin which ended on 18 September 2012. The council was intended to meet monthly with the three branches of Lonmin, to discuss issues that had arisen. The idea was that branches would give a report to the council, and the council would advise where necessary. The council and the branches would then collectively 'combine everything and then plan a way forward'.[68]

Zakhele (see Chapter 3), the chairperson of the council, described the logic behind its formation:

> the elderly workers like us met and said since we have left NUM and now joined AMCU on our return [to work] from the mountain, it's now

a worker thing. And we thought perhaps had AMCU been there before, people would not have died in the manner they did. And if older guys like us were in leadership, because we have a great deal of experience on the movements in mines, we would have been able to call people in order to talk and agree as leaders. So we decided that even if we are not in AMCU, there is a need for a structure called the Greater Lonmin Workers' Council that will deal directly with the leaders [of AMCU] and not depend entirely on the union even though we are affiliated to the union. That was how we will be able to monitor the union and hold them to account, you see?[69]

Members of the council had a vast experience as both informal and formal leaders in the mines, including inside the NUM. Most importantly, the members had their fingers on the pulse of the rank and file. Some had even witnessed the rise and demise of the NUM as it became a tool of management. While it was once an 'insurgent trade union' acting as an engine of working-class power, it became defunct. But, why did this happen? Zakhele and other founders of the GLWC suggested that one core reason was that it did not have an independent council to ensure it was accountable to the rank and file:

Zokwana's union died because the branches took over and the members were not in control. Yet we have been there for too long and we know what happened .... When I came to the mines in 1981 the NUM was our thing. We fought for it. We walked with Ramaphosa and them, but today they have turned against us.[70]

'When the NUM left,' he recalled, 'we were aggrieved with the R14,000 [per month] the leaders were getting paid. That is what made us not progress and [be] unsustainable because it [exorbitant payment] was being used by management [to prevent workers from having their demands addressed]'.[71] The branches in the mines are clearly the focal point – and arguably the core organisers – of any union at the platinum mines. They therefore play a key role in determining the extent to which a union is driven from below, or controlled from the top down. The GLWC was a response to many years of shortcomings of the NUM branches, which became disconnected from their members, particularly following the transition to democracy.

Unlike the situation at Amplats, the branch committees at Lonmin were elected in 2013 in an extremely hostile environment. Workers and their families were traumatised by the infliction of state violence on 16 August 2012, and with the continuation of violence in the area, levels of fear and distrust undoubtedly reached a plateau. Some of the negotiators following the massacre were already leaders of the AMCU, while other leaders died, were injured and went to hospital, or were accused of murder by the South African state. Based on his communication and involvement with a wide range of worker leaders (both informal and informal), Bheki summarised the process through which the branch committees at Lonmin were elected:

> Those comrades after the 22 per cent [was given to the workers], they called a mass meeting in different shaft[s]. Those who are vocal enough, they would come with a list in those mass meetings and say… 'Here is a list of the people. Here is the chairperson in the shaft committee.' And call them [the mass of workers and ask], 'who oppose[s] this'? Tell me at that time who [is] going to oppose this because everyone is afraid? … So all the office [bearing members of AMCU], it was not democratic, it was imposed and even AMCU [NEC] has got no time [to deal with this issue].[72]

Bheki, who attended their meetings and worked directly with the GLWC in an attempt to ensure that it was sustained and empowered to achieve its objectives, further pointed out that there was a strong tension created by what he called the 'opportunist' AMCU branch leaders and the GLWC. While the GLWC appeared to undertake a programme which meant they would act as genuine representatives of the workers, the branch officials were not historic leaders of the 2012 strike and were arguably 'bribed' by their salaries and prone to taking orders from the AMCU NEC or from management, either of which would serve to undermine and eventually eclipse independent voices.

According to Bheki, the defining feature of the council was its dedication to the workers who had fought and died on the mountain. When the strike ended, workers at Lonmin had heard about the worker committee at Amplats, which was independent from union affiliation and more structured than the somewhat elusive committee(s) at Lonmin. When workers decided to end their strike, these older leaders committed themselves to 'continue and serve the legacy of Mambush and all those leader[s] who have fallen. We want justice to be done until to the end.' Bheki who was part of the initiative, further resolved the spirit with which the GLWC sought to move forward:

We want to counsel our [branch] leaders who are in the union [AMCU] now. To understand that they don't abandon … the thing that happened in the mountain. As much as they will be serving in the union, but they must know that the union was brought here by the blood [of the workers]. So that blood; it need[s] to be take[n] care of.[73]

'The blood' here is referring to the spirit of independent militancy which was spilled on the day of the massacre – 16 August 2012. The council viewed the 34, and also those who stood firm on the mountain in 2012, as heroic figures who had fought for their rights. They were involved in issues related to the commission, given that it would largely decide the outcome for those 271 mineworkers who had been arrested and charged with murder on the basis of an Apartheid 'common purpose' law.

Thus, when it was announced that funding for the workers' lawyers would not be provided by the state, the GLWC, alongside the MSC and with the EFF's support, began to plan a march to Pretoria (which was to take place on 12 September). On Sunday 8 September, Bheki met with Joseph Mathunjwa and Dumisani Nkalitshana – the national organiser – at Dali Mpofu's office in Sandton. Night shift workers could come to the march with no hesitation if they wished, but the day shift would need the day off in order to attend. It was decided that Joseph Mathunjwa would inform the branch leaders of a march to Pretoria which would take place the next week. However, he did not do this. Furthermore, when Seoka went to Lonmin management to ask for a day off, it was not granted.

The MSC nevertheless continued mobilising. It paid R1,000 to have two cars patrolling around Marikana to alert people that there was going to be a mass meeting that day (11 September) and a march which was intended to include all of Lonmin the following day. It also created a pamphlet which was distributed at the mass meeting, which took place at the mountain and included an impressive 10,000 workers. Bheki remembered that 'the pamphlet, it was ringing in the minds of the workers'.[74] From their perspective, they were the ones who were attacked and killed by the police, and yet the state was refusing to grant their lawyers funding to represent them. At the meeting, logistics were of central concern, as workers needed to be mobilised since buses had already been booked by the GLWC.

When both the branches and the GLWC were set to address the masses that day, Bheki sensed that there was 'going to be tension' and he therefore decided to 'meditate' between the two parties. He recalled, 'When I tried to call them altogether the branch secretary of the union sang a song that was anti-me.'[75] The song asked questions like: who is this outsider? Where is he coming from? Through a song, the branch leader questioned why Bheki wanted to be part of something that was for workers, while he was not a worker himself. He could have backed down at this stage in fear of being attacked, based on the fact that indeed he was not part of the mobilisation which had culminated in the massacre at the mountain more than a year earlier, nor was he a worker at Lonmin or any mine. However, Bheki had become a part of the struggle in Marikana, he knew it and many of the workers did as well. He therefore responded antagonistically to the leader, believing that regardless of where he was coming from, his political position in the matter was the correct one:

> No comrade, don't even do that. I'm coming a long way with the struggle and everything. If you want to fight me directly physically, not ideo-logically, that one [where] you can put aside idea[s], then we can fight physically. Even myself, I'm a man, I can face you. That's the way that we do [it] in Africa isn't it? That if you are challenged by a man without idea[s and] he challenge[s] you physically, you must say that you are a man too [by fighting]. If you are a man, you must show it.[76]

The secretary, according to Bheki, then 'shut up, he shut his mouth'. When Bheki looked to the others, 'you can see the whole [of the] branches, their face[s], they were fuming'. Even the mass of workers could see that there was a division between the men who were about to address them.[77]

The GLWC then addressed the meeting, explaining that 'we were in a meeting with Mathunjwa and our lawyers on Sunday to prepare for a march to Pretoria because they don't want to pay our lawyers. So AMCU had applied to [the] company and … [it] refused to give us a day off.'[78] The workers then became silent until, without raising their hands, they said, '*futsek asiyi*' (Zulu slang for 'Fuck off, we are not going'). The mood signified that workers were refusing to go to work, and were adamant that they must attend the march the following day.

Bheki and some others could see that 'the branches have calculated [that workers could come to this conclusion]. They [branches] have their own people that they have planted within the mass meeting.'[79] One worker raised his hand. When called upon, he questioned why the workers' council was addressing the workers instead of the office-bearing branch officials who had been elected to represent them. The chairperson responded that the agenda for the meeting was to discuss the march, not to discuss who was addressing them. The workers were pleased with this explanation.[80]

AMCU branch officials, however, told the workers to go to work that evening, and that the next day, people should also go to work and not on the march. As one official put it, 'The company has told us that they want the production.'[81] A branch secretary at Karee, who coincidentally was not on the mountain on the day of the massacre, warned workers that if they did not attend work the next day, they could be fired:

> OK comrades, we as AMCU cannot allow you not to report on duty tomorrow. Listen here comrades. In Karee in 2011, we went on strike. There was a case of 283 people who were dismissed ... that case is still on. We are fighting it. Comrades, second thing is [that] which happened on the 16th of August, it's still on. It's on the shoulders of the union. Now if you take a resolution of not going back to work tomorrow, who's going to represent you?[82]

Bheki remembered thinking that rather than standing alongside the workers, 'these people are representing the employer now'. He recounted the way in which another branch leader stood up and commented:

> No, I want to open my chest. I want to speak out like the first comrade who have commented that 'Why are our leaders not there?' .... These people, we know them, we have elected them to be Lonmin Workers' Council but now what they are doing? ... It's not what we have been mandating them [to do]. Some of them they want ... to take us out from the branch office in order for them to be resuming power .... And then in the pamphlet that was produced it's written ... [Zakhele] and Bheki. That Bheki never worked in a mine.[83]

Bheki then stood up. The workers responded positively towards Bheki and said, 'We know this person.' According to him, they then asked, 'Why now he's been badmouthed?' The meeting became disorderly and a group of workers, seeing the potential for others to turn against him, took Bheki away quickly to his car.[84] No decision was taken regarding whether or not people should go to work or attend the march the following day. The march nevertheless was successful and included a larger number from Amplats than from Lonmin.

The following Monday, 16 September 2013, Mathunjwa held a meeting with the branch and the GLWC at 11 am, again in Sandton. However, the influential leaders of the council, including the secretary and the chairperson, were not present. Instead, according to Zakhele, a few members arrived, and were told by Mathunjwa that he had done some research and concluded that 'in Anglo, [the council there] has been disband[ed] because the people … end up to form another union which wants to be against AMCU. So that must be one structure [only].'[85] Zakhele further summarised:

> We had gone to him [Mathunjwa] as old men to ask him to hear out the GLWC and he said, 'Oh, you are the guys that have formed a new union there?' We said, 'No there is no new union, a new union will only be formed on the day we die.' … But he did not come to us – what he did was meet up with the leaders [of the branches] after that. So we heard that they [branches] were pointing at the shacks saying, 'There is a new structure starting that side, don't get misled by these people.' We then saw that we are being targeted. So we left it [the council], but we are still members of AMCU.[86]

Zakhele reflected on the violent culture in the mines which appeared to be on the verge of taking his own life: 'They ended up wanting to kill us for opening a new union and it became clear that some of us were going to be murdered at their homes, but they [the prospective killers] found them not there. So this is what happens at Lonmin.' He resolved that 'it's not even the NUM [that is the problem any more] because we removed NUM from [the] office as workers'.[87] The struggle to ensure that the new union, the AMCU, is accountable to and represents the concerns of the vast majority of mineworkers continues. Without the council, however, the possibility of the branches whitewashing the demands of the masses remains much greater. An articulate and long-standing worker representative pointed out, 'AMCU capitalised on the mistakes of the NUM. It also must not forget that it too is prone to that same mistake.'[88]

Without a council to ensure that the AMCU remained on the right track, it was not evident to former leaders such as Zakhele that the union would do so. When Siphiwe interviewed Zakhele in early November 2013, he pressed us to 'Make it clear to the people':

> I don't like AMCU because of Mathunjwa but it's because I can see that

I will benefit something from it. I have lots of kids. My child in matric wants to be a doctor and I don't have money to take him there [to school]. You see I can't just love another man for nothing. They must do something for us for us to like them. That's why I like him because I believe he will do the right thing and get us the money. But if he doesn't get it right we must tell him, he must not hear from his office bearers alone, but also from us workers as well.[89]

AMCU BRANCHES CALL FOR 'ZERO' REDUNDANCIES

While initially Amplats had proposed to make 14,000 workers redundant, they had backed down by September 2013 and planned to cut only 4,800 jobs, laying off 3,300 workers. On 27 September Amplats workers went on strike to demand 'zero' redundancies.[90] The branch leaders had become committed to the idea that no worker would be sacked under their new watch. Earlier in the year Makhanya had been elected as the prestigious AMCU branch chairperson position, and was generally perceived by Amplats workers in the Rustenburg region to be their foremost leader. He did not let this go to his head. Rather than distancing himself from the workers given the new perks which he received, he strove to remain embedded in his worker constituency. On the first day of the strike, he could be seen striding out with workers on a long walk to Thembelani, where branch leaders – including himself – would address a mass meeting. When asked why he did not obtain a lift in a car like the other leaders, he responded, 'No. I must be with the workers.'[91]

At the mass meeting, workers' adoration of the new union, and its president turned spokesperson, was displayed. Jonathan (introduced in Chapter 4) addressed the crowd and told the meeting, 'Eh Mathunjwa, pray. Elder Mathunjwa pray. We never saw a beautiful AMCU like this, so pray.' A chorus of workers responded, 'We are seeing beautiful AMCU, so Mathunjwa pray.' While the reputation of the AMCU was beginning to solidify as a militant union which represented the needs and aspirations of the mineworkers, the NUM continued to be vilified. The time for negotiating single-digit wage increases under the NUM was over. Mineworkers wanted a greater share of the resources which they were risking their lives to bring up from underground.

The meeting was ready to start and Jonathan, who was not an official AMCU leader himself, welcomed the office bearers and asked them to address the masses. Makhanya stood in the centre of the workers in the back of a truck so that he, along with the other leaders, was in full view. Makhanya chanted, 'Phansi [down] 8 per cent phansi!', 'Down with Zokwana! Down!' to which the crowd responded, 'Phansi!'[92]

He then told the workers that if the branch leaders were done with summarising the ongoing negotiations with management, people would be prompted to ask questions, and proceeded:

> We know that you have been here since 7 am. Comrades, we are apologising we arrived late … it's not because us we are [purposefully] coming late, it's because the meeting started late yesterday around 8 pm. And the meeting ended just now in the morning around 9 am. When you are in a meeting from yesterday the whole night until today in the morning [it is tiring] …. We sat with the Anglo management from yesterday until today in the morning and the other thing is, I am going to apologise that Mathunjwa is not here, we were with him the whole night until the morning. So when we left around 9 am after the meeting, Mathunjwa was phoned that he must come to union building in Pretoria to meet with Vice President Motlanthe and Susan Shabangu. Yeah, we are just apologising for that and we don't know if he is going to come this side today [the workers grumbled, '*Hayi* [no] Mathunjwa').[93]

The last general strike at Amplats had been the unprotected strike of 2012, a year earlier. Workers had therefore become accustomed to police interventions given the illegal nature of the actions which sometimes accompanied the strike. Makhanya clarified further that this strike was protected, or, in his words:

> legal … there will be no police that is going to stop you. As you are going on the road, make sure you don't close the road, don't carry sticks, as you are coming here at Siza [hostel at Thembelani] from Jabula … wherever there is an AMCU members [sic], it can be smelters or other shafts, no one is supposed to go to work.[94]

At the meeting, the workers agreed to stop AMCU employees from clocking in, but to leave alone members of the other unions, the NUM and UASA.

On 10 October, however, an agreement was reached which saw a small number of the workers made redundant, and the following day employees picked up tools again. The available evidence suggests that this agreement witnessed Mathunjwa negotiating directly with management without consulting branch leaders, and also conceding that some workers would indeed be let go. As we shall see, this move sowed divisions among the AMCU leadership.

DEEPENING CRACKS IN THE AMCU LEADERSHIP

The relationship between the AMCU NEC and branch committees at Amplats became steadily more antagonistic, and by late 2013 individuals from the branches – and even the North West region as whole – began to challenge the leadership style of the national structure. A letter directed to the head office in early November 2013 claimed that the AMCU regional organiser of the North West, Alfred Phanyana, had been unfairly expelled from the union: 'You have decided to suspend CDE Phanyana without involving other mines including ANGLO platinum... [this] is where you as [the] national office created disrepute within [the] organization without proper consultation.'[95]

The letter highlighted several other issues, including a preference for bottom-up rather than top-down approaches to decision making in the AMCU. It also requested the minutes of the NEC meeting that had unilaterally resolved to suspend Phanyana, as well as a clear outline of how and where he had failed to fulfil his duties as an organiser in the region. The letter concluded by questioning the integrity of the union, and also by beginning to make a comparison to its arch-rival:

> But if AMCU is a one man show like NUM, please explain to us directly so that we know there is no need of [the] constitutional structure to exist, it means that AMCU operates like a business whereby there [is] no need for consultation [but] only instruction .... It seems as if the union does not have [a] political agenda to drive [the] union forward but [that] it has a discrimination/personal agenda.[96]

When approached by Anglo branch leaders regarding the suspension, a currently disgruntled AMCU branch leader nicknamed Mabanana remembers Mathunjwa abruptly responding that 'I hired Phanyana. You don't know how come Phanyana came to AMCU.'[97]

Mabanana reflected that in meetings with the NEC, 'We were always arguing about things,' and that when shop steward councils were held at Amplats, debates were stifled by the president. He recalled one meeting in which 'When he comes to us he is shouting at us like all of us, like "Some of you are corrupt here! Some of you are doing bad things and I know all those stories! What is going to happen is that one day I am going to get one person [who is being a problem]."[98] At another meeting Mabanana described a situation in which the chairperson of Khomanani's shaft raised his hand to request some assistance from the national office and Mathunjwa began to shout. He proceeded to ask, 'You never raised your hands with Zokwana while he was speaking, [so] why are you doing that to me?'[99]

Edwin, from Bathopele, also became disenchanted with Mathunjwa's leadership style in 2013. As a former worker committee member (see Chapter 4), he helped bring the AMCU to the mines and also became branch chairperson at Bathopele. Edwin also believed that Phanyana was unjustly removed from his position in the AMCU. Like Gaddafi and Mabanana, he is of the opinion that he was victimised by Mathunjwa because:

> We were a threat to him. Truly speaking, because we were questioning [him], when was the congress where he was elected and where are the minutes of the congress he was elected [at]? And then [we also asked], how long should his term be because we know that according to the Labour Relations Act, it's all about terms organisationally. Even a president, after a certain time there must be elections. [We questioned] 'When will those elections be conducted?' And then he [Mathunjwa] started thinking that maybe we wanted to contest him.[100]

Essentially, Edwin resolved to go back to the NUM, which he viewed as a better union. He reflected on his previous job as a shop steward for the NUM:

> It was a very good experience, different than AMCU. It was perfect because we had many things like [an] education desk, health and safety .... The only thing that was a mistake was the leadership from above from the regional office. Those are the people that killed NUM because their problem is that they did not want to take the mandate from the workers and the workers to control the organisation. So when the people raised a complaint, they failed to resolve those complaints in a fair way.[101]

While Amplats workers had gained formal recognition for the AMCU and subsequently had fought against redundancies, as we have seen, the struggle for recognition at Lonmin had taken place in the aftermath of the police massacre and the 2012 strike. Leaders were victimised and in some cases tortured. Both NUM and AMCU members were being killed. With the final seal of AMCU recognition at Lonmin, the new GWLC committee was formed, but this too was broken up. .

Painting a somewhat bleak future for AMCU, Bheki, like a number of others, blamed the AMCU NEC for crushing the same workers' organisations that had brought it into power. He summarised the process through which the union became recognised at various platinum and gold mines:

> Even the union itself, you can see that they wish that something of the mountain [of militant and independent working class power], it can be something of the past, it can be something that no one is talking about as something that happened in 1996 [when several workers were killed in Sefikile, Northam during an Amplats strike] and no one knows about it. It's like the approach of the union officials is ... to say this thing of the mountain is like something that can take away their focus on the union issues. But mind you, those people at the mountain are the one[s] who made the union come to Lonmin. Even you can come to [the] worker committee at Anglo, [they] are the ones who organised AMCU. You can go to union comrade[s] from Impala, you can go to them to Carletonville, you go to whatever mine where AMCU is, you find that there is no national organiser who organised them .... It's organised by workers. But now, what is the union doing? All those efforts of the workers are being compromised in the manner of the same rule of the NUM, 'subscription forward, then workers back'.[102]

As a practical reflection of the near inevitability that is claimed in orthodox literature on trade unions and Marxism, it would appear that the emerging independent working-class power that was harnessed by the committees in 2012 was short-lived.

The culture of militancy displayed by the vast majority of workers at the platinum mines seemed to be in the process of being usurped and institutionalised by AMCU's trade union bureaucracy. However, as the next chapter demonstrates, this was not the case. Following a defensive struggle in 2013 against the imposed retrenchment at Amplats, and despite the need for worker leaders to attend the commission at Lonmin (since they were up on murder charges), the ongoing determination by workers to gain AMCU majority status continued at both mines. The year 2014 witnessed one of the longest and most important strikes in South African history. This strike and the immediate events leading up to it are the subject of the next chapter.

6

Insurgent Trade Unionism and the Great Strike of 2014

This strike did not begin in January this year. It started in 2012 at the moment when our brothers were massacred by the police.[1]

Since the brutal killings of mineworkers by the police in 2012, the insurgence of mineworkers had been bubbling beneath the surface. While it had lain in abeyance in 2013, conditions had not changed and neither had mineworkers' perspectives regarding the amount of compensation that they deserved for their work. S. K. Makhanya, the former IFP councillor, truck driver, and then winch operator at the Khuseleka mine, was at the forefront of 70,000 mineworkers based at the three largest platinum mining companies in the world.

Having formulated the R16,070 demand in the changing rooms after work in mid-2012, with the older working-class stalwart Chris, he was now AMCU branch chairperson for one of the most militant shafts in the belt. He had attended Socialist Workers Party annual conferences in Britain on more than one occasion, and he was not only schooled in working-class politics based on his experience with struggles, but was now also a self-proclaimed socialist. As keynote speaker and the 'official' mineworker from South Africa, Makhanya was met with applause by the international audience when he exclaimed, 'I am not just only the mineworker, I am the socialist, I am the freedom fighter.'[2] The struggle was no longer simply about individuals or solely about economistic concerns, but rather became at least symbolically about justice and the well-being of present and future generations:

S. K. Makhanya, arguably the quintessential leader of the contemporary mineworkers' movement, stands outside his Reconstruction and Development Programme (RDP) house. He is now an ordinary AMCU member who works underground in the same job that he had prior to the strike wave. (Photo by Luke Sinwell.)

As the youngest mineworkers that have worked in South Africa, we have seen our father, our grandfather, even ourselves, working on the mines and becom[ing] poor. We said, 'We are the last generation who are going to become poor in South Africa.' [crowd applause] Our previous strike[s] which took place last year [2012], have opened our minds to realise we have power to demand everything .... So we said in our next election [2014], we want to vote out this capitalism [sic] government. In this next election, we want to see a better life to all .... It's not just [the people who died at Marikana]. [At] different mines in South Africa they shoot and kill the mineworkers. Our last demand that we have put on the table is not just for the mineworkers. We are hopeful, in this next negotiation that we have already opened, we will end up [finalising] around September [2013], [that] there is some better living wage that we are going to receive. Or else there is a huge strike that we are going to see in South Africa.[3]

On the eve of the great strike, however, things did not look promising to many who had hope in the idea that workers would again unite to put effective pressure on the bosses of the three largest platinum mining companies in the world. (Workers from Amplats, Impala and Lonmin had now united under one union, the AMCU.) In January 2014 I wrote in my journal that 'As long as Mathunjwa is at the helm, AMCU will oppose the self-emancipation of workers. But he is clever, an organic intellectual linked to the everyday realities of the mineworkers.'[4] Splinters in the union appeared at first to undermine the unity of the workers, resulting in a situation where dissident AMCU branch leaders at Amplats in particular chose three different paths: forming a new union, attempting to re-establish the NUM, or remaining inside the AMCU. The last of these was, most importantly, the choice of the vast majority (including Makhanya). The refusal of Joseph Mathunjwa to let NUMSA representatives speak to a mass rally of workers meant that the chances of other unions, from different sectors, uniting in solidarity action with the platinum mineworkers seemed unlikely.

Mathunjwa was left with two choices. With the pressure put on by the ANC government alongside the negative portrayal of strikes in the mainstream media, he could succumb and end the strike early without ruffling too many feathers. This would likely mean he would be removed from his prestigious position by rank and file workers who had become disgruntled with a top-down leadership. Or he could be led by the workers in their ongoing quest for a living wage.

As is demonstrated below, there appeared to be a contradiction in Mathunjwa's approach to dealing with workers. On the one hand, his leadership style within AMCU had not changed since he was asked by workers at Douglas Colliery to form the union more than a decade earlier. He had ordained himself as the sole spokesperson and decision maker, and refused to be challenged by any other representative. This led to an undemocratic approach which denied branch leaders (especially former worker committee members at Amplats) the opportunity to express their opinions. On the other hand, he took the lead from the former committees of 2012 (and the rank and file which acted in unison with them) in order to uncompromisingly demand a living wage. Mathunjwa chose to ride the tiger of working-class insurgency while simultaneously acting personally to complete a spiritual journey. He proclaimed himself called by God to his holy task of leadership. The union, taking the lead from below, would not bow out of the strike until the mass of workers decided that it was time to do so.

THE GREAT 2014 STRIKE BEGINS

On 19 January 2014 the AMCU held a mass meeting of a few thousand workers from Amplats, Lonmin and Impala. Although official strike action did not begin until 23 January, this meeting took a decisive move that would lead to the longest strike in South African mining history. The mood signalled that action was imminent, but none were entirely aware of the uncompromising spirit that would fuel the workers for the next five months. Makhanya addressed the large crowd in the Olympia Stadium in Rustenburg which was a central place where mass meetings are sometimes held by workers from Impala, Amplats and Lonmin. Others had introduced themselves after being prompted by the master of ceremonies, but when it was Makhanya's turn to speak, he told the crowd that 'If you do not know me by now, then you are a spy.'[5] Indeed, few rank and file mineworkers and even fewer shop stewards of AMCU in the platinum belt covering the area from Rustenburg to Northam did not know this young man, who had been at the forefront of the struggle since mid-2012.

Soon afterwards Joseph Mathunjwa arrived with his coterie, which included AMCU officials and bodyguards. They did so in style, in expensive BMWs. An ovation spread like wildfire – the workers appeared to be in awe. At the outset of Mathunjwa's eloquent one-hour-long speech, he greeted the workers, thanked God for what they had received in life, and apologised sincerely for arriving late. He then exclaimed:

> Comrades, today is a big day, and it's not Mathunjwa's day, but AMCU's because you the workers are AMCU. AMCU is not a company, but it belongs to the workers. AMCU was not born out of the board room, but came from the workers in the mines who stayed ten days without food saying we are tired of NUM! ... If you think that AMCU is a company that was opened in board rooms and caucuses [then] you got it wrong. It comes from the grassroots and the belly of the earth and God blessed it on earth and in heaven. Hence today we are meeting, the workers here have found their home in AMCU![6]

The crowd responded with loud applause. Mathunjwa spoke passionately and persuasively, as if he was a preacher. From his perspective, God was on his and his union's side and nothing therefore could stand in their way. The workers continued to cheer when he explained in an obvious reference to AMCU's antagonism to close-knit political parties and trade unions (the ANC and the NUM):

> We saw on the belt [first hand] that if unions collaborate with political parties, workers will get hurt .... when we took this decision of being apolitical they said, 'Have you ever seen a union that survives without a political party?' I said [in response] 'God has agreed and if God has agreed I don't care what anybody says because He is Alpha and Omega.'[7]

Although Mathunjwa did not want to be viewed by the ANC as its archenemy, he could not avoid it, as we shall see later. During his speech he attempted to avert this when he claimed that the AMCU was not opposed to the ANC by calling the president the 'Honourable President Jacob Zuma'.[8]

Mathunjwa dealt with the idea of forming a new union – the Workers Association Union (WAU) – with the same venom that he used against his arch-enemy the NUM. He exclaimed, 'Down with the traitors, down!', 'Down with WAU, down!' to which the workers answered enthusiastically, 'Down!' He went so far as to personalise and identify specific individuals who had once been staunch AMCU branch leaders and former worker committee members. He had suspended, in total, about nine of them. In his speech, Mathunjwa elaborated, 'Let's talk about this man called

Thebe who is nowadays famous on TV [for defaming Mathunjwa]. We know, comrades, that any person who has anything bad to say about AMCU will be given a lot of play on TV and radio.'9

He proceeded to blame Thebe, in front of all the workers, for getting 5,000 workers dismissed at Thembelani mine for undertaking an unprotected strike. He further said, regarding others who had been disgruntled with his top-down leadership approach, that they had received R1,000 over the December holidays while they were in the Eastern Cape to go to a meeting which would lead to the formation of a new union. Thebe had then, according to Mathunjwa, 'appeared on TV barking like a demon'. Mathunjwa told workers who viewed him as a heroic figure, often referring to him as 'the lion', that these others had devised a plan to 'disgrace' him in public.[10]

It was not only the new union WAU which he sought to discredit. Referring to the former worker committee at Amplats, he indicated:

Comrades as the issue proceeded there were three groups during your strike here at Anglo. There was a group that wanted the workers to join any union from COSATU, like for example NUMSA. Others said a new union must be formed. The third said they did not want to join COSATU or form a new one but they wanted to go to AMCU. After that when we wanted to get your stop orders the striking committee said it was not going to release your forms and gave us conditions that we must give it money. We said, no problem, we will call mass meetings and ask the workers if they are for sale, and how much are they? And they backtracked and said, 'No, don't do that, we just wanted to talk a little bit you know' .... Comrades you know that during the strike these committees were in private talks with COSATU, did you know that?[11]

Other aspects of his speech are worth quoting at length since, like Julius Malema and the EFF, Mathunjwa is able to effectively link anti-capitalist ideology to the needs and aspirations of a vast majority of workers in the platinum belt:

Comrades, our future was determined even before we were born by the capitalists. By the time our mothers were expecting babies, the capitalist class was very jubilant because another slave was on its way. We [are] the slaves. Comrade, it's up to us that we continue the way the things are continuing, or we change the course .... [The employer] cannot differentiate [between] being a human being and mining equipment. We the workers are just taken to be tools to extract the mineral wealth of the country and not as people. How many workers have been killed in the mines? But I have never seen any manager or CEO being arrested or charged. Always it is the workers who went into a place that is not safe .... Who is benefiting from the economy? It's the politicians and the capitalists. And this thing that when we go on strike we are sabotaging the government is not true. We want to realise a better life for all. Comrades, 20 years [of democracy] has been wasted in the mining industry. After 1994, the so-called big unions ... sat cosily with the capitalists in their boardrooms.[12]

Again, treating the former union as an enemy of the mineworkers, he suggested that the NUM's approach to wage negotiation was to become a thing of the past: 'They [the NUM] were happy with the status quo and were happy that every time they went to negotiations, they just requested 6 per cent or 8 per cent for a mineworker who got paid R5,000.'[13]

Mathunjwa gave a similarly impressive speech at the two-year commemoration of the Marikana massacre on 16 August 2014. Activist-academic Trevor Ngwane told him that he sounded like the late civil rights spokesperson Dr Martin Luther King Jr.[14] The AMCU president's conclusion on 19 January was, 'Comrades, let's intensify the struggle for decent salaries. Let us strengthen our campaign so that we get the results that make us dignified people.'[15]

But all was not as straightforward as this speech presented at face value. Profound disgruntlement with the president's leadership style continued to bubble beneath the surface, particularly among shop stewards at Amplats. Mathunjwa had already mentioned workers who he said were ringleaders in the formation of another union. Thebe Maswabi, the AMCU branch chairperson of Thembelani, and another shop steward at the shaft, Lovers Mkhwa, were the ringleaders.[16]

According to Zandisile Mlindi, the AMCU chairperson of Swartklip mine at Northam in Limpopo, 'Thebe called me on December 29. I was at home in Mthatha, but he said I must get on a flight the next day to attend a meeting with Mathunjwa in Johannesburg.'[17] They missed the flight and instead drove up in a luxury BMW X1, along with others including George Tyobeka, who took a separate car. Gaddafi Mdoda was also among those involved. However, the meeting in fact 'was being held to establish an alternative union for platinum mineworkers. They [those invited] were told the breakaway union was being formed because

Mathunjwa was dominating AMCU and had made no information available about its financial affairs.'[18] Makhanya was invited to the meeting, but he explained to me that he 'refused, really, when they called. I said my father is in bad condition going to hospital so I am going to hospital.'[19]

Mabanana was among those who were singled out at the mass meeting at Olympia Stadium. He had arrived at the stadium, but then decided to flee as things took a turn for the worse:

> I got the call from one of the guys I am working with that 'Godfrey, can you please guys not go there.' Then I asked, 'What is wrong?' [Because] I was there. He said, 'The president is going to talk bad things about you guys.' Then I was confused. He even told me that for your safety's sake, you must not be there. And I did manage to come out of the stadium before he made his meeting. And we found out during his speech that [Mathunjwa said] we sold [out] the workers. He even mentioned our names, that me Godfrey, Gadaffi, George ... Thebe, that we betrayed the workers, we are the ones who signed that these two shafts, these three shafts must be closed and we are the ones that signed that the workers must be forced [sic] retrenched. And [he said] we were being given R4 million by the mine management. To bribe us so that we agree that these peoples must be forced retrenched. And now as I am speaking the community is angry at me, the workers are angry at me. They are saying that the president has spoken it loudly in front of everyone that you betrayed the workers .... Because the workers are confused, according to the statement that was made by the president .... Even the workers they are not even ashamed of telling us that 'You betrayed us, we are gonna deal with you.' I have got several calls from the workers, telling me that I am going to die at any time.[20]

The unity amongst former worker committee members who collectively decided to join and become leaders of AMCU was now crumbling. Inter-union rivalry and violence between the AMCU and the NUM was in danger of being intensified by the launch of the new union. It appeared that Mathunjwa, for his part, was contributing to this in order to maintain the strength of his own union.

Edwin had also become disillusioned with the AMCU NEC, and about a week later he and ten others received letters of termination regarding their union membership. According to Edwin:

> They [AMCU] just wrote the letter to the company so that they won't deduct our subscription fee for the union. They said we were no longer

AMCU members because we put the union into disrepute and we talked about our president in the media. Of which we were just giving the reality …. What we wanted to do was to get that guy to come closer because what we wanted was truth and justice.[21]

He responded vehemently, and indeed spitefully, when he said, 'If you look at Marikana, many people were killed there and when we dig deeper we referred back to find that the main cause of the death of those people was the president, Joseph Mathunjwa.' Edwin further maintained that bloodshed and unemployment had resulted from the AMCU's involvement in the platinum belt.[22]

The eight or nine workers who it was claimed had put AMCU into 'disrepute' were now speaking out against the 2014 strike. Having previously been a negotiator on behalf of the worker committee in 2012 for the living wage of R16,070 at Amplats, Edwin, for example, now appeared to be contradicting himself when he used the logic of the economy in order to oppose the workers' demands for R12,500 in 2014:

We said we don't want the people to go on strike now, we need the other option to be taken before the strike, because, one, if we are on strike we are not only thinking about the company here but we are thinking broader including the country at large, because when you are on strike it's going to be no work, no pay – it's going to affect many people. And then the 12,500 is going to be impossible for the company to give to the workers because if you think properly for the business you can't pay out the profits simply because you have the money to do so. If my profit is R10, then I cannot pay everybody R9 and am left with R1 – the business will die …. Again this year if we strike for just two days it will have a huge impact on the company …. Now for the benefit of everybody not just ourselves we need to think properly about the strike and not just demand 12,500.[23]

In opposition to the spirit which resonated in the hearts and minds of AMCU members across the platinum belt, he concluded that 'At Marikana they were demanding 12,500, the people were on the mountain, 34 people were killed but they did not get that 12,500 …. Now again they must go on strike and climb the mountain again to be killed, it's a dirty game.' In February 2014, he boldly declared 'We are actually about to bury AMCU. AMCU is dead already. It won't live until March and the president, I hope he will be arrested.'[24]

At the core of the former worker committee members' grievances was the fact that Mathunjwa was considered to be an authoritarian leader who had hijacked the same struggle that the worker committees had adopted as their own in 2012. Mabanana reflected on the situation:

> He never wanted us, that's why he did what he did to the masses ... and he knew that the masses, they believe in us. They listen to each and everything that we say. What he managed to do is that he made sure that ... [he] divide[s] these young boys .... Because to be honest, before we met Mathunjwa we were united, we were [the] worker committee. Then we told him that 'Comrade, can you be our umbrella? Please can you help us with that?'[25]

From Mabanana's perspective, the AMCU and the worker committee had met each other on equal ground, but Mathunjwa had then proceeded to betray and undermine the committee. He persisted, 'He is a sell-out. He makes sure he gets all the powers ... . He wins the souls of the masses, after that he is trying to destroy us.' However, in his view there was still hope since 'some workers they do see that ah, no, no, no, no, there is something wrong here.'[26]

The divergent paths taken by the DSM and DLF at this juncture told volumes about the approaches that they took during their time on the platinum belt. The DSM, in response to these allegations of authoritarian leadership in the AMCU, held a press conference to give a platform to the disgruntled mineworkers, with some of whom its activists had worked closely during the strike of 2012. As an organisation that promoted the independent power of the working class, and the building of unions and worker committees from the ground up, it too had been blacklisted by the AMCU leadership. The press conference involved disgruntled members from the three major platinum mines, some of whom including Gaddafi expressed concern, like Mabanana, that they had been victimised and unjustly removed from their position in the AMCU. The DSM, for its part, maintained that:

> The real reason for the witch-hunt is that these comrades have been at the forefront of calling for the democratisation of AMCU and the accountability of its leadership. Amongst the complaints is the AMCU leadership's failure to organise even basic democratic structures in Rustenburg that would give workers a genuine voice in their own union.[27]

Members of the DLF were also approached but chose not to associate themselves directly with these ostracised leaders. Rehad Desai, on hearing that workers were forming another union, responded decisively, 'They are making a mistake. You can't form another union if the workers are not behind it.'[28] Perhaps because of their more direct link to the ongoing grassroots organising in the platinum belt, DLF activists were aware that Mathunjwa, and more importantly the AMCU, was deeply engrained in the hearts and minds of the workers. As they were preparing to go on their first major strike, the DLF and others concluded that the last thing they needed was to be divided. While the DLF intervened to some extent in the platinum belt during the 2014 strike, it is less clear that the DSM did so.

The WAU was officially launched on 2 March 2014 in Rustenburg. There was a mere 200 people present.[29] Amid rumours that the ANC was bribing the dissident AMCU leaders to build a new union – given the non-feasibility of reviving the NUM in the Rustenburg platinum belt following the Marikana massacre – trucks labelled with ANC symbols dropped mass quantities of fast food off for those attending. There were more T-shirts available than people, and one observer indicated that there were more school kids than actual workers.[30] This suggested that the WAU itself had greatly inflated its membership estimates. The leaders of the WAU included the former NUM deputy of health and safety, Adam Salaledi. The NUM's previous regional chairperson, Elphas Ngoepe claimed the WAU had about 8,000 members.[31] As suggested earlier, the leaders of the WAU sought to end the strike being waged at the three platinum mining companies. Ngoepe, for example, told the press that 'Our members want to go back to work …. We cannot sit back when our members are condemned to hunger by an indefinite strike.'[32]

In addition to the fact that at the dawn of the 2014 strike in January, a new union was set to be formed, a further concern emerged about the AMCU's relationship to the broader working class. Makhanya had invited the NUMSA, which had broken its direct ties to the ANC the previous month, to speak at the rally:

> Before I invite NUMSA to the rally, I write an email to the head office [of AMCU], to the GS [General Secretary] and to the administrator there to notify them that NUMSA is coming to our meeting to support so that we can start a strike together in solidarity with us. One of these two said, 'I

don't see any harm with them coming' so I continued with the invitation of NUMSA. They [then] come to the mass meeting of AMCU.[33]

He recalled thinking that the head office of AMCU was confused since some had thought that he joined the WAU, and yet now he was inviting the NUMSA to speak. They weren't sure:

> whether they can attack me for WAU or NUMSA and then I make him [Mathunjwa] to hear the point that we have been with NUMSA since from 2012 in your absence. As AMCU workers know NUMSA since from 2012, they won't join NUMSA now that we have invited them to our mass meeting.[34]

Directly after the rally ended, as workers were leaving the stadium in preparation for strike action, I managed to speak to Makhanya. He lamented that the president of NUMSA, Andrew Chirwa, had been prevented from speaking. For Mathunjwa, it seemed it was either the AMCU or nothing, and yet Makhanya's previous experiences organising workers independently had taught him that 'a worker is a worker' regardless of political affiliation, or the trade, and that their strength lay in their power to unite with each other. He put it simply when he told me, 'When workers come to support other workers, they must be given a chance to speak.'[35]

Mathunjwa's practices reflected a belief that while mineworkers should join and be united within the AMCU in order to fight the bosses, the AMCU should not unite with any other political organisation or union. With what seemed like a top-down leadership intent on crushing any individual shop steward who challenged Mathunjwa's control, and the AMCU closing its boundaries to other formations, there was reason to conclude that workers would now also be bound by the same heavy chains as before, but enslaved by a union master – with a new dress code of green instead of red.[36]

THE STRIKE THAT WILL NOT DIE

By early March, the strike was in full swing. On 6 March, thousands of AMCU workers marched to the union buildings in Pretoria to highlight their demands. Two days earlier, they had conceded that the demand for R12,500 could rather be met over four years (instead of having immediate effect), but the platinum producers claimed that even this deal was unaffordable. One marcher from Lonmin seemed to capture the essence of the spirit of the mineworkers when he stated that 'Our fellow workers died for a living wage. I cannot betray them .... Our journey for a living wage is strong than before .... I am prepared to go on strike for future mineworkers to earn a decent wage.'[37]

As the mass stay-away rolled into late April, leading 15 weeks of strike action, desperation was beginning to set in. No one had been paid since the end of January. Thapelo Lekgowa, who was largely based in Rustenburg at the time, particularly at Marikana, conveyed the mood in a text message sent to me on 27 April: 'Shit is bad here. People are hungry.'[38] Workers nevertheless remained determined to achieve, if not R12,500, then something near it. One key factor which contributed to this determination was the fact that, in accordance with the LRA, they were protected by membership in a union. As Mofokeng reflected:

> You know what motivated these people. Was one thing, that is Mr. Mathunjwa's certificate, it does not expire. It does not get expired. That's why you see we were so strong because this certificate. We saw that this certificate does not expire. That's why we have seen that we cannot be expelled from work.[39]

At a meeting held by an organisation called 'Sidikwe! Vukani' in Johannesburg, workers from Amplats and Lonmin exemplified this determination. Although people were unmistakably hungry (and indeed financially broke), their spirit remained seemingly unshaken. They sang and danced as a collective, enthusiastically declaring to those in attendance and to each other, 'Asijiki' (We will not retreat).[40]

Makhanya, for his part, signalled to me during this time that he and others had been unaware that the strike could last this long. In a sense, even the leaders had miscalculated the workers' resolve to emerge victorious:

> My estimation and my budget, it was only two months. The maximum time I put on my side is two months. So this month it was the first month to me to strike without food and other things because my budget was if I can have the money for food for February, March ... so going forward from April it's where I get surprised and it is now too much for me.[41]

By early May, however, it was clear to him that the rank and file would not back down.

As the strike became more and more prolonged, the ANC government – concerned about foreign investment and the price of the rand – intervened more forcefully. At the COSATU Workers' Day rally held in Polokwane, President Zuma reportedly 'urged unions to "act in good faith" and avoid resorting to "blackmail as a negotiating tool"'.[42] Earlier in the week, the home of an ANC councillor in Marikana and the ANC office in Nkaneng were set alight. Zuma intended to speak in Marikana the following Tuesday, but the trip was cancelled because it was deemed unsafe. At the COSATU rally, Zuma hit hard against the 70,000 or so mineworkers on strike when he suggested they were being irrational: 'Unions must always be alive to the realities that endless strikes are not in the interests of the workers, not in the interest of the economy .... exercising the right to strike must never be allowed ... to degenerate into anarchy.' He continued, 'The methods of engagement employed by trade unions must always appreciate that we now have a democratic government put in place by an overwhelming majority of our people, most of whom are workers.'[43]

President Zuma and his coterie were correct to be concerned given their interest in maintaining the status quo and curtailing strike action, but their calls fell on deaf ears. Based on Makhanya's deduction, the workers had become more committed than they had been in 2012: 'You know now the strike will last so long. I cannot even estimate how long because when you see the morale of the people they were too emotional now. Our strike is too [sic] militant than before. People attend [mass meetings] in numbers and numbers.'[44]

Each of the shafts would hold a mass meeting on a daily basis every day with the exception of Sunday. On average, at Jabula, the meetings would consist of between 2,000 and 4,000 workers. 'I used to tell them that they know me from 2012 and I am their child,' Makhanya explained. He elaborated on the purpose of the meetings:

> Sometimes I must just come and greet them and tell them there is nothing and we go back, or we just sing that day and knock off [leave the area] ... so when we are in a strike we must come and see each other and see whether or not we are still in the strike collectively. That is the purpose of coming to the meetings. It's not to bring feedback. So people must understand that when we go to the mass meeting it is not that we have something to discuss, we are just going to see each other.[45]

The workers were arguably more united than they had ever been. The cracks in the leadership at Amplats had barely, if at all, extended to the rank and file. Certainly, the three mines – Amplats, Impala and Lonmin – which had gone on unprotected strikes at different times during 2012 (and in the case of Impala and Lonmin, beginning with merely one category of workers), were now working together as one. Referring to the way in which this unity grew over time, Makhanya pointed out that:

> To be in a strike at the same time it assist[s] us because previous[ly] we never got to meet with each other with these rules and boundaries that if you are working at Anglo you must just stick at Anglo. And we found that these two companies, Lonmin and Impala, they were having [the] wrong information …. So [they thought] Anglo is arrogant, they want to rule … the head office. So now they start[ed] to understand [who we really are] so we usually communicate with them. And anything that we want to do, anything that we prefer to do we must address from the head office collectively. So that is one thing that we have achieved as branches. Now we are able to communicate and understand each other.[46]

Makhanya had a habit of having informal conversations with workers as a strategy to gauge their ongoing commitment or lack thereof to the strike action, or as he said, 'checking their morale'. One day he was visiting the community of Sondela, near Khuseleka. He recalled that he 'interviewed different people one by one and just asked him as an ordinary person about how the feeling is about the strike'. He summarised the response of these individuals, who told him: 'Now it's where we are in the strike because we cannot say we are in a strike but I still have money, still have food in the house. So now it's where we feel the feeling of striking.' They further affirmed that they 'cannot return to work empty handed'. On the one hand, he explained that 'we all had [the] feeling [that] it was too much now'. On the other, he outlined the logic of continuing with the strike:

> We spend almost 15 weeks saying we are in a strike and we're not waiting for 1 per cent [only]. Remember the company put the offer of 9 per cent in the first week of January. So from January until now, it's April, I mean [4] May. If the company comes with the offer of 1 per cent, workers said for the whole four months we were waiting for just 1 per cent? That's where they said, 'No we must refuse this 10 per cent. We can't take it because we were waiting for 1 per cent all along.' But they are able to say if the company can put an offer on the table they can take it.[47]

The strike was not only taking place in Rustenburg. In Ditshaba, in Northam, workers were continuing to strike. In part because of the media coverage, the public perception was essentially that mineworkers and their families were starving. At a mass meeting in Ditshaba, in response to these concerns, Makhanya was told:

> They must stop panicking about our child and wife at home whom they think will die at home of hunger. Just tell them simply that we have committed ourselves to going on a strike now. So if they feel these pains that our children will die of hunger they must leave our child [to] die at home. After this strike we'll go and make another child, so there is no need to panic about the child at home.[48]

In addition to the mineworkers' internal strength and unity, external agents intervened to provide solidarity at a critical time when money and therefore food and other basic necessities were scarce. The Gauteng Strike Support Committee (GSSC) was one of the most important platforms through which the platinum mineworkers were assisted. The GSSC was founded by the DLF in January 2014 following the NUMSA's call for a united front of action to take place on 26 February (it was later postponed until 19 March) to protest, among other things, against labour brokers and e-tolls. The DLF built this alternative committee through which to unite community-based organisations (which worked under its umbrella) and the NUMSA's local branches. However, the committee shifted its focus as the platinum belt strike continued to gain momentum. The DLF and the GSSC had attempted to obtain the support of the NUMSA and other unions, but to no avail. As Ngwane, a key activist inside the committee, concluded, 'Sometimes the [working] class is just not ready.'[49]

By May, building upon food collections initiated by two students at the University of Johannesburg (UJ) who were undertaking research in the platinum belt, the GSSC had developed a plan to collect food and money outside malls, in communities (such as Soweto) and at universities (including Wits and UJ). As food and donations began to mount, the committee undertook investigations about the AMCU strike relief fund. In the minutes taken at the GSSC on 18 May 2014, it was noted, based on observations from workers who attended the meeting, that:

> workers are hungry, but do not want to show this. The delivery of food

by the University of Johannesburg team over the weekend boosted their morale …. it was clarified that this [AMCU] account is used for emergencies faced by workers such as funerals, the money for food must [therefore] be deposited into the Marikana Support Campaign account and all the money would be used for food.[50]

As collections intensified, 17 different shafts in the platinum belt were identified, and mineworkers from each shaft were selected as leaders who would be responsible for distribution. The GSSC relied on the pre-existing informal networks that the DLF had built with mineworkers over a period of nearly two years.

By the end of the month, Gift of the Givers (GOG) had been approached by the committee and bought into the idea, and they agreed to match any donation which was raised. Tens of thousands of families of striking mineworkers received food parcels. The spokesperson for GOG, Emily Thomas, announced that on one day alone, Saturday 24 May in Wonderkop, 'hungry and starving men, women and children ululated as 2,300 families received food parcels, 6,000 were fed a hot meal, over a thousand were treated by a 25-member medical team and 300 were given blankets and tinned food in an attempt to give something to everyone of the 10,000 desperate people who turned up'.[51] Eventually, food was no longer collected by the committee given the logistics of distribution, and money raised rather went directly into a GOG account. Volunteers then purchased, packed and distributed the food themselves, making it difficult to quantify the amount that was actually raised through the intervention of the GSSC. According to a personal communication from Jim Nichol after the strike, Mathunjwa had been unaware that this initiative was prompted by the committee and the DLF.[52]

With solidarity activities bourgeoning and mineworkers remaining committed to their cause, it seemed as if the strike might never end. However, by mid-June the tide finally turned. The company put down an offer of R800 for the first year. In line with the newly established radical tradition which mirrored that of the worker committees, Mathunjwa and others brought this offer back to a mass meeting of workers. Bheki recalled that 'Workers were literally crying when they heard that offer, saying the shafts should rather close and the companies go back home'.[53] They had come too far to settle for what they considered to be a mere pittance. Makhanya further elaborated, 'Everyone was doubting the point.

We go back to the workers and we tell them that the company has said ... "800 is the maximum money that we can give you."[54] The workers thought the AMCU officials had sold out, and responded by 'threatening all the leadership'.[55] As is the lot of trade union representatives, they found themselves between a rock and a hard place, and needed to respond to the workers immediately in order to maintain their legitimacy (and even safety).

Perhaps more important than the fact that the three companies were united in their common demand under the protection of their union was the radical democratic practice of the AMCU, which was maintained during the 2014 strike. Although Mathunjwa undermined branch leaders who offered opinions conflicting with his own, the union simply did not make decisions without consulting the mass of workers. Reiterating what other workers had deduced prior to the strike, Mofokeng later confirmed that:

> We were so strong and we were being motivated by him that it can happen that we can get this money, but he [Mathunjwa] wanted to get a mandate from us. Whether he signed that money they gave him before this 1,000 rand. It's where we said, 'We want that 12,500. We don't want anything [else]'. So he just take[s] our mandate as it is.[56]

According to Makhanya, 'We went to the caucus and look[ed at] what we can do. We take it back to the workers and say to them "Now the company said they won't offer any [other] price and [that] this is the maximum price."' He noted that 'It's where the workers have show[n] their strength.'[57] They said [waving their fingers at the AMCU officials who were negotiating on their behalf], 'It seems as [if] you leadership, you have agreed now in this 800 rand. Before we take our struggle going forward I think we need to kill this leadership.'[58] The workers gave one final push, showing trade union leaders and the company their willingness to continue. As Makhanya put it, 'I think that's where the company has realised ... the workers, they won't retreat. One day after, they put a better offer of R1,000 on the table. That's where I realised the workers they may not be educated [but they know how much their labour is worth].'[59]

Bhele, an AMCU shop steward at Lonmin who was involved in the strike from August 2012 (see Chapters 2 and 3), reiterated Bheki's observation: 'At some point, our rallying cry was "Rather we starve as unemployed men than starve at work." We had to maintain unity despite our colleagues being provoked by SMSs and all sorts of tricks.'[60]

As the strike was coming to an end, the political strategist Makhanya did not waste any time. He offered a sober assessment of the strike when he commented that 'Workers don't lack power, they lack leadership.'[61] He was constructively critical when he lamented, 'We did not prepare well also because it was difficult for us to understand how far the capitalist class can go.' There was not a strong enough awareness of the fact that 'your enemy [the capitalist] has the upper hand.'[62] Makhanya had premised his organising on the principle that:

> You know when you are in a strike there is no good negotiator. The strike is the issue of power, to have power between the labour and the capitalist. Someone who's going to feel the pain or who has the power; one of them will win .... But after the strike even if you can take anyone who is not even educated to demand 12,500 from the company and end there. If the company feels the pain they will come back tomorrow and say, 'OK we don't have 12,500 but we have so much.' So now it's just trying to get a settlement because both parties failed to negotiate. So the only time we will win is when the company feels the pain and find a reason to give us our demands. If we don't change our position we will win, it's not about having extra energy or anything else we can do to negotiate.[63]

As the 2012–14 platinum belt strike wave – and I hope this book – has demonstrated, it is the power and unity of the class that matters. 'Next time', he concluded, 'we need greater working-class alliances because at the end of the day we are fighting one enemy [capitalism].'[64]

In preparation for the next strike to come, 'money must come out of AMCU stop orders for the strike that is to come in two years' time'. Workers would not settle for less that the R1,000, or the 20 per cent increase which they obtained in the great strike of 2014. As the strike came to a close we were not witnessing the beginning of the end, but an ongoing class struggle in which mineworkers have become unwilling to accept slavery wages any longer. In a continued attempt to assess the strike, Makhanya concluded that:

> Yes, we have win [sic] the struggle of the living wage, but we didn't win the struggle of the working conditions. We're still working in the condition where it's not good for the mine or for the human being ....

we're still living in the condition where it's not good for the human being. We are still living in the shacks, in the squatter camp, but we are producing the platinum – 80 per cent in the world. So that's why I am saying ... maybe we have achieved 20 per cent increase, but we still have some challenges ... we still go underground ... up to 3.5 kilometres, come up with diseases like silicosis ... TB, deformity of water in the lungs. So meaning we still have a fight, we still have a long way to go as the mineworkers.[65]

Throughout the course of this research, a key concern raised by the mineworkers was that they were essentially victims of apartheid education, although informants did not always use this phrase. The bosses were white, they did not go regularly underground, and when they did, they received a risk allowance. Unable to finance their education mostly in rural areas, young black men went to the mines because it was the best option for them, even though it meant subjecting themselves to sub-human working conditions. I once heard Joseph Mathunjwa speaking to this reality when he asked rhetorically, with a smirk on his face, 'Do you know why managers get paid more money?' He paused, and then responded to his own question. 'Because they are white.'[66] Mineworkers have sought to convince their children to get an education so that they do not need to go into the mines like their fathers. Similar responses were reportedly given to Makhanya as they settled for the R1,000 offer tabled by the company. They told him, 'When we move out here, we need to check. We need to take our child out from the bedroom, they must go to the boardroom. We need to take our child out from the club-room, they need to go to the classroom. So that tomorrow they cannot come here and got [sic] the lower salary like ourselves.'[67]

The worker committees that were formed at Lonmin in 2012 were temporary structures merely intended to negotiate wage demands and never designed to defeat capitalism as such. However the committees (and the workers at Lonmin who went on strike) have had long-lasting effects which reverberate in the platinum sector and among the South African working class more generally. What is clear is that the workers have been unwavering in their commitment to a 'living wage', regardless of whether they have been under the umbrella of a committee or a union. Workers' resolve to demand R12,500 at Marikana soon spread to other sectors, including gold mining. Moreover, the demand for R12,500 has been adopted not only by mineworkers around the country, but by communities who call for a living wage for all. The ability of workers to provide a challenge to capitalist hegemony extends far beyond the outcomes of the 2012 and 2014 strikes. They gave confidence to and were a victory for the working class. The spirit of Marikana – which is defined by independent working-class power – will continue to reverberate in the lives of South Africans, in both communities and workplaces, for many decades to come.

Postscript

The end of this book has brought me back to its beginning – 'the spark underground', those individual leaders who started it all. Once ordinary workers, they became (like, I would argue, the rank and file and others who joined them) working-class heroes. While both Mofokeng and Makhanya had approached workers about a living wage demand in a similar manner at their own shafts (Karee and Khuseleka) prior to the unprotected strikes of 2012, they took on profoundly different roles under the banner of the new union, the AMCU. Makhanya's voice coloured the pages of the last chapter because he played a pivotal role in terms of the interface between rank and file workers and the office bearers in the union. The insurgency of the rank and file prevented shop stewards or branch committee office bearers from being co-opted by management. Conversely, something inside leaders like Makhanya kept them from bowing to the relatively luxurious lifestyle of a steward who no longer has the burden of working underground. Stewards often find themselves in a contradictory location as their lives may become more difficult during a prolonged strike (which ironically would serve the interest of their members).

In mid-2013 he pronounced, 'I am still believing that I am not this kind of leader who is going to come and address in the boardroom as I am here today. I believe that when there is a shooting, when there is a struggling, my body must become dead in the ground.'[1] On several days during the great strike (and during the strike against retrenchments in September/October 2013), we could see his eyes beginning to roll over because of sleep deprivation. A genuine 'pastoral' leader, this did not stop him from addressing masses of workers in fields and elsewhere, particularly outside of Jabula where he was the emblematic spokesperson. When he arrived home in Siraleng, where he lives near his trusty political partner Bheki, he would simply eat and then sleep. In an interview he lamented that he was now like a 'slave'. Perhaps this is the fate of genuine activists who become leaders inside insurgent trade unions.

'I have been a leader in other organisations', he later explained, but 'it is too difficult to be a leader especially in mining'. Makhanya suggested that if he was nominated to be a leader in a different company in the future, 'I will refuse.'[2] During 2012, however, it was more 'painful' because he was largely considered to be the chairperson of all the operations on strike, including to a certain extent Swartklip and Amandelbelt in Northam:

> Khuseleka nominated me and when I'm organising all these operations to join the strike they end up nominating me for [dealing with] all these operations. So I used to have this pain of knowing each and everything that is supposed to happen and driving the strike for all these mines and people depended on me.[3]

On occasion, though, he struggled to maintain his own family's wellbeing. He borrowed money from his brother so he could pay for petrol to travel to other operations. In addition:

> Other workers who are not able to get a single cent from the[ir] families, when you go to the mass meeting they will ask you whether or not you have some cash to lend them to do this and you find that you don't have it at all. You find that you don't have anything to survive with while you want the same things. And going to the mass meetings daily for a period of four months and [you are] having nothing to say. There is so much pressure because people expect you to have something to say to them that day. Other people just come and ask when the strike will end. So now it seems like it is your own strike.[4]

As the final stage of the research for this book was coming to a close, I ran into Bheki and Makhanya (on 23 October 2014) during a meeting of the Marikana Support Campaign in Braamfontein, Johannesburg. I questioned Makhanya: 'Did you really draft the demand for R16,070 in the changing rooms?' He clarified, 'I drafted the demand at my house. I brought it to Mbobo in the changing rooms after work and we sold it to the workers.'[5]

When I returned to Marikana almost exactly two years after I had first set foot on that fateful soil (two days after the massacre), the town's mood seemed to have been transformed. The back road leading to the infamous mountain had been long cleared for cars to pass, as had the once rugged area which lay before it. The drive was now relatively smooth. Individuals, as well as the community as a whole, also seemed to have started afresh. The spilled blood of their brothers had left gaping wounds inside the souls of the surviving mineworkers at Lonmin. These wounds were now healing over.

As Siphiwe and I approached Nkaneng, which had two years earlier been the refuge toward which workers had run to avoid being slaughtered by the police, and also arguably the site of some of the most important events in working-class history (where workers decided to unite following the massacre), I saw a young, sturdy man in an AMCU T-shirt waiting for one of his comrades. Coincidentally, as we moved closer, I realised it was the same worker who I had initially met (while with Thapelo Lekgowa) in 2012 during our first detailed interaction with the former Lonmin worker committee. Once understandably stern and protective of what had become a sacred space of resistance that he and his fellow workers carved out and defended, he now seemed at ease as he grinned and shook our hands. Up ahead as we passed the settlement on our right, we saw Mofokeng whom we had arranged to meet. He entered our car and told us, 'Just for now':

> Everything now is ok, because as AMCU gave us R1,000 which is [an] increase. Yes, that's what I can say because AMCU came with R1,000 which is not [a] percent[age], which is increase [of] R1,000. Yes. So things came down. Everything now yah, I think it's ok now because there is nothing happening, even now if you can see these days, there's no violence.[6]

The increase is a great improvement, 'even though', as Mofokeng reflects, 'being a machine operator is [still] not good'.[7]

This quietly composed man chose not to vie for a position inside the AMCU, and at times found himself tiptoeing around the newly elected branch leaders at Lonmin (from 2013):

> when it's just that when you just talk something or you just ask something which maybe sometimes you can find that ... these people don't like this thing [that you are saying]. Yes, it happens that you find that this thing just makes these people not happy by just asking .... It was just one day when I had, I know about how much money they get [as branch officials], they earn, just to know about the recognition agreement which

[even] Mathunjwa did not hide [and I knew the details behind it]. So when you try to talk about it, it's where just I was called and I was asked questions, 'Where did I get this [information]? Why did you say to the workers that we get so much money?' I saw that they think that I think I influence these workers somehow. It's where I thought it's better not to be like this [how I was] before [in 2012]. I know because it's me now [who] started this thing here at Karee. It's me who made this thing spread to Lonmin. So I said I have to be like other people, like other employees I am working my work just my life like before.[8]

He concluded that 'Other people have just heard it's just 12,500. They don't know and how it came [to be]':

They credited themselves because they fought for it. I created this thing so they just took that thing. You know there is one of the leaders in Karee who I always see. This guy he is just naughty because he just sees that I am a machine operator, but [he knows] I created this thing. Even [Karee manager] Mike Da Costa today, he is asking how come I don't see this guy [Mofokeng]? Where is he? Because he knows I was the first person to talk to these guys. And I was even now chosen that time ... even though people don't know the idea, this creation is created by me, what they got it's created by me, whether they like it or not. It's my idea. It's just that to those who know they know that this thing is done by myself. Even some of the leaders of AMCU there, they know. Because some of the days I used to go there and just share.[9]

With 'great man' theories of history abounding, I am hesitant to ask: what if Mofokeng and Makhanya had not taken it upon themselves to initiate the action that led to the 2012 strikes at Amplats and Lonmin? What if they had never gone to those specific mines in search of work? Would we be witnessing the same political developments that we see today in South Africa? In other words, if they had not carefully approached individuals who became susceptible to their intended intervention, would there have been a significantly, if not qualitatively, different outcome? These questions are intended to be rhetorical: indeed, we will never have a definitive answer. As I contemplate the last words of this book, I am reminded of the fact that no uprising is ever exclusively spontaneous. It is indeed correct that the structural conditions for mass mobilisation must be intact. The masses must be ready to go. What is also essential is that leaders must be prepared to lead them.

Appendix A
Interview Methodology

The researcher was encouraged to explore, rather than merely ask questions. The core issue which was addressed is: what did the mineworkers do to organise and sustain the historic strikes during the period under investigation? To answer this, the researcher needed to pay particular attention to chronology.

This series of prompts was used to structure interviews.

Personal Background

When were you born? Where? Level of education? Where did you attend school? When? Were you involved in any leadership activities in school? Do you have kids, brothers, sisters, a wife (and do you look after them financially?)? What did you do after school? When did you come to the mine(s)?

Did you belong to a union? Which union? Why? When exactly did you join that union? Did you shift to another union? Which one? Why did you join? When exactly did you become a member of that other union (exact dates needed). Were you a leader in the mine (like a shop steward?). When was that? What is the difference between AMCU and NUM? What do you think of NUM (when did it first betray the workers, if at all?)? Which shaft do you work in? What is your specific job (e.g. RDO)?

The Strike

Exact dates are very important here.

When did the strike begin? Who started the strike (a specific group of people within the mine? A union, a committee?) What were the issues that drove the strike? Demands? When did you first hear about the demand for R12,500 or R16,070? How were these demands determined (and by whom?)? How did management respond? How did NUM and

AMCU respond? How long did the strike last? How did they workers manage to stay on strike for that long? Why did the strike end? Was the strike violent? Who caused the violence and what happened? Were there important strikes or other issues that preceded or followed the strike?

The Strike Committee

We learned that these were more generally called 'worker committees' to reflect that they were not merely about striking, but about workers' grievances. (In fact, it can be argued that members of these committees went on strike in consultation with workers as a last resort.)

When was the committee formed? What is its objective? What was its name? Did it serve its purpose? Was there one committee, or several committees in each shaft? What is the difference between the strike committee and the unions? How was the committee formed? Were there any important events that preceded (or followed) the formation of the committee? Did the leadership or organisation of the committee change during the strike? Did it become smaller or larger (how? And why?)?

How did you become part of the committee? Who selected you? Why did they choose you to be a leader? When exactly was this (exact date)?

After the strike ended, what happened to the committee? Does the committee still meet? Has it collapsed (in AMCU?)? When (exactly) did it stop meeting (and why)? What is the difference between the strike committee and AMCU? Is there still a need for an independent strike committee?

What is the difference between shaft committee and shop steward?

Political and Other

Was the committee (or the strike more generally) affected by what happened at any of the other mines (specifically, Amplats, Implats or Lonmin?)?

What do you think of ANC? ANCYL? COSATU? DLF? Zuma? Malema?

Will you vote in 2014? What do you think of the EFF? (Ask follow-up questions if possible.)

Is there anything else that you would like to share with us?

Appendix B
Workers' Secretary's Notes of a Meeting with Karee Management, 21 June 2012

NOTES MEETING WITH VP

0001: CLAIM TO REQUEST INCREASE OF R12,500 DUE TO HARD LABOUR

0002: WORK HARDER IN LUST AREA (MISERY) - INCREASE OF BASIC IS RAISED. (ALL KAREES ...) EXPLAINED THAT THIS IS NOT LONMIN PROCESS. EXPLAINED THAT PROMISE TO GO THROUGH CHANNELS. EXPLAINED THAT THIS ISSUE IS DURABLE AS IT MENTIONED BEFORE

0001: NOT A STRIKE, BUT A MATTER OF GRIEVANCES
MANAGEMENT THAT THE INCREASE ARE DISCUSSION AT WAGES NEGOTIATIONS.

0003: UNDERSTANDS WAGE NEGOTIATIONS IS FOR EMPLOYERS AND THIS SPECIFIC FOR RDOS DUE HARD LABOUR.
01: SUBMITS THE MEMO BECAUSE OF LUTCHMAN LOUISE.
VP: QUESTIONED "WHAT THE CURRENT BASIC RATE OF PAY."
0001: RECENT R5800 EXCLUDING THE BONUS
VP: WANTED TO KNOW WHAT INFORMED R12,500 DEMAND
0003: ... TO WORK CONDITIONS, AND HARD LABOUR
WANTED TO KNOW IF THEY WILL BE PAID MORE THAN THOSE T/LABOUR

0002: NOT ABLE TO DISCUSS OTHER ISSUES. INTENTION IS NOT TO ADDRESS NEGOTIATIVE IMPACT ON PRODUCTION. PERSON WHO APPROACHES TOLD MANAGEMENT.

VP: CONSULT WITH TOP MANAGEMENT. AS THE DEMAND IS UNREASONABLE TOUGH ECONOMIC CONDITIONS LED CLOSURE OF OTHER MINES.
0003: THIS IS IN LINE WITH VPS ISSUES. WANTED TO KNOW HOW WILL THEY
VP: FEEDBACK.

SECRETARY: RAMPELA MOHOLWANE
CHAIRMAN: ... GABBEN ...

B.J. TYE
M. DA COSTA
M. ... Cele

170

Appendix C
Memorandum from Khuseleka 1 and 2 to Management

MEMORANDAM

FROM KHUSELEKA 1# & 2#

TO

MANANGEMENT

* BESIC R10.000
* LIVING OUT ALOWANCE R2000
* KLOKING IN RISK R500 PER MONTH
* MONTH SEPT BONUS- R1500
* CAR / PETROL ALOWANCE -R60 DAY
* MAEL / FOOD ALOWANCE-R30 A DAY

Notes

1 Introduction

1   These are the three largest platinum mining companies in the world, located in the Bushveld complex which stretches from Rustenburg in North West South Africa to Limpopo and into Zimbabwe. The area contains more than 80 per cent of the world's platinum. For an extensive discussion of the political economy of the rise, and indeed 'boom', of the South African mining platinum industry from the mid-1990s until the late 2000s, see G. Capps, 'Victim of its own success? The platinum mining industry and the apartheid mineral property system in South Africa's political transition' (2012). For a critique of the development state paradigm and an exploration of the way in which systems of accumulation relate to the shifting nature of the political economy in South Africa (understood as the minerals energy complex – MEC), see S. Ashman, B. Fine and S. Newman, 'Systems of accumulation and the evolving South African MEC', in Fine, Saraswati and Tavasci (2013). For the authoritative collection of essays on platinum mining in South Africa, see the special issue of *Review of African Political Economy* edited by G. Capps, D. Moodie and R. Bush, 'White gold: new class and community struggles on the South African platinum belt' (2015). It is beyond the scope of this book to explore these essential scholarly works in detail.

2   'R' is the abbreviation for Rand, the official South African currency.

3   The book was written by myself, Luke Sinwell. When I am not writing from the mineworkers' own perspective, the text appears in the first person. In addition, Botsang Mmope, Thapelo Lekgowa and Bongani Xezwi conducted preliminary research for this project. Siphiwe Mbatha undertook indispensable research without which this book project would be of a different quality. Siphiwe did research on his own and at other times we conducted fieldwork together.

4   See e.g. F. F. Piven, *Challenging Authority: How Ordinary People Change America* (2006). See also the classic by F. F. Piven and R. A. Cloward, *Poor People's Movements: Why They Succeed, How They Fail* (1977).

5   Pocket unionism refers to a situation in which unions are in the pockets of management and therefore cannot represent the interests of workers.

6 I. Ness and D. Azzelini, 'Introduction' in their *Ours to Master and to Own: Workers' Control from the Commune to the Present* (2011).

7 See e.g. S. Buhlungu, *A Paradox of Victory: COSATU and the Democratic Transformation in South Africa* (2010); K. Forrest, *Metal That Will Not Bend: The National Union of Metalworkers of South Africa, 1980–1995* (2011); G. Adler and E. Webster (eds), *Trade Unions and Democratization in South Africa, 1985–1997* (2000); for a particularly significant exception see K. von Holdt, *Transition from Below: Forging Trade Unionism and Workplace Change in South Africa* (2003).

8 Buhlungu (2010). For a discussion of the fragmentation of labour struggles in South Africa and a critical analysis of the limitations and potential of achieving liberation in the country, see: A. Beresford. *South Africa's Political Crisis: Unfinished Liberation and Fractured Class Struggles*. New York and Hampshire: Palgrave Macmillan (2015).

9 See V. L. Allen's trilogy *The History of Black Mineworkers in South Africa, 1871–1994* (2005), which provides a detailed account of this extensive phase.

10 P. Frankel, *Between the Rainbows and the Rain: Marikana, Migration, Mining and the Crisis of Modern South Africa* (2013), p. 5.

11 See e.g. A. Bezuidenhout and S. Buhlungu, 'Union solidarity under stress: the case of the National Union of Mineworkers in South Africa' (2008).

12 J. Saul and P. Bond, *South Africa: The Present as History, From Mrs. Ples to Mandela & Marikana* (2014).

13 B. Silver, 'Theorising the working class in twenty-first-century global capitalism' (2014), p. 46. See also her *Forces of Labour: Workers' Movements and Globalization since 1870* (2003). For an insightful and unromanticised historical account of the impact of working-class struggles on the political reconfiguration of the African continent see P. Dwyer and L. Zeilig, *African Struggles Today: Social Movements Since Independence* (2012).

14 Silver (2014), p. 46.

15 Silver (2014), p. 46.

16 G. Capps, 'Local battle in a global wealth war', *Sunday Times*, 25 May 2014, p. 23.

17 M. Taal, S. Patel and T. Elsley, 'A mineworkers' wage: the only argument against the R12,500 is greed, *Amandla Magazine*, issue26/27 (September 2012), p. 23. These authors concluded that 'the average worker would … need to work 325 years to earn the value of the CEO's remuneration in 2011!' The price of platinum had also skyrocketed by 350 per cent between 2002 and 2008, leaving the three major platinum mines (Amplats, Impala and Lonmin) to reap the benefits without substantially increasing the price of labour.

18 See C. Chinguno, 'Marikana and the post-apartheid workplace order' (2013).

19 P. Stewart, '"Kings of the mine": rock drill operators and the 2012 strike wave on South African mines' (2013).

20 For an incisive historical account of RDOs' role in mining and the argument

that this category of workers must be given more careful consideration when comprehending the roots of the 2012 strikes in the platinum belt in South Africa, see Stewart's "'Kings of the mine'". For a structural analysis of the way in which the migrant labour system contributed to the 2012 platinum belt strike wave see G. Hartford, 'The mining industry strikes: causes – and solutions?' (2012).

21 P. Bonner, 'History and the here and now' (2013), p. 160.

22 A. Giddens, *The Constitution of Society: Outline of the Theory of Structuration* (1984).

23 C. Barker, L. Cox, J. Krinsky and A. G. Nilsen, 'Marxism and social movements: an introduction', in their *Marxism and Social Movements* (2013), p. 13.

24 Barker et al. (2013).

25 A. Gramsci, *Selections from the Prison Notebooks of Antonio Gramsci* (1971), p. 9.

26 M. Baud and R. Rutten, 'Introduction', in their *Popular Intellectuals and Social Movements: Framing Protest in Asia, Africa, and Latin America* (2004), p. 6.

27 Baud and Rutten (2004), p. 7.

28 A related issue here is that organisations – rather than individuals – have tended to be the focus of social movement studies.

29 C. Barker, A. Johnson and M. Lavalette, 'Leadership matters: an introduction', in their *Leadership and Social Movements* (2001), p. 1.

30 Barker et al. (2001), pp. 18–19.

31 D. Moodie, 'Becoming a social movement union: Cyril Ramaphosa and the National Union of Mineworkers' (2010), p. 172.

32 For a journalistic account of the Marikana strike and massacre which dedicates an entire chapter to Mambush, see F. Dlangamandla, T. Jika, L. Ledwaba, S. Mosamo, A. Saba and L. Sadiki, *'We are Going to Kill Each Other Today': The Marikana Story* (2013). While claiming a certain degree of objectivity, the book arguably contributes to the demonisation of striking mineworkers at Marikana.

33 T. Cliff and D. Gluckstein, *Marxism and Trade Union Struggle: The General Strike of 1926* (1986), p. 21. A close reading of much of the available Marxist scholarship indicates that although trade unions are in a contradictory position between capital and working-class resistance, and also highlighting that trade unions tend to be part of a conservative element in labour struggles, one of the core underlying factors which in fact determines the nature of a given union is the politicisation and militancy of the rank and file. For a contemporary example, see R. Darlington, 'The rank and file and the trade union bureaucracy' (2014).

34 See also L. Sinwell, "'AMCU by day, workers' committee by night": insurgent trade unionism at Anglo Platinum (Amplats) mine, 2012–2014', *Review of African Political Economy*, 42(146), (2015), pp. 591–605.

35 In R. Hyman, *Industrial Relations: A Marxist Introduction* (1975), p. 151.

36   P. Alexander, L. Sinwell, T. Lekgowa, B. Mmope and B. Xezwi, *Marikana: A View from the Mountain and a Case to Answer* (2013).

37   See G. Isaacs, 'Can the platinum producers afford the wages demanded?' *Daily Maverick Online*, 11 June 2014, www.dailymaverick.co.za/opi nionista/2014-06-11-can-the-platinum-producers-afford-the-wages-demanded/#.VvOqidJ95D9

38   For an analysis of the relationship of the political economy of mining to the Marikana massacre, see S. Ashman and B Fine, 'The meaning of Marikana' (2013).

39   D. Moodie with V. Ndatshe, *Going for Gold: Men Mines and Migration* (1994). For a discussion on power dynamics within the compound see D. Moodie, 'The moral economy of the black miners' strike of 1946' (1986).

40   For an alternative account see Chinguno (2013).

41   Greg Marinovich, *Murder at Small Koppie: The Real Story of the Marikana Massacre,* Cape Town: Penguin (2016).

42   B. Busch, 'Introduction', in B. Busch, L. Busch and K. Press, (eds), *Interviews with Neville Alexander: The Power of Languages Against the Language of Power* (2014).

43   D. Graeber, *Direct Action: An Ethnography* (2009).

44   M. Burawoy, 'Teaching participant observation', p. 291 in M. Burawoy, A. Burton, A. A. Ferguson, K. J. Fox, J. Gamson, N. Gartrell, L. Hurst, C. Kurzman, L. Salzinger, J. Schiffman and S. Ui (eds), *Ethnography Unbound: Power and Resistance in the Modern Metropolis.* Los Angeles, Calif.: University of California Press (1991).

45   Unless noted otherwise, all interviews conducted in 2013 and 2014 were undertaken by Siphiwe Mbatha and/or myself. While many interviewees chose to speak in English, interviews were often conducted in African languages or the language of the interviewee's choice. The most important interviews with key leaders were transcribed and (where necessary) translated by Siphiwe and me together.

2   The Spark Underground

1   Interview, Mofokeng, Rustenburg, 28 September 2013.

2   E. Batstone, I. Boraston and S. Frenkel, *The Social Organization of Strikes* (1978), p. 1.

3   Batstone et al. (1978), p. 1.

4   Interview, anonymous mineworker, Rustenburg, 28 October 2013.

5   G. Marinovich and T. Lekgowa, 'Marikana: Fear and terror at the unions' battlefield', Daily Maverick, 14 May 201, www.dailymaverick.co.za/article/2013-05-14-marikana-fear-and-terror-at-the-unions-battlefield/#.VDzwGNSUc00 (accessed 14 October 2014).

6   Marinovich and Lekgowa, 'Fear and terror'.

7   Interview, Tholakele 'Bhele' Dlunga, Wonderkop, 20 May 2013.

8   Interview, Dlunga.

9   Interview, anonymous mineworker.

10 Marinovich and Lekgowa, 'Fear and terror'.

11 NUM Rustenburg Region, unpublished document in NUM's bundle in the Marikana Commission of Inquiry referred to in the witness statement of Erick Gcilitshana. Undated, p. 7.

12 Vusi Sampula, senior manager (employee relations), Lonmin, unpublished document in NUM's bundle in the Marikana Commission of Inquiry referred to in the witness statement of Erick Gcilitshana, 20 May 2011, pp. 8–9.

13 Interview, anonymous mineworker.

14 Marinovich and Lekgowa, 'Fear and terror'.

15 Interview, anonymous mineworker.

16 Sampula, unpublished document, p. 9.

17 Marinovich and Lekgowa, 'Fear and terror'.

18 Interview, Joseph Mathunjwa, in Alexander et al. (2013), pp. 46–7.

19 Same interview, p. 47.

20 Same interview, p. 50.

21 Same interview, p. 51.

22 Same interview, p. 51.

23 Interview, anonymous mineworker.

24 Interview, anonymous mineworker.

25 Da Costa, Michael Gomes, vice-president Karee mine, Lonmin. Supplementary statement to the Judicial Commission of Inquiry into the events at Marikana Mine in Rustenburg. Unpublished and undated, p. 149.

26 Interview, Mofokeng, Rustenburg, 28 September 2013.

27 Interview, Mofokeng. 2013.

28 Interview, Mofokeng, Marikana, 19 September 2014.

29 This point is drawn from the insightful historical research done by Paul Stewart (see Stewart, 2013). Based on his own thorough and unique observations of drillers with and without assistants, he indicated that 'A key job of the rock driller's assistant was to hold the drill bit against the face to start drilling a shot hole. I have seen the drill bit slide and slip when there is no assistant to help. I remain personally convinced that the accuracy of drilling is strongly related to the assistant's role …. working alone is a qualitatively different experience to having company and may well be a contributing factor to the collective anger expressed by rock drillers on the platinum mines where the issue of one-handed drilling (again) arose during current strikes' (p. 60). As Mofokeng suggests, Stewart was right.

30 Interview, Mofokeng, 2013

31 Interview, Mofokeng, 2014.

32 Interview, Mofokeng, 2014.

33 Interview, Magqabini, Rustenburg, 15 August 2013.

34 Interview, Magqabini.

35 Interview, Mofokeng, 2013.

36 Interview, Mofokeng, 2013.

37 Interview, Mofokeng, 2013.
38 Interview, Mofokeng, 2013.
39 Interview, Mofokeng, 2013.
40 Interview, Mandla, Marikana, 9 August 2013.
41 Interview, Mandla.
42 Interview, Mofokeng, 2013.
43 Interview, Mofokeng, 2013.
44 Interview, Mofokeng, 2014.
45 Michael Gomes Da Costa, vice-president Karee mine, Lonmin. Witness statement to the Judicial Commission of Inquiry (to be chaired by Justice Farlam), 23 November 2012. Unpublished, p. 67.
46 Da Costa, 'Witness statement', p. 68.
47 Da Costa, 'Witness statement', p. 77.
48 Da Costa, 'Witness statement', p. 68.
49 Interview, Mofokeng, 2013.
50 Da Costa, 'Witness statement', p. 69.
51 Da Costa, 'Witness statement', p. 69.
52 Interview, Mofokeng, 2014.
53 Interview, Mofokeng, 2014.
54 Interview, Magqabini, 2013.
55 Da Costa, 'Witness statement', pp. 71–2 (emphasis in the original).
56 Interview, Mofokeng, 2014.
57 Interview, Mofokeng, 2014.
58 Da Costa, 'Witness statement', p. 72.
59 Workers' secretary's notes of a meeting with Karee management, 21 June 2012 (see Appendix B).
60 Da Costa, 'Witness statement', p. 73.
61 Da Costa, 'Witness statement', p. 74.
62 Da Costa, 'Witness statement', p. 75.
63 Interview, Magqabini.
64 Interview, Magqabini.
65 Da Costa, 'Witness statement', p. 78.
66 Da Costa, 'Witness statement', p. 78.
67 Da Costa, 'Witness statement', p. 79.
68 Da Costa, 'Witness statement', p. 80.
69 Da Costa, 'Witness statement', p. 80.
70 Interview, Mofokeng, 2013.
71 Da Costa, 'Witness statement', p. 81.
72 Interview, Mofokeng, 2013.
73 Interview, Mandla.

3   The Spirit of Marikana is Born

1   Interview, Kaizer Madiba, in S. Masombuka and T . J. Strydon, 'Miners choose death over slavery', 20 August 2012, www.timeslive.co.za/thetimes/

2012/08/20/miners-choose-death-over-wage-slavery (accessed 15 October 2014).

2   Interview, Mofokeng, Rustenburg, 28 September 2013.
3   Interview with Thomas (a pseudonym), Wonderkop, 18 August 2013.
4   Interview, Thomas.
5   Interview, Tholakele 'Bhele' Dlunga, Marikana, 10 November 2012 (by Thapelo Lekgowa).
6   Interview, Dlunga. See also Simphiwe Booi, Revised witness statement in the Marikana Commission of Inquiry, February 2013, p. 2.
7   TEBA is the recruitment agency that links local mining and rural communities to mining jobs and thus plays a central role in maintaining the migrant labour system. Formerly TEBA was the only recruitment agency for the mines, but in the contemporary period traditional authorities play some role in recruitment.
8   During the 'funeral benefit' strike at Impala in 2003, the NUM negotiated a settlement that included low-interest loans from management.
9   Interview, Zakhele (a pseudonym), Wonderkop, 3 November 2013. The NUM had a quite generous scholarship fund for the children of mine-workers, but of course it presupposed a decent high school education and was quite competitive.
10 Interview, Zakhele.
11 Interview, Mofokeng.
12 Interview, anonymous mineworker, Marikana, 2012. Evidence in fact indicates that although the NUM did shoot and injure two workers who were sent to the hospital, neither of them died.
13 Interview, anonymous mineworker, Marikana, 2012.
14 Xolani Nzuza, Witness statement in the Marikana Commission of Inquiry, February 2013, p. 1.
15 Interview, Thomas.
16 Interview, Thomas.
17 Interview, anonymous mineworker, Marikana, 2012.
18 Interview, anonymous mineworker, Marikana, 2012.
19 Interview, anonymous mineworker, Marikana, 2012.
20 Interview, anonymous mineworker, Marikana, 2012.
21 Alexander et al. (2013), p. 32.
22 Interview, anonymous mineworker, Marikana, 2012.
23 Interview, Ntandazo (a pseudonym), Marikana, 2012.
24 Interview, Ntandazo.
25 Interview, Sobopha, Marikana, 19 September 2012 (by Thapelo Lekgowa).
26 Interview, Sobopha.
27 Interview, Thomas.
28 Interview, Sobopha.
29 Joseph Mathunjwa, 'Witness statement in the Marikana Commission of Inquiry', quoted in Dlangamandla et al. (2013), pp. 129–30.

Notes

30 Mathunjwa, 'Witness statement', p. 130.
31 Mathunjwa, 'Witness statement', p. 130.
32 Speech, Joseph Mathunjwa, 16 August 2014, Marikana (as summarised to me by Trevor Ngwane who was present during it).
33 Reverend Johannes 'Jo' Thomas Seoka, Witness statement in the Marikana Commission of Inquiry, 12 November 2012, p. 1.
34 Seoka, 'Witness statement', p. 2.
35 Seoka, 'Witness statement', p. 4 (this quote is Seoka's paraphrase of what he remembers being told by Mr Mokwena – the emphasis is in the original).
36 Seoka, 'Witness statement', pp. 4–5.
37 Interview, anonymous woman, Wonderkop, 12 November 2012.
38 Interview, anonymous woman.
39 Interview, Cebisile (a pseudonym), 2013.
40 Interview, Thomas.
41 Interview, Cebisile.
42 Interview, Mofokeng.
43 Interview, Cebisile.
44 Interview, anonymous mineworker, Marikana, 2012.
45 Interview, Cebisile.
46 Interview, Cebisile.
47 Interview, Thobile (a pseudonym), 2012 (by Thapelo Lekgowa).
48 Interview, Thobile.
49 Interview, Andile (a pseudonym), 2012 (Fox Pooe assisted with translating).
50 Interview, Andile.
51 Interview, Andile.
52 Interview, Bongani (a pseudonym), 2012 (Fox Pooe assisted with translating).
53 Interview, Bongani.
54 Interview, Bongani.
55 Interview, Bongani.
56 Frans Baleni, videotaped message. Retrieved from B. V. Auken, 'South African miners defiant in face of government, company threats', World Socialist Website, www.wsw.org.en/articles/2012/08/safr-a21.html (accessed 15 October 2014).
57 DSM website, 'Who we are', www.socialistsouthafrica.co.za (accessed 15 October 2014).
58 Interview, Mametlwe Sebei, University of Johannesburg, 21 February 2013.
59 Obituary for Kemela Ernest Mokgalagadi, written by M. Sebei, 'a genuine working class fighter and a revolutionary socialist', 10 June 2013.
60 Interview, Mametlwe Sebei, in K. Sosibo, 'Cheeky newcomers challenge union giants', Mail and Guardian Online, 2 February 2012, mg.co.za/article/2012-02-17-cheeky-newcomers-challenge-union-giants (accessed 15 October 2014).

61 Interview, Mametlwe Sebei, University of Johannesburg, 21 February 2013.
62 Interview, Sebei, in K. Sosibo, 'Mine workers' hope lies in mass action', Mail and Guardian Online, 19 October 2012, mg.co.za/article/2012-10-19-mine-workers-hope-lies-in-mass-action (accessed 15 October 2014).
63 Personal communication with Bheki Buthlezi, Siraleng, 6 May 2014.
64 Interview, Bheki Buthelezi, Siraleng, 17 October 2013.
65 Interview, Siphiwe Mbatha, Johannesburg, 23 October 2013.
66 Interview, Buthelezi.
67 Interview, anonymous worker, Marikana, 2012.
68 Democratic Left, 'Civil society to launch its own independent inquiry into the Marikana massacre', press release, 19 August 2012, www.democraticleft.za.net/index.php?option=com_context&view=article&id=131:civil-society-to-launch-its-own-independent-inquiry-into-the-marikana-massacre (accessed 15 November 2014).
69 Rehad Desai speaking at the Annual General Meeting of the Marikana Support Campaign, Johannesburg, 20 October 2013.
70 Interview, Buthelezi.
71 Interview, Buthelezi, Rustenburg, 17 September 2013.
72 Interview, Magubane Sohadi, nicknamed 'Rasta', Nkaneng, 20 May 2013.
73 Interview, Molefi (a pseudonym), 2012.
74 Interview, Molefi.
75 Interview, Molefi.
76 Interview, Molefi.
77 T. Lekgowa, 'Heartfelt, hard, painful songs of Marikana', Daily Maverick Online, 28 January 2013, www.dailymaverick.co.za/article/2013-01-28-heartfelt-hard-painful-songs-of-marikana#.VD-eqluUc00 (accessed 16 October 2014).
78 Song sung in March during the 2012 strike following the massacre. In Lekgowa, 'Heartfelt, hard, painful'.
79 Lonmin Plc, 'Update on Marikana illegal strike', 17 September 2012, www.bloomberg.com/article/2012-09-17/aqDkux1Hq1U4.html (accessed 16 October 2014).
80 Text of the Lonmin Marikana Peace Accord, 6 September 2012, www.politicsweb.co.za/politicsweb/view/politicsweb/en/page71651?oid=324570&sn=Detail&pid=71651 (accessed 16 October 2014).
81 Interview, Molefi.
82 S. Hlongwane, 'The worthless Marikana peace accord', Daily Maverick Online, 10 September 2012, www.dailymaverick.co.za/article/2012-09-10-analysis-the-worthless-marikana-peace-accord (accessed 16 October 2014).
83 Speech given by Joseph Mathunjwa, mass meeting at Olympia Stadium (Rustenburg), 19 January 2014.
84 T. Poloko, 'Man in the green blanket mourned', iol News, 10 September 2012, www.iol.co.za/news/crime-courts/man-in-the-green-blanket-mourned-1.1379101 (accessed 16 October 2014).

85 Interview, anonymous mineworker, Marikana, 2012 (by Botsang Mmope).

86 Interview, anonymous mineworker.

87 Statement, Simon Scott, Lonmin CEO, www.lonmin.com/downloads/media_centre/news/press/2012/Lonmin_RNS_-_Marikana_Update_-_17.09.2012_-_FINAL.pdf, 17 September 2012 (accessed 18 August 2014).

88 Media briefing, Jeff Radebe, justice minister, quoted in F. Parker 'Radebe: mines will settle down – or else', Mail and Guardian Online, 14 September 2012, mg.co.za/article/2012-09-14-radebe-mines-will-settle-down-or-else (accessed 16 October 2014).

89 S. Hlongwane, 'Reporter's Marikana notebook: police intimidation 1, abandoned community 0', Daily Maverick Online, 17 September 2012, www.dailymaverick.co.za/article/2012-09-17-reporters-marikana-notebook-police-intimidation-1-abandoned-community-0/#.VD-0s4uUc00 (accessed 16 October 2014).

90 Paulina Masutlho, quoted in SABC, 'Woman's death in Marikana prompts march', SABC online, www.sabc.co.za/news/a/57633c004ccf33729a3fdbb8fcf576/Womans/death-in-marikana-prompts/march-20120922 (accessed 16 October 2014).

91 Primrose Sonti, quoted in 'Woman's death in Marikana'.

92 Resident of Marikana, quoted in 'Reporter's Marikana notebook'.

93 Jo Seoka, quoted in 'South African police crack down on striking miners', *Taipei Times*, www.taipeitimes.com/News/world/archives/2012/09/17/2003542992, accessed: 16 October 2014.

94 Interview, anonymous mineworker, Marikana, 2012.

95 Personal communication with anonymous mineworker, Marikana, 18 September 2012.

96 Sithembile Sohati, quoted in M. Molakeng, 'South Africa's Lonmin miners accept pay rise to end strike', Reuters, 18 September 2012, www.reuters.com/article/.../us-safrica-mines-idUSBRE88H0R420120918 (accessed 16 October 2014).

97 Zolisa Bodlani, quoted in Molakeng, 'South Africa's Lonmin Miners'.

4 Amplats Carries the Torch

1 Interview, Bheki Buthelezi, Siraleng, 17 October 2013.

2 Interview, Evans 'Bax' Ramokga, in P. de Wet and N. Bauer, 'Amplats "not like Marikana"', *Mail and Guardian*, 20 September 2012, p. 2.

3 Interview, Zukile Christopher Mbobo (Chris), Freedom Park, 27 August 2013.

4 Interview, Chris.

5 Interview, Chris.

6 Interview, Chris.

7 A hippo in this context is an armoured police vehicle used by the South African state primarily to quell black township protests until the late 1970s,

when they were replaced by Caspirs. So Chris may be referring to a Caspir. These were both larger, and presumably more intimidating than the Nyala (police vehicle) mentioned in chapter 3.

8 Interview, Chris.
9 Interview, Chris.
10 Interview, Chris.
11 Interview, Chris.
12 Interview, Zukile Christopher Mbobo (Chris), Freedom Park, 8 June 2013.
13 Interview, S. K. Makhanya, Siraleng, 9 August 2013.
14 Interview, Makhanya.
15 Interview, Makhanya.
16 Interview, Makhanya.
17 Interview, Chris, 8 June 2013.
18 Interview, S. K. Makhanya, Siraleng, 4 May 2014.
19 Interview, Makhanya, 2013.
20 Interview, Makhanya, 2014.
21 Stop orders are forms that workers fill in and sign stating that they are a member of a particular union and that money can be deducted from their salary each month to pay for the union's activities. They can also be described as an application to become a member of a particular union.
22 Interview, Makhanya, 2014.
23 Interview, Chris, 8 June 2013.
24 Interview, Chris, 8 June 2013.
25 Interview, Makhanya, 2013.
26 Interview, Makhanya, 2014.
27 Interview, Tumelo (a pseudonym), Rustenburg, 17 August 2013.
28 Interview, Tumelo.
29 Interview, Tumelo.
30 Interview, Tumelo.
31 Interview, Makhanya, 2014.
32 Interview, Tumelo.
33 For this latter point, see Stewart's "'Kings of the Mine'" (2013).
34 Interview, Tumelo
35 Interview, Tumelo.
36 Speech, S. K. Makhanya, 'South Africa after Marikana', at Marxism 2013: Hosted by the Socialist Workers Party, London, published on You Tube, 22 August 2013, www.youtube.com/watch?v=a3uOYFvLi-Y (accessed 14 October 2014).
37 Speech, Makhanya.
38 Speech, Makhanya.
39 Speech, Makhanya.
40 Interview, Makhanya, 2013.
41 Interview, Makhanya, 2013.
42 Interview, Evans Ramokga, in M. Magome, 'More mines shut down as strikers dig in their heels for pay hike', *The Star*, 13 September 2012, p. 2.

43 Interview, Tumelo.
44 Interview, Makhanya, 2014.
45 Interview, Makhanya, 2013.
46 Interview, Makhanya, 2013.
47 Interview, Makhanya, 2014.
48 In an Anglo American letter signed by CEO Chris Griffith on 25 September 2012 to Rustenburg Mining Operations Employees entitled, 'Disciplinary action leading to potential dismissals to commence on Thursday, 27 September 2012', the CEO acknowledged that 'some employees have been awaiting the outcome of the Khuseleka Mine CCMA matter before returning to work. We can confirm that this matter went before the CCMA on Tuesday, 25 September 2012.' As noted in the previous section, the outcome of this matter a month earlier (on 25 August) prompted the workers to engage in strike action in unity with the other shafts.
49 Interview, Lazarus Khoza, Rustenburg, 26 May 2013.
50 Interview, Lazarus.
51 Interview, Makhanya, 2013.
52 Interview, Makhanya, 2013.
53 Interview, Daniel (a pseudonym), Rustenburg, 9 June 2013 (by Botsang Mmope).
54 Interview, Daniel.
55 Interview, Daniel.
56 Interview, Makhanya, 2013.
57 Interview, Makhanya, 2014.
58 Interview, Buthelezi.
59 Interview, Tumelo.
60 Interview, Makhanya, 2013.
61 Pamphlet entitled 'Meeting', 8 September 2012.
62 Interview, Jonathan (a pseudonym), Rustenburg, 28 October 2013.
63 Interview, Jonathan.
64 Interview, Jonathan.
65 Interview, Jonathan.
66 Interview, Jonathan.
67 Interview, Jonathan.
68 Interview, Desmond (a pseudonym), Rustenburg, 17 August 2013.
69 Interview, Desmond.
70 Interview, Desmond.
71 Interview, Desmond.
72 Interview, Tumelo.
73 Interview, Tumelo.
74 Interview, Godfrey Lindani (nicknamed 'Mabanana'), Rustenburg, 18 September 2013.
75 Interview, Gaddafi Mdoda, Rustenburg, 24 February 2013.
76 Interview, Gaddafi.
77 Interview, Buthelezi.

Notes

78 Interview, Buthelezi.
79 Interview, Buthelezi.
80 Interview, Buthelezi.
81 Interview, Gift (a pseudonym), Rustenburg, 28 October 2013.
82 Interview, Gift.
83 Interview, Gift.
84 Interview, Elias, Rustenburg, 30 October 2013.
85 Interview, Elias.
86 Interview, Elias.
87 Interview, Elias.
88 Interview, Elias.
89 Interview, Elias.
90 Interview, Mabanana.
91 Interview, Mabanana.
92 Interview, Edwin (a pseudonym), Rustenburg, 18 February 2014.
93 Interview, Edwin.
94 Interview, Edwin.
95 Interview, Lazarus.
96 Interview, Lazarus.
97 Magome, 'More mines ...' (2012).
98 Interview, Evans 'Bax' Ramokga, in Magome, 'More mines ...'.
99 Statement by Chris Griffith, in Magome, 'More mines ...'.
100 Interview, Godfrey Lindani, in Magome, 'More mines ...'.
101 S. Mkhwanazi and L. Mkentane, 'Zuma warns instigators', The New Age Online, 14 September 2012, www.thenewage.co.za/mobi/Detail.aspx-?NewsID=62169&CatID=1007 (accessed 29 October 2014).
102 M. Magome, 'Striking platinum miners play tough', The Star, 14 September 2012, p. 2.
103 M. Mofokeng and J. Maromo, 'Mineworkers take their protest underground', Sunday Independent, 16 September 2012, p. 4.
104 Press conference, Jeff Radebe, quoted in Mofokeng and Maromo. 'Mineworkers take their protest ...'.
105 Interview, Makhanya, 2013.
106 See A. Flak, 'Two mines reopen, but situation remains tense', The New Age, 18 September, p.15.
107 Interview, Sebei, in Flak, 'Two mines reopen...'.
108 Interview, Cynthia Carroll, in L. Steyn and E. Glokos, 'SA's biggest miner locks its gates', Mail and Guardian, 20 September 2012, p. 2.
109 Interview, Lesiba Seshoka, in Steyn and Glokos, 'SA's biggest miner locks its gates', p. 2.
110 Interview, Sebei, in P. de Wet and N. Bauer, 'Amplats "not like Marikana"', Mail and Guardian, 20 September 2012, p. 2.
111 Interview, Lucas Rapai, in de Wet and Bauer, 'Amplats "not like Marikana"', p. 2.

185

112 Interview, Sfana Chauke, in de Wet and Bauer, 'Amplats "not like Marikana"', p. 2.
113 Interview, Ramokga, in de Wet and Bauer, 'Amplats "not like Marikana"', p. 2.
114 Sapa, 'Strikers swell to 100 000', *The Citizen*, 28 September 2012, p. 23.
115 Statement by Chris Griffith, 'Amplats taking action against workers', *The New Age*, 28 September 2012, p. 1.
116 See S. Bega and Sapa, 'Mines may follow Amplats in dismissing strikers', *Saturday Star*, 6 October 2012, p. 4.
117 Interview, Tumelo.
118 Interview, Makhanya, 2013.
119 Interview, Makhanya, 2013.
120 Interview, Makhanya, 2013.
121 P. Tau, 'Violence breaks out at Limpopo mine', *The Star*, 10 October 2012, p. 6.
122 Interview, Makhanya, 2013.
123 Mametlwe Sebei, 'Marikana wildcat strike leaders meeting: Mametlwe Sebei of the DSM', public speech at press conference, published 14 October 2012, www.youtube.com/watch?v=U4CVzts6SIQ.
124 Interview, Tsietsi Mofokeng, in O. Mooki, 'Workers hold Rustenburg to ransom', *The Star*, 3 October 2012, p. 7.
125 Interview, anonymous mineworker, in B. Tshehle and K. Mabuza, 'Angloplats workers stick to their guns: violent protests will go on until demands are met', *Sowetan*, 4 October 2012, p. 2.
126 Interview, Tumelo.
127 Interview, anonymous mineworker, Rustenburg, 27 September 2013.
128 Interview, anonymous mineworker, Rustenburg, 28 October 2013.
129 Interview, Makhanya, 2014.
130 Interview, Makhanya, 2014.
131 Interview, Ishmael (a pseudonym), Rustenburg, 5 July 2013.
132 Official document, 'Anglo American Platinum offer return to work by 30 October 2012', regarding a meeting held on 26 October 2012.
133 Official document, 'Anglo American Platinum offer'.
134 Official document, 'Anglo American Platinum offer'.
135 Interview, Bheki Buthelezi, Rustenburg, 17 September 2013.
136 Interview, Buthelezi, 2013.
137 Interview, Buthelezi, 2013.
138 G. Marinovich, 'War: COSATU vs Amplats strikers. Battlefield: Rustenburg', Daily Maverick Online, www.dailymaverick.co.za/article/2012-10-27-war-COSATU-vs-amplats-strikers-battlefield-rustenburg/ (accessed 30 October 2014).
139 Interview, Buthelezi, 2013.
140 Marinovich, 'War: COSATU vs Amplats strikers'.
141 Interview, Buthelezi, 2013.
142 Interview, Mabanana.

143 Interview, Buthelezi, 2013.
144 Interview, Buthelezi, 2013.
145 Interview, Buthelezi, 2013.
146 Speech by Trevor Ngwane, 'Message to the Amplats mineworkers rally in Rustenburg delivered by Trevor Ngwane, Democratic Left Front, November 10 2012', www.politicsweb.co.za/politicsweb/view/politicsweb/en/page71654?oid=339465&sn=Detail&pid=71654 (accessed 30 October 2014).
147 Speech by Ngwane, 'Message to the Amplats mineworkers'.
148 Sapa, 'Amplats deadline extended', The Times Live, 12 November 2012, www.timeslive.co.za/local/2012/11/12/amplasts-deadline-extended (accessed 8 August 2014).
149 According to the attendance register for 'Meeting between COSATU and the Amplats Strike Committee 12th November 2012'.
150 Interview, Buthelezi, 2013.
151 Interview, Mabanana.
152 Interview, Buthelezi, 2013.
153 Interview, Buthelezi, 2013.
154 Interview, Buthelezi, 2013.
155 Interview, Makhanya, 2013. He has a copy of the agreement which was signed by the various parties including the committee itself. Also see an AngloAmerican document, 'Rustenburg Platinum Mines Limited: Interim Access Guidelines for the Own Mines Managed Operations', p.1 which states that 'The company, NUM, NUMSA, UASA and the Interim Committee entered into a "Return to Work Agreement"(RTWA) on the 15 November 2012', no date, p. 1.
156 Interview, Makhanya, 2013.
157 Interview, Daniel.

5 The Rise of the AMCU and the Demise of Worker Committees

1 Interview, Tumelo, Rustenburg, 17 August 2013.
2 Interview, Desmond, Rustenburg, 17 August 2013.
3 Interview, 'Rasta', Marikana, 29 September 2013.
4 Personal communication with Bheki Buthelezi, 20 September 2013.
5 AngloAmerican, 'Interim Access Guidelines', p.1.
6 AngloAmerican, 'Interim Access Guidelines', pp.1–2.
7 AngloAmerican, 'Interim Access Guidelines', pp.1–2.
8 Interview, Bheki, Rustenburg, 17 September 2013.
9 Interview, Desmond.
10 Interview, Chris, 8 June 2013.
11 Interview, Ishmael, Rustenburg, 5 July 2013.
12 Interview, anonymous mineworker, Rustenburg, 27 September 2013.
13 Interview, Lazarus Khoza, Rustenburg, 26 May 2013.

14   Interview, Makhanya, Siraleng, 9 August 2013.
15   Interview, Mabanana, Rustenburg, 18 September 2013.
16   Interview, Mabanana.
17   Interview, Gaddafi, Rustenburg, 24 February 2013.
18   Interview, Gaddafi.
19   Interview, Gaddafi.
20   Interview, Tumelo.
21   Interview, Tumelo.
22   Interview, Daniel, Rustenburg, 9 June 2013 (by Botsang Mmope).
23   Interview, Lazarus.
24   Interview, Makhanya.
25   Interview, Makhanya.
26   Interview, Trevor Ngwane, in K. Sosibo, 'The co-option of AMCU's radical heart', The Con Online, www.theconmag.co.za/2013/08/30/the-co-option-of-AMCUS-radical-heart/ (accessed 30 October 2014).
27   Direct observation by Luke Sinwell, 23 February 2013.
28   Paraphrased words of Mametlwe Sebei, 'Notes taken by Luke Sinwell', 23 February 2013.
29   Paraphrased words of Gaddafi Mdoda, 'Notes'
30   Paraphrased words of Tumelo, 'Notes'.
31   Paraphrased words of Gaddafi, 'Notes'.
32   Paraphrased words of Sebei, 'Notes'.
33   Paraphrased words of Liv Shange, 'Notes'.
34   Press conference, Mpumi Sithole. In Miningmx, 'Amplats signs AMCU recognition pact', www.miningmx.com/pls/cms/iac.page?p_t1=3085&p_t2=7933&p_t3=0&p_t4=0&p_dynamic=YP&p_content_id=1536774&p_site_id=83 (accessed 30 October 2014).
35   Press conference, Joseph Mathunjwa, in 'Amplats signs AMCU recognition pact'.
36   P. De Vos, 'Marikana, no common purpose to commit suicide', Constitutionally Speaking blog, 30 August 2012, http://constitutionallyspeaking.co.za/marikana-no-common-purpose-to-commit-suicide/ (accessed 30 October 2014).
37   Interview, Thomas, Wonderkop, 18 August 2013.
38   Interview, 'Rasta', Marikana, 18 May 2013.
39   Interview, Tholakele 'Bhele' Dlunga, in G. Marinovich, 'Marikana: police torturing their way to intimidation', Daily Maverick Online, www.dailymaverick.co.za/article/2012-11-02-marikana-police-torturing-their-way-to-intimidation/ (accessed 30 October 2014).
40   Interview, mineworker, in Marinovich, 'Marikana: Police torturing'.
41   Interview, Tholakele 'Bhele' Dlunga, Marikana, 10 November 2012 (by Thapelo Lekgowa).
42   P. Tau, 'Lonmin miners back at work after brief strike', The Star, 6 March 2013, p. 4.

43 Interview, Joseph Mathunjwa, in N. Marrian and A. Seccombe, 'AMCU wants "majority status" at Lonmin', *Business Day*, 6 March 2013, p. 2.

44 Message from Joseph Mathunjwa in L. Mkentane, 'Find the killers – union', *The New Age*, 14 May 2013, p. 3.

45 Message from Jack Khoba, in O. Molophanye and L. Mkentane, 'Miners' truce', *The New Age*, 16 May 2013, p. 1.

46 Speech, Joseph Mathunjwa, in M. Magome, 'AMCU starts to flex its muscles', *Sunday Independent*, 19 May 2013, p. 6.

47 Response from Lesiba Seshoka, in Magome, 'AMCU starts to flex', p. 6.

48 P. Tau, 'Murder takes place during peace talks', *The Star*, 4 June 2013, p. 4.

49 Statement by Mildred Oliphant, in Tau, 'Murder takes place during peace talks', p. 4.

50 Statement by Oliphant, in Tau, 'Murder takes place during peace talks', p. 4.

51 Statement by Joseph Maqhekeni, in Tau, 'Murder takes place during peace talks', p. 4.

52 Speech, Joseph Mathunjwa, in P. Tau, 'AMCU issues Marikana strike ultimatum', *The Star*, 6 June 2013, p. 4.

53 Tau, 'AMCU issues Marikana strike ultimatum', p. 4.

54 Statement by Natascha Viljoen, in 'Lonmin "needs help to quell violence"', *Business Day*, 7 June 2013, p. 2.

55 Direct observation by Luke Sinwell, small church in Pretoria, 8 August 2013.

56 Statement by Joseph Mathunjwa, direct observation.

57 Statement by Trevor Ngwane, direct observation by Luke Sinwell, St Albans Cathedral, 10 August 2013.

58 Statement by Joseph Mathunjwa, direct observation, St Albans.

59 Statement by Bheki Buthelezi, direct observation, St Albans.

60 Statement by unknown mineworker, direct observation, St Albans.

61 Personal communication with Mametlwe Sebei, Marikana, 16 August 2013.

62 Speech at Marikana, in Julius Malema, 'Malema's hero welcome at Marikana', 16 August 2013, published on YouTube, www.youtube.com/watch?v=ccBpxz9AA8k (accessed 31 October 2014).

63 Speech, Malema, 'Malema's hero welcome at Marikana'.

64 Speech, Malema, 'Malema's hero welcome at Marikana'.

65 Interview, 'Rasta'.

66 Interview, 'Rasta'.

67 Siphiwe and I attempted to contact Lonmin's branch leaders (at Eastern, Western and Karee) on many occasions, but they refused to talk and/or used delaying tactics. As such, I rely primarily on Bheki Buthelezi's narrative of events with regards to the practices and ideas of these AMCU office bearers since he engaged directly with them on a regular basis.

68 Interview, Zakhele, Wonderkop, 3 November 2013.

69 Interview, Zakhele.

70 Interview, Zakhele.

71 Interview, Zakhele.

72 Interview, Bheki, Siraleng, 17 October 2013.
73 Interview, Bheki, 2013.
74 Interview, Bheki, 2013.
75 Interview, Bheki, 2013.
76 Interview, Bheki, 2013.
77 Interview, Bheki, 2013.
78 Interview, Bheki, 2013.
79 Interview, Bheki, 2013.
80 Interview, Bheki, 2013.
81 Interview, Bheki, 2013.
82 Interview, Bheki, 2013.
83 Interview, Bheki, 2013.
84 Interview, Bheki, 2013.
85 Interview, Bheki, 2013.
86 Interview, Zakhele.
87 Interview, Zakhele.
88 Interview, Zakhele.
89 Interview, Zakhele.
90 'The Mineworker: a DLF publication', pamphlet, 2013.
91 Personal communication with Bheki Buthelezi, 27 September 2013.
92 Direct observation and transcription of a tape recording of the AMCU mass meeting held outside Thembelani mine, 27 September 2013.
93 As note 91.
94 As note 91.
95 AMCU document, Limpopo and North West region letter to NEC entitled, 'THIS A DEMINDS LIMPOMPO AND NORTH WEST REGIRN LEADERSHIP OF THE UNOIN [sic], 2013.
96 AMCU, 'THIS A DEMINDS.'
97 Interview, Mabanana, Rustenburg, 28 January 2014. Another particularly trusted worker told me – without being prompted and as a matter of fact – that he took two full days to heal emotionally after being reprimanded by the president. We also heard Mathunjwa telling workers at a mass meeting at Jabula that they should not listen to what other people have to say about the strike: 'Turn off the television after you have heard me, or watch soccer.'
98 Interview, Mabanana, 2014.
99 Interview, Mabanana, 2014.
100 Interview, Edwin, Rustenburg, 18 February 2014. Edwin further asserted that the day after Steve questioned when Mathunjwa would hold a congress where the position of president would be contested, he was killed. While there is no clear-cut evidence in this regard, he also alleged that 'it is unlikely that it was NUM or someone from outside [who killed him]. It's within AMCU. Many deaths are from AMCU itself.' It should be noted that it is possible Edwin came to this conclusion as a result of the extent to which he was disgruntled with AMCU as an organisation.

101 Interview, Edwin.
102 Interview, Bheki, 2013.

6 Insurgent Trade Unionism and the Great Strike of 2014

1   Speech, anonymous mineworker, 2014.
2   Speech, Makhanya, at Marxism 2013 closing rally.
3   Speech, Makhanya, at Marxism 2013 closing rally.
4   Journal notes, Luke Sinwell, 19 January 2014.
5   Speech, Makhanya, at Olympia Stadium, Rustenburg, 19 January 2014.
6   Speech, Mathunjwa, at Olympia Stadium, Rustenburg, 19 January 2014.
7   Speech, Mathunjwa.
8   Speech, Mathunjwa.
9   Speech, Mathunjwa.
10 Speech, Mathuinjwa.
11 Speech, Mathunjwa.
12 Speech, Mathunjwa.
13 Speech, Mathunjwa.
14 Trevor Ngwane, personal communication with Luke Sinwell, 17 August 2014.
15 Speech, Mathunjwa.
16 J. De Lange, 'Inside AMCU's secret mutiny', City Press Online, 26 January 2014, www.citypress.co.za/news/inside-AMCUs-secret-mutiny/ (accessed 3 November 2014).
17 Zandisile Mlindi, quoted in Lange, 'Inside AMCU's secret mutiny'.
18 Lange, 'Inside AMCU's secret mutiny'.
19 Interview, Makhanya, Siraleng, 4 May 2014.
20 Interview, Mabanana, Rustenburg, 28 January 2014.
21 Interview, Edwin, Rustenburg, 18 February 2014.
22 Interview, Edwin.
23 Interview, Edwin.
24 Interview, Edwin.
25 Interview, Mabanana.
26 Interview, Mabanana.
27 Edited version of wasp, 'Statement on the latest strikes', *The Socialist Newspaper*, 29 January 2014, www.google.co.za/url?sa=t&rct=j&q=&esrc=s&frm=1&-source=web&cd=2&ved=0CCYQFjAB&url=http%3A%2F%2Fwww.socialistparty.org.uk%2Farticles%2F18076&ei=Bl9XVNX0Ac-N7Abdx-IHACg&usg=AFQjCNEtY9MyaQhFMyZUOMzJPgKvY9CYl-g&sig2=iT5EkGr8AJ2ApcymIT_mZA (accessed 3 November 2014).
28 Rehad Desai, personal phone communication with Luke Sinwell, 19 January 2014.
29 Notes by Siphiwe Mbatha, based on observation of WAU launch, 2 March 2014.

30 Thapelo Lekgowa, personal phone communication with Luke Sinwell, 2 March 2014.
31 Interview, Elphas Ngoepe, in 'Workers' Association Union launched in Rustenburg', Mail and Guardian Online, 3 March 2014, http://mg.co.za/article/2014-03-03-workers-association-union-launched-in-rustenburg (accessed 3 November 2014).
32 Interview, Ngoepe, in 'Workers Association Union'.
33 Interview, Makhanya.
34 Interview, Makhanya.
35 Makhanya, personal communication with Luke Sinwell, Rustenburg, 19 January 2014.
36 NUM T-shirts are red, while AMCU T-shirts are green.
37 Interview, Jukulunga Joka, in Sapa, 'AMCU marches on Union buildings', Mail and Guardian Online, 6 March 2014, http://mg/co.za/article/2014-03-06-AMCU-marches-on-union-buildings (accessed 4 November 2014).
38 Thapelo Lekgowa, text message to Luke Sinwell, 27 April 2014.
39 Interview, Mofokeng, Rustenburg, 19 September 2014.
40 Launch of 'Sidikwe! Vukani!', Witwatersrand University, 15 April 2014.
41 Interview, Makhanya.
42 Speech, Jacob Zuma. In N. Marrian, A. Seccombe and K. Gernetzky, 'Zuma warns over strikes descending into anarchy', Business Day Live Online, 2 May 2014, www.bdlive.co.za/national/labour/2014/05/02/zuma-warns-over-strikes-descending-into-anarchy (accessed 3 November 2014).
43 Speech, Zuma, in Marrian et al., 'Zuma warns over strikes'.
44 Interview, Makhanya.
45 Interview, Makhanya.
46 Interview, Makhanya.
47 Interview, Makhanya.
48 Interview, Makhanya.
49 Trevor Ngwane, personal communication with Luke Sinwell, Johannesburg, 20 June 2014.
50 GSSC minutes, meeting held at Witwatersrand University, 18 May 2014.
51 Interview, Emily Thomas, in Sapa, 'We're not giving food parcels only to AMCU members: Gift of the Givers', Times Live Online, 25 May 2014, www.timeslive.co.za/local/2014/05/25/we-re-not-giving-food-parcels-only-to-AMCU-members-gift-of-the-givers (accessed 3 November 2014).
52 Jim Nichol, personal communication with Luke Sinwell, Johannesburg, 14 September 2014.
53 Interview, Bheki Buthelezi, in K. Sosibo, 'AMCU shifts strike goalposts', Mail and Guardian Online, 20 June 2014, http://mg.co.za/article/2014-06-19-AMCU-shifts-goalposts-of-striking (accessed 3 November 2014).
54 Makhanya, 'What's next for South Africa?' speech at Marxism 2014 closing rally, London, published 25 July 2014, www.youtube.com/watch?v=fZ41EC uus8Q (accessed 3 November 2014).

55 Makhanya, 'What's next for South Africa?'
56 Interview, Mofokeng.
57 Makhanya, 'What's next for South Africa?'
58 Makhanya, 'What's next for South Africa?'
59 Makhanya, 'What's next for South Africa?'
60 Interview, Tholakele 'Bhele' Dlunga, in Sosibo, 'AMCU shifts strike goal-posts'.
61 Makhanya, 'What's next for South Africa?'
62 Makhanya, personal communication with Luke Sinwell, Rustenburg, 21 June 2014.
63 Interview, Makhanya.
64 Makhanya, personal communication with Luke Sinwell.
65 Makhanya, 'What's next for South Africa?'
66 Direct observation by Luke Sinwell, small church in Pretoria, 8 August 2013.
67 Interview, Makhanya.

Postscript

1 Speech, Makhanya (2013).
2 Interview, Makhanya.
3 Interview, Makhanya.
4 Interview, Makhanya.
5 Makhanya, personal communication with Luke Sinwell, Johannesburg, 23 October 2014.
6 Interview, Mofokeng.
7 Interview, Mofokeng.
8 Interview, Mofokeng.
9 Interview, Mofokeng.

Selected Bibliography

Books, Journal Articles and Reports

Adler, G. and E. Webster (eds) (2000) *Trade Unions and Democratization in South Africa, 1985–1997*. Johannesburg: Witwatersrand University Press.

Alexander, P., L. Sinwell, T. Lekgowa, B. Mmope and B. Xezwi (2013) *Marikana: A View from the Mountain and a Case to Answer*. London: Bookmarks.

Allen, V. L. (2005) *The History of Black Mineworkers in South Africa*, 3 vols, 1871-1994, Great Britain: Moore Press.

Ashman, S. and B. Fine (2013) 'The meaning of Marikana', *Global Labour Column*, no. 128 (March), www.global-labour-university.org/fileadmin/GLU_Column/papers/no_128_Ashman_Fine.pdf (accessed 27 October 2014).

Ashman, S., B. Fine, and S. Newman (2013) 'Systems of accumulation and the evolving South African MEC', in B. Fine, J. Saraswati and D. Tavasci (eds), *Beyond the Developmental State: Industrial Policy into the Twenty-First-Century*. London: Pluto Press.

Barker, C., L. Cox, J. Krinsky and A. G. Nilsen (2013) 'Marxism and social movements: an introduction', in C. Barker, L. Cox, J. Krinsky and A. G. Nilsen (eds), *Marxism and Social Movements*. Leiden, Netherlands and Boston, Mass.: Brill.

Barker, C., A. Johnson and M. Lavalette (2001) 'Leadership matters: an introduction', in C. Barker, A Johnson and M Lavalette (eds), *Leadership and Social Movements*. Manchester and New York: Manchester University Press.

Batstone, E., I. Boraston, and S. Frenkel (1978) *The Social Organization of Strikes*. Oxford: Blackwell.

Baud, M. and R. Rutten (2004) 'Introduction', in A. Baud and R. Rutten (eds), *Popular Intellectuals and Social Movements: Framing Protest in Asia, Africa, and Latin America*. Cambridge: Cambridge University Press.

Beresford, A. (2015) *South Africa's Political Crisis: Unfinished Liberation and Fractured Class Struggles*. New York and Hampshire: Palgrave Macmillan.

Bezuidenhout, A. and S. Buhlungu (2008) 'Union solidarity under stress: the case of the National Union of Mineworkers in South Africa', *Labour Studies Journal*, Vol. 33, No. 3.

Bonner, P. (2013) 'History and the here and now', *Social Dynamics*, Vol. 39, No. 2.

Buhlungu, S. (2010) *A Paradox of Victory: COSATU and the Democratic Transformation in South Africa*. Scottsville, SA: UKZN Press.

Burawoy, M. (1991) 'Teaching participant observation', p. 291 in M. Burawoy, A. Burton, A. A. Ferguson, K. J. Fox, J. Gamson, N. Gartrell, L. Hurst, C. Kurzman, L. Salzinger, J. Schiffman and S. Ui (eds), *Ethnography Unbound: Power and Resistance in the Modern Metropolis*. Los Angeles, Calif.: University of California Press.

Busch, B. (2014) 'Introduction', in B. Busch, L. Busch and K. Press (eds), *Interviews with Neville Alexander: The Power of Languages Against the Language of Power*. Pietermaritzburg, SA: UKZN Press.

Capps, G. (2012) 'Victim of its own success? The platinum mining industry and the apartheid mineral property system in South Africa's political transition', *Review of African Political Economy*, Vol. 39, No. 131, pp. 63–84.

Capps, G., D. Moodie and R. Bush (2015) 'White gold: new class and community struggles on the South African platinum belt', *Review of African Political Economy*, Vol. 42, No. 146.

Chinguno, C. (2013) 'Marikana and the post-apartheid workplace order: working paper: 1', unpublished document, April.

Cliff, T. and D. Gluckstein (1986) *Marxism and Trade Union Struggle: The General Strike of 1926*. London: Bookmarks.

Darlington, R. (2014) 'The rank and file and the trade union bureaucracy', *International Socialism*, No. 142 (Spring).

Dlangamandla, F., T. Jika, L. Ledwaba, S. Mosamo, A. Saba and L. Sadiki (2013) '*We are Going to Kill Each Other Today': The Marikana Story*. Cape Town, SA: Tafelberg.

Dwyer, P. and Zeilig, L. (2012) *African Struggles Today: Social Movements Since Independence*. Chicago, Ill.: Haymarket.

Fine, B., J. Saraswati and D. Tavasci (eds) (2013) *Beyond the Developmental State: Industrial Policy into the Twenty-First-Century*. London: Pluto.

Forrest, K.. (2011) *Metal That Will Not Bend: The National Union of Metalworkers of South Africa, 1980–1995*. Johannesburg, SA: Wits University Press.

Frankel, P. (2013) *Between the Rainbows and the Rain: Marikana, Migration, Mining and the Crisis of Modern South Africa*. Bryanston, SA: Agency for Social Reconstruction.

Giddens, A. (1984) *The Constitution of Society: Outline of the Theory of Structuration*. Cambridge: Polity Press.

Graeber, D. (2009) *Direct Action: An Ethnography*. Oakland, Calif. and Edinburgh: AK Press.

Gramsci, A. (1971) *Selections from the Prison Notebooks of Antonio Gramsci*. London: Lawrence & Wishart.

Hartford, G. (2012) 'The mining industry strikes: causes – and solutions?', unpublished document, October.

Hyman, R. (1975) *Industrial Relations: A Marxist Introduction*. London: Macmillan.

Moodie, D. (1986) 'The moral economy of the black miners' strike of 1946', *Journal of Southern African Studies*, Vol. 13 No. 1, pp. 1–35.

Selected Bibliography

Moodie, D. (2010) 'Becoming a social movement union: Cyril Ramaphosa and the National Union of Mineworkers', *Transformation*, No. 72/73, p. 172.

Moodie D. with V. Ndatshe (1994) *Going for Gold: Men Mines and Migration*. Johannesburg, SA: Witwatersrand University Press.

Ness, I. and D. Azzelini, (2011) 'Introduction' in I. Ness and D. Azzeleni (eds), *Ours to Master and to Own: Workers' Control from the Commune to the Present*. Chicago, Ill.: Haymarket.

Piven, F. F. (2006) *Challenging Authority: How Ordinary People Change America*. Lanham, Md.: Rowman & Littlefield.

Piven, F. F. and R. A. Cloward (1977) *Poor People's Movements: Why They Succeed, How They Fail*. New York: Vintage.

Saul, J. and P. Bond (2014) *South Africa: The Present as History, From Mrs. Ples to Mandela & Marikana*. Johannesburg, SA: Jacana.

Silver, B. (2003) *Forces of Labour: Workers' Movements and Globalization since 1870*. Cambridge: Cambridge University Press.

Silver, B. (2014) 'Theorising the working class in twenty-first-century global capitalism' in M. Atzeni (ed.), *Workers and Labour in a Globalised Capitalism: Contemporary Themes and Theoretical Issues*. Basingstoke: Palgrave Macmillan.

Stewart, P. (2013) '"Kings of the mine": rock drill operators and the 2012 strike wave on South African mines', *South African Review of Sociology*, Vol. 44, No. 3, pp. 42–63.

Von Holdt, K. (2003) *Transition from Below: Forging Trade Unionism and Workplace Change in South Africa*. Scottsville, SA: UKZN Press.

Newspapers, Magazines and Online News Sources

Assorted issues of:

Amandla Magazine: Taking Power Seriously
Business Day
The Citizen
City Press
Daily Maverick online
Democratic Left Front official website
Democratic Socialist Movement official website
Lonmin official website
Mail and Guardian
Mail and Guardian Online
Miningx
The New Age
The New Age Online
Reuters
Saturday Star
South African Broadcasting Company Association official website

Sowetan
The Star
Sunday Independent
Sunday Times
The Times

Index

Index

Index

Index